ABOUT THE AUTHOR

ROSIE JONES MCVEY has a natural talent for horse training. She has trained horses professionally since she was a teenager. At 21, she became the youngest ever Recommended Associate of Intelligent Horsemanship. She has ridden in demos for Kelly Marks and Monty Roberts. Her passion for finding the best solution to horse-training problems is infectious, and she never loses the perspective of a student, keen to learn from any direction and willing to share her experiences. She remains refreshingly open to new ideas and honest about her own internal debates surrounding horse-training choices. She is currently undertaking a PhD in horse/human interaction at Cambridge University.

GLOBETROTTING

A travelogue exploring horsemanship in far-flung places

ROSIE JONES MCVEY

J. A. ALLEN • LONDON

First published in 2015 by
J. A. Allen
Clerkenwell House
Clerkenwell Green
London EC1R 0HT

J. A. Allen is an imprint of Robert Hale Limited
www.allenbooks.co.uk

ISBN 978-1-908809-40-7

British Library Cataloguing in Publication Data
A catalogue record for this book is available from the British Library

Edited by Jane Lake
Printed and bound in Great Britain by CPI Group (UK) Ltd

Disclaimer of Liability
The author and publisher shall have neither liability nor responsibility to
any person or entity with respect to any loss or damage caused or alleged to
be caused directly or indirectly by the information contained in this book.
While the book is as accurate as the author can make it, there may be errors,
omissions, and inaccuracies.

CONTENTS

ACKNOWLEDGEMENTS

Hannah and I wish to say thank you to all the kind strangers and helpful people who were part of our travels but whose names we do not know and therefore we cannot thank personally.

Thank you to the people who feature in the book. You took a chance on us, often after an out-of-the-blue email, trusted us and welcomed us with good food, good humour and good horse stories. None of it would have been possible without such generosity.

Thanks also to those who put us up, and for being part of our horsey adventures but not appearing in the final book: Madison and Melissa Whitfield, Ros Rowe and Leg Up Trust, Marilyn and Elder Jenks who run Kaimanawa Heritage Horses, Tracey Harland who helped with our New Zealand travelling links, Sarah MacIntyre and her family (who also gave us a family Christmas away from home).

For extra help with accommodation, our thanks go to Sally Charkos, 'The General' and his wife, and Matt and Joanna Rankin.

For a first-aid kit that could equip a field hospital, we were grateful to Tim and Cynthia McVey.

Special thanks to the people who helped with the writing and photos: Allison Sixsmith, Hannah's mum Cynthia, my mum Mandy.

Thank you also to Lesley Gowers and the team at J A Allen for all their help in turning my scribbled jottings into a real book.

I also wish to extend my personal thanks to particular people.

To Jim Goddard, for looking after my horse Harvey while we were away, and to Harvey (who hates most men) for not savaging Jim during my absence.

To my parents for letting me flounce around being a horse whisperer instead of making me get a real job and, more specifically, for putting us up for a while when we arrived home penniless, smelly, and tediously full of our own stories.

To IH student Tim for coming up with the name for the book.

Thank you to all my friends and teachers who have contributed to my horsey education so far, and who have been so generous with their own ideas and skills, many of which I have adopted and discussed in this book (and hopefully referenced you all appropriately in those instances). Particularly, Kelly Marks, Ian and Sandy Vandenberghe, Sandra Williams, Jim Goddard, Linda Ruffle, Julia Fisher and Sue Palmer.

And, Hannah, I can't thank you enough. This book is a reflection of just a small part of our adventures together, and I am endlessly grateful that your energy, imagination, and insightful wisdom permeate this book as well as the rest of my life.

PREFACE

M Y NAME IS ROSIE JONES MCVEY, and I train horses. Or rather, horses and I train each other, which is really what it's all about. Of course, anyone who has anything to do with horses is a horse trainer too, because horses are learning all the time – and not always what you want them to. As a child I remember inadvertently teaching a pony called Chester to gallop when he heard the countdown '3 - 2 ...' I never did get to 1 after that first time. I began deliberately training horses as a teenager. I managed to get the slow ones to speed up and the fast ones to slow down enough to give me a bit of a reputation, which grew into a career, and a lifelong addiction for trying to understand what exactly goes on between those big ears.

There have been ground-shaking changes in the international horse world over the last twenty years regarding the way that horses are under-stood and trained, and Britain has been one of the places at the epicentre of those tremors. A new wave of alternative systems for interacting with horses has emerged, including clicker trainers, 'horse whisperers', and natural horsemanship gurus. This has prompted a tumultuous discourse within the magazines, internet forums, and tack rooms while people try to negotiate the enticement of new systems with their loyalty to old. In fact, while it might *feel* like a battle of the new versus the old, many of the 'newer' systems have descended directly from lineages of age-old horsemanship ideas, and of course, many 'traditional' ideas have been evolving in one way or another all the time. What *is* different now, is the scale of the feeling of change; it would be almost unthinkable to ride and train horses today without coming across an article, or hearing of a new technique that unsettles your own assumptions, causing you to wonder: Is there a better way? Am I doing the best job possible for this horse? There is a trend in today's equestrian culture for rigorous evaluation of the techniques everyone uses, and the impact they might be having on the horse's welfare and success. While this has been a brilliantly exciting time for horse training, the downside is that it seems to have resulted in some horse people developing either an absolute commitment to a particular new or old technique, along with a resentment for those who don't share it, or, on the other hand, total confusion to the point of almost decision-making paralysis when it comes to knowing what is the best thing to do.

I have been lucky enough to 'grow up' into my equestrian profession amidst this wave of, some might say, new-fangled horsemanship ideas, through the relationship I have formed with Intelligent Horsemanship. IH is a horse-training organisation run by Kelly Marks, a former champion jockey and show jumper, now better known for her approachable teaching and writing style and her practical knowledge of horse and human psychology. At eighteen years old, having bought and sold a few horses and ponies to help pay for a horsey addiction in a non-horsey family, I made the bitter-sweet decision to sell my beloved Ocean, a chestnut thoroughbred show-jumping mare whom I worshipped. The reason I parted with her was to raise the funds to attend courses with Intelligent Horsemanship. It was a difficult decision that changed my life for the better. Through those courses I accelerated my addiction to horse training, refined my training skills and nurtured a network of friends and colleagues that has been the underpinning of the horsey life I have lived and loved since.

I was lucky enough to live fairly close to Intelligent Horsemanship's office (in Lambourn, Berkshire) and teaching yard (Hartsop Farm near Witney, Oxfordshire) and so I took up the tactic of returning repeatedly, trying to be useful as often as possible until eventually Kelly gave me a job. She even took me on as her tour rider, which kept me happily busy alongside my self-employed horse training work and a trip to

Colorado to work with rescued wild mustangs one summer.

At twenty-one, I became the youngest ever Recommended Associate of Intelligent Horsemanship (IH). Becoming an RA was a very proud moment for me; it meant joining a list of people I deeply respected – talented horse trainers, lovely people and all around 'good eggs'. IH has a close link with the American horse trainer Monty Roberts, because IH runs Monty's UK demonstrations and teaches his techniques on courses. Monty Roberts was a key instigator, if not *the* key instigator, in the monumental shift in thinking about the way we train horses in Britain.

Join-Up® is the name that Monty Roberts gives his technique that claims to talk to the horse in the horse's own language – the language of body gestures. These gestures are used in such a way that first moves the horse around the pen ahead of you, and then encourages the horse to follow you.

While Monty's techniques and terminology might have sounded unfathomably strange when he began demonstrating them internationally in the 1980s, once his demonstrations received the Queen's endorsement, they gained credibility. Thousands of British equestrians began taking Monty seriously and watching his training demonstrations in awe. While not everybody adopted his techniques, word spread widely and his influence was massive; he unsettled previous norms surrounding the way people talk about horses, and he opened the door for a plethora of alternative ideas about how we should understand horse behaviour.

At twenty-five, I became the first woman to ride untrained horses in Monty Roberts' demonstrations, and felt incredibly honoured to be part of a growing revolution in horsemanship. I felt on top of the world, and while I didn't think I got things perfectly right all the time, I was pretty confident I knew what 'right' looked like and how to get better at achieving it. That was before social anthropology caused me to question life so thoroughly I no longer knew which way was up.

My fascination with people, and particularly with the way people relate to animals, led me to take a social anthropology degree at Sussex University as a mature student. I gained a first-class degree, writing a dissertation on human-horse relationships, alongside continuing my work helping all sorts of horse people with all sorts of horse behavioural problems on a daily basis. Social anthropology specialises in studying groups of people by spending time living with, working with and observing them. My studies led me to realise how much variety there is in the world, how many different ways there are of relating to one another, or to animals. My horizons were broadened to the extreme, and my respect for unfamiliar ways of living was nurtured. While I have always *felt* like I was an open-minded horse person, during my studies I began to realise how little I really knew.

The thing is, none of us really know how horses think and feel. We can only guess, to the best of our knowledge, using whichever concepts and language make the most sense to each of us. I think it is hard enough knowing the mentality of other people. Think, for instance, about choosing Christmas presents. It's a nightmare, even though you have language and species familiarity on your side. Yet people seem all too willing to narrate the specific complex train of thought and emotion they think their horse is having, or worse, ask me to. While there are times when I feel I am right on the ball with my translations of equine behaviour, sometimes I quite like the fact that the mysteries of their exact thought processes are inevitably a bit of an enigma.

Science isn't yet in a place where it can fully help us to know the horse's mind, with many recent experiments focusing on the horse's ability to identify various shapes or push buttons – which is some way off being able to sit them on a chaise longue and ask about their foalhood. Add to that the horse's very different sensory experience from ours, and that we don't know for sure which bits of them are or aren't hurting, or how far ahead they are able to speculate, for instance. Then we get on the horse's back, with all our own emotional baggage and physical limitations, and try to teach him to trot on the spot, or jump over things he could clearly just go round, or whatever else we have lined up. Furthermore we want to do that in the most ethical way, not that any two horse people can agree on exactly what 'ethical' is, and in the most successful way, but neither can we all agree on exactly what that means. It is no good pretending to myself or anyone else that I know where to find all the answers. I don't even think I have all the right questions yet. But I find it absolutely fascinating to uncover and evaluate the different tactics that people have developed for interacting with their ultimately ineffable, unknowable horses.

Hannah, my travelling companion, who since this book was written has become my wife, is a brave and beautiful explorer. It's in her blood. The only time she is homesick is when we actually move in to a house to live in it long-term. She is the sort of person who can walk straight through an airport without even glancing about, and just suck all the information about flights and buses and baggage straight into her brain. She can also conjure up French onion soup and Welsh cakes for twenty-five wildlife sanctuary volunteers on a Bunsen burner in the Bolivian jungle. She has a Velcro-like quality for interesting people, whatever walk of life they come from; she needs only to pop into a pub to use the loo and will come out with a woman who owns a yacht and has offered us a ride to exactly where we need to go.

My growing interest in learning from the unfamiliar, and Hannah's propensity to sigh longingly at the sight of any plane heading to foreign lands without her, meant that by the time I graduated, we were brimming with excitement at a trip we had planned. When I say planned, I am using the loosest sense of the term. We had booked a round-the-world plane ticket, and decided on most of the countries we would be visiting, but beyond that, our exact mission and itinerary were unclear. I knew that several months away from horses would be detrimental to my mentality, as well as probably damaging to our ~~relationship~~ (since I am pretty hard to live with unless I spend time near horses on a regular basis), but Hannah loves animals and relished the chance to make our trip vocational and productive, so we were aiming to find horses wherever we could.

I was desperately hoping I might be able to share learning with people from some very different spheres of horsemanship, but we knew this might prove idealistic and difficult to arrange in the places to which we were heading. We had absolutely no idea, when we left, that our vague hopes and optimism would turn into a snowball of unreal equine adventures. Our journeys were often to wonderfully remote places, and involved unbelievably unique characters. One profound encounter led onto the next; we became swept up in the gathering momentum of our equine odyssey, and the growing interest our internet travel-blog was receiving. Hannah spent many late nights arranging travel or accommodation on our meagre backpackers' budget, emailing new contacts and thanking past ones, while I typed up blog entries in sticky internet cafes, dingy hostel rooms or on lakeside beaches.

During our travels, while we might not have discovered the definitive answers to the world's horse-training problems, we had the company of some extraordinary individuals in discussing some of the most pressing horsemanship questions. I arrived home feeling a little wiser, a little poorer, and a little dirtier than I left, with a collection of stories I will always treasure. Some of those stories are shared with you here. The first step of our journey took place in India, where we found three, very welcome little messages that our exploits were going to be worthwhile.

✦

CHAPTER ONE

OPTIMISM

In Dharamsala and Rajasthan, India

Aᴼᴛᴇʀ sᴛᴀʀɪɴɢ at the back of a seat for eight hours on the plane, breathing in the scentless dry cabin air, and eating the tasteless food, we took a moment in Delhi airport to prepare ourselves for the sensory overload that awaited us on the streets of Delhi. I had seen *Slumdog Millionaire* and so I felt I probably knew exactly what I was getting into. Sleepily, I unfurled my travel-crumpled limbs, and got ready to leave the cocoon of familiarity behind, and brave the raucous, vibrant and potentially dangerous world outside. I was trying very hard not to look like this was my first time in India. I was hoping this would a) impress Hannah and b) avoid mugging/conning/other dangers listed in the Lonely Planet travel guide.

But, luckily for us, we were saved from negotiating the slippery streets that surround Delhi airport, and were treated to a much nicer welcome. The night before we left we had a call from Hannah's father to let us know that a rather unlikely connection with someone's father-in-law in India had come good. The offer of a shower and meal before catching our train to Dharamsala, a city in the northern Indian state of Himachal Pradesh, was too good to miss. What we didn't know was that the gentleman in question was pretty high up in the Indian army. An important-looking uniformed man with a sign with our names on was waiting for us, on the wrong side of passport control. We were whisked through and ushered into a 1950's white Jeep with a flag on the front. We were taken straight to the house of our host: a man we referred to as 'the General', who greeted us with the type of charming attention and genteel etiquette that I have only witnessed in black and white British movies. This included carefully poured tea in the best china, and the assignment of a continually head-bowing chap at our beck and call. The concept of white women travelling alone was tantamount to madness in the eyes of most locals, so on hearing our travel plans, the General immediately announced that he had a better solution. We were assigned two drivers, Tenzin and Shankar, and a rickety army Jeep for our journey out of the capital and up north to the mountains.

Tenzin was a kind, caring Tibetan with a fairly maternal streak, and he was very concerned for our health and safety. As we drove, he told us repeatedly about the various scams and difficulties that we must avoid. The best thing about him was his wide smile, which crinkled his eyes. He was tirelessly jolly and he regularly tried to tell us all about his life in very stilted English and mime – with roars of laughter every time he got to a curious bit about jumping out the window. He was mildly amused by my interest in horses. I tried to show him pictures of my horse Harvey, in the hope he would understand my mission and take me to meet some horse people, but he just laughed 'Yes, horse!' Tenzin and Shankar soon got used to the fact that I wanted to photograph every mule we passed on the journey and ask questions about the blinkers and saddles, though they kept warning me that mules might kick. They simply didn't seem to understand the concept of a horse trainer at all or certainly didn't recognise one in me, anyhow.

During our journey, we made a slight detour to visit Tenzin's family. Children and relatives seemed thrilled by the unexpected visit. I guessed that as Tenzin lived far away, this drive to his home town was a rare and precious event. Tenzin, in stilted English, managed to communicate that he wanted me to talk to his uncle about horses. I got the impression this must be the horseman of the family. I found a moment with 'Uncle' (I never did catch his name) to try to find out more about local training ideas, hoping, perhaps, that he would whisk me off to meet a Tibetan horse whisperer or take me riding in the blue-grey mountains. I asked him whether horses are easy to train. 'Some are easy, some are not,' he said. 'They are as different as people, but they are not as good as Jeeps.' Ever enthusiastic for these first few encounters with foreign equine cultures, I thoughtfully wrote this down in my notebook: Hmmm ... Not as good as Jeeps ... very interesting indeed.

I was beginning to worry that horsey contact was going to be harder to make than I had thought, but I decided to focus on what I could learn out the window while we waited for various email trails to lead somewhere fruitful.

I had been aware before we left that we would witness some heartbreaking sights as we encountered the life of working horses in India. I had seen the campaigns of the charity The Brooke Hospital for Animals and I know that these horses work incredibly hard, often in awful conditions in order to support their owners' struggling livelihoods. So I wasn't surprised when I did see thin horses or harness rubs, and heard of long working hours. But I am not going to home in on those things here, and I hope you don't feel I am downplaying these issues while I focus instead on something positive that I recognised in the working horses. I was actually impressed by some aspects of the horses' behaviour, for instance, the way they reacted to traffic. Or rather, didn't; 'traffic proof' doesn't even nearly cover it.

As we hurtled down the wide roads at night, somehow surviving despite the apparent lack of road rules, it was not at all unusual for a pony and trap to suddenly appear out of the darkness, tottering down the highway as though it was a village lane. Our driver would swerve round them at breakneck speed, his hand rammed onto the horn, which seemed to be the normal way to let other road users know you were alive and awake. The horses looked entirely unfazed as they were once more swallowed up into the darkness, or bombarded again by the colossal honking of an overtaking juggernaut lorry. One group of donkeys meandered along the roadside carrying packs and grazing as they went, following a well-worn track with no bridles or headcollars on at all. After work was done, there were many horses left to wander the village streets till they found a cool spot, perhaps a traffic island or similar, to climb up on to and go to sleep despite the blasting horns, chaotic driving and revving engines. At one point we were held up as a car driver had to lean out the window to literally shove out of the way a sleeping donkey's bottom that was blocking the road.

As I watched a young horse tied to the back of a trap, trotting along behind his mother who was pulling it, it was clear that this youngster would grow up quite habituated to the world in which he would be expected to work. While I worried for his safety and felt for his welfare, it was a good reminder that the bomb-proofness of the Indian horses was partly because they grew up, grazed, wandered, rested, slept and then worked in the same type of environment, so they had every chance to get used to the mind-boggling chaos of the streets and surroundings.

This might sound like an obvious comment to make, but sometimes it's a new perspective that makes you realise you are not making best use of the common-sense chances to improve your horse's behaviour. Recently, back in the UK, I encountered a small group of horses who had a water tray incorporated into their yard environment so that they sploshed through it of their own accord on a daily basis whenever they brought themselves into the yard for hay or water. I have also seen the way the Spanish Riding School of Vienna allow their mares and foals to meander in the arena as the seats fill with crowds to become used to the show environment. These, like the Indian horses, are examples of making good use of the horse's downtime to allow him to train himself.

• The first message that our journey had given me was to remember that it is important for horses to spend plenty of time, quality time, including resting time, eating time and free time, in the type of environments within which we expect them to act as though they are at home. ♦ Just to show them 'spooky objects' a few times when working them in hand or under saddle isn't nearly enough. They should also be allowed

to feel truly at home with the noise level in which we expect them to •
relax and concentrate. This might be better achieved by looking at how
they spend their rest time, rather than simply what we do with them
during their short working hours. Grazing a horse near pigs, or between
spooky jump fillers, or near a busy road, twenty-four hours of the day,
is going to do much more for your riding safety and enjoyment, and all
handling of the horse, than if you try to work on these fears during a
twenty-minute slot here and there.

As I reflected on the responsibility of keeping horses safe, and keeping
horses *feeling* that they are safe, it was clear that these are definitely two
different things. More often than not, in the UK, we keep our youngsters
somewhere tranquil, and far away from the competition centres and
busy highways they will come across later. This might well make us less
spooky about their safety and welfare but them much spookier in the
long run.

These thoughts filtered through my mind as we drove on that orange
road at sunset, through a small village of tin-roofed huts, weaving
between the donkeys and cattle, listening to the shrill chanting of
Hindi-pop and experiencing a timeless moment of total euphoria. Our
spirits were high and our sanitary expectations were low, which seemed
to be an excellent tactic for backpacking in India. Even these low expectations were not always met, in surprisingly varied and colourful ways.
But having so far navigated public toilets with the appropriate amount
of instant sanitiser, deflected bed bugs and avoided dysentery, I was
feeling competent enough to keep myself alive and well. This in itself
was immensely satisfying, for someone who hadn't travelled in this part
of the world before. I felt a sense of accomplishment for simply being
in that spot at that moment, and knowing that months of adventure lay
ahead. The Hindi-pop tune began its thirtieth repeat, and I felt my mood
brightening as I realised the trip was already giving me new perspectives. Even without getting my hands on a horse, I was getting a new
angle, a new way of thinking, a new lesson, or rather, an old lesson put
in a new way. I was full of lentil dahl and optimism.

Attitudes to animals and animal welfare in Dharamsala were varied.

A strongly Buddhist influence encouraged compassion to all animals. I loved the Buddhist teaching that insisted that since all sentient beings are reincarnated many times, every animal may have been your mother in a past life, and should therefore be loved and respected. Treating animals as though they might have been your mother once is a pretty nice ethos to have. As part of the religion, vegetarian food was so popular that many places didn't even serve a meat option and those that did had only one item on the menu and referred to it collectively as 'non-veg'.

In general, when it came to the handling of working animals, I didn't actually see any anger or deliberate violence towards animals, who seemed to be of exactly the same health and weight as their owners. There was no animosity towards the stray dogs that roamed the streets in Macleodganj, and if a cow stole a cauliflower, she was just cussed at and pushed away to move on to the next stall. However, this was in the shadow of the residence of the Dalai Lama, with orange-robed monks shuffling in sandals down every cobbled street. We were in the middle of the mountains and people were unavoidably close to nature. I wondered how things would change when we moved into other regions and bigger cities.

A few days later, on returning to Delhi, ready for the next leg of our trip, I was still having trouble making meaningful equine links. Strange, but it was as though India had other priorities, and wasn't really that bothered about a travelling horse trainer and her obsession with the insides of horses' heads. Go figure. When we finally left the General's care to head out on our own, I was disheartened that even such a friendly, helpful and resourceful link had led to nothing in terms of real horse-based contact. We had done everything possible to encourage some equine networking, and the lack of anything to show for it left me feeling powerless. As we were driven out of the army compound, I caught sight of a military equine facility – thirty horses at least, some being ridden in an arena with jumps. I am not proud of it now, but I have to tell you I became a little bit unhinged at that point. I would love to blame it on the heat, but the truth is I began to worry that if the General hadn't been able to sort us out a meeting with the military horses 500 yards from his door, then perhaps I was never going to get to meet horse people during our travels at all. What if I ended up with several months of no riding and horses altogether?! I had frankly gone cold turkey on my equine addiction, which was not a pretty sight, and Hannah mopped the snot up and tried to cheer me up by pointing at a mule out the window as she reminded me that it wasn't all meant to be about horses, and that it had, after all, only been a week.

The following day we snoozed on the train to Jaipur and when we woke and looked out of the window, it was like we were on a different continent. Dharamsala had been green and blue mountains, Buddhist prayer flags hung like bunting, and teeming waterfalls. In contrast, Rajasthan, India's largest state, some 490 miles south of Dharamsala, was a hot windy sandscape, with a plentiful population of working camels, and the rich colours of dyed fabric at the markets.

After a dedicated research stint we made a link with Durga and Davendra Singh, cousins, local landowners, descendants of Maharajas, and big-time breeders and traders of the Marwari horse. A reply came through that by chance there was a lift going to their main stables and country home, three hours from Jaipur. So, we seized the chance and packed up, cancelled our other plans and headed to the stables in the desert town of Nawalgarh.

As we turned off the road and through the impressive gateposts, we caught each other's eyes with disbelief. Davendra's country home was magical, and more than a little larger than we had expected. The beautiful yet imposing yellow palace was adorned with pretty windows outlined with white paint, and huge doors made of heavy, old, wood. And best of all, as we walked through the substantial formal gardens, I became excited by the reassuring horsey noises coming from just beyond the glittering swimming pool.

At first I don't think Davendra quite knew what to make of me. He was a sunglass-wearing, blacked-out-Jeep driving, chino-clad business-man with an air of elegant, casual confidence that I felt I somehow lacked as I stooped to tie my shoelace, whilst counterbalancing my backpack and trying to think of questions that would be interesting to him and sound intelligent. The first couple of attempts didn't go too well. After hearing that the horses have to eat a seasonal variety of foods, I asked 'And do you find the changing diet affects the temperament?' He paused, and looked seriously at me from above his sunglasses. 'The story with that,' he said, using a turn of phrase that I would come to learn was a favourite of his, 'is that you English are making it too complicated. You look at things in too much detail because you just want something new to say. Horses behave like horses.'

He held my gaze above his sunglasses for a little too long before laughing it off and I laughed nervously with him. If he wasn't going to be up for a bit of horse chatter then I wasn't quite sure what on earth I was going to do with him.

To my relief, once we were around the animals he softened up, I got a grip and relaxed, and I realised we were getting on like a house on fire. Within an hour Davendra had introduced me to his herd and showed me how to recognise a good Marwari. By lunchtime he had begun to enthusiastically share horsey anecdotes and tips, and by evening we had really hit it off and rode Marwari horse after Marwari horse together until it was so dark we couldn't see what colour horse we were riding next.

The Marwari breed is incredibly old and beautiful, something like an Anglo-Arab to look at, but with more distinctive ears that curve right around in an arc and touch each other at the top. Marwaris can come in any colour, though most were bay or chestnut. The smallest we saw was about 14hh, and the largest about 16.1hh, and Davendra really knew how to show off the breed. He waited until evening, when the orange sun mixed with the dust, making the air as think as soup. Then he told us where to stand, and sent a boy to open a gate. We waited for a good few minutes listening to strange birdsong in the cool twilight, and then the heavy noise of galloping hooves drumming on the ground announced an imminent arrival. The first one to appear from behind the scrubby trees was grey. She changed canter lead as she skipped around the corner, sun-drenched dust-smoke up to her knees, pearly light on her coat, exquisite ears curling like a crown above her face. Behind her were about fifteen others, racing around the corner alone or in pairs or threes: bays, browns, blacks, all reflecting different shades of gold and running on clouds of sunlight. Each did a circuit or two of the yard before heading into the communal barn for their grain. Hannah and I grinned in appreciation of their beauty.

Davendra kept a real menagerie of animals, and went to great lengths to introduce us to all of his favourites, including Daisy the sheep, Sky the bulldog and an ancient camel they used to pull the manure cart, though he was perhaps most smitten with his golden Jersey cow. Of course he also showed us all his favourite horses, and there were many. Davendra collected more than he sold. He told us that at most he has had around 100 horses at his place, though when we visited there were probably forty or fifty. He was incredibly passionate about his horses' welfare, making sure they all had adequate turn-out, rest and feed. He had even built them a lake in their paddock so they could wade in and keep cool.

Most impressive of all was the bit donation scheme that he was involved in. In India, what might look like a simple iron snaffle from the outside was often crafted into razor-sharp edges and spikes inside the horse's mouth, or filed into what I can only describe as a meat tenderiser. The bit scheme encouraged horsemen at horse fairs across India to swap these rough bits for donated snaffles, most of which come from England. Davendra told me that they manage to replace around 1000 rough bits for good ones every year.

Amongst other things, Davendra shared with me his talent for naming horses. The horse's names all had beautiful meanings, like 'Loved by the Emperor', 'That which is Closest to My Heart', 'Body of a Flower', or 'Miss Flamboyant'. Davendra also waited until his horses were rideable before naming them: 'How do you know them until you ride them? And how can you name them if you do not know them?' he exclaimed. I muttered that in England we just give them names we like when they are little and hope that one day they might live up to them. The naming should have given us some warning about the type of ride Hannah was going to get when she mounted up on 'Double Barrel' – who we later learned 'goes like she has been fired out of a gun'. Hannah, who was still a fairly novice rider, coped amazingly well with what Davendra later assured us was his 'best horse' because she 'goes so fast and won't stop all day'.

Under saddle, Davendra insisted all his riders leave the horse's heads alone by giving them plenty of loose rein. They were allowed to move freely forward, in big loose sweeping movements around the school. I also liked his exercise of settling a young horse by facing them to a wall and waiting until they can stand patiently and relax before moving off – he makes sure all his horses can do this as part of the process of being started, because it helps them to become 'settled'.

Of all the horses I rode while we stayed with Davendra, I felt most honoured to be allowed to ride Albella, his favourite stallion. Albella was about 15.2, and very dark bay, like a polished mahogany surface, with a mane so glossy it could have been used for shampoo adverts. He was compact and strong, with a deep girth and wide chest, and a long neck that had the natural curve of a swan's. His manners on the ground were impeccable; you would never have known he was a stallion. To ride, he was very sure-footed, responsive and willing. He was extremely forward-going and forward-thinking – to the point that his attitude would be seen as rushing and perhaps even rudeness in England but was prized as hard-working and enthusiastic in the world of endurance that Marwari's are often bought and bred for. To be fair, Albella stopped beautifully as soon as I asked him to, and waited patiently while I organised my stirrups when I first mounted, but once you were on the move he really powered along, swinging his back left and right to get good long strides in and pricking his ears forward eagerly as he ate up the ground. It was like being on a horizontal airport escalator; the world swam by effortlessly.

As I learned more about Davendra's approach, I was astounded that you can travel halfway around the world and find so many similarities with the native systems at home. The techniques employed at Davendra's place were largely the same as those found on most breeding and dealing yards of a similar size in Britain. There was the same proportion of farrier issues, face pulling, nipping and napping, and his boys seemed to deal with these issues with a fairly typical mix of patience and firmness – though not necessarily much in the way of innovative tactics or training strategies. Perhaps the similarities were because many of the equine traditions in India come from British colonialism.

It must also be a factor that most successful horse people will have figured out the same fundamental tools for getting along with the same species. It was good to watch Davendra using 'pressure and release', body language and timing while trying to teach a young colt to lead, even though he didn't describe his actions using these terms that are familiar to me. I was initially impressed when I heard him say that he had 'no problems with behaviour whatsoever', but I soon learned this was simply a matter of perspective. This was partly because Davendra accepted that 'horses are horses' and didn't expect perfect behaviour all the time from every horse. In fact Davendra told us a joke about a horse trader who is asked to find a horse for a buyer that won't kick, bite, run off and will never disobey. He asks the buyer to sit on a wall. The buyer waits and waits and asks 'Where is my horse?' The trader says 'The wall is your perfect horse!' Davendra had a point. Life is somehow more relaxing if you just come to terms with the fact that dealing with equine behaviour isn't necessarily a 'problem' at all, but is an inevitable part of the sport and lifestyle. The 'no behaviour problems' fallacy that Davendra maintained was also confounded by the fact he had staff to do every-thing around his horses. Therefore, what he meant was no behaviour problems bothered him since, other than riding his favourite horses when he felt like it, his 'boys' dealt with all the handling, settling, training and exercising.

And boy, could those boys ride! They had the most amazing ability to sit to the horses' movement smoothly, with superb core stability and balance. They all looked as composed and elegant as dressage star Carl Hester, even when they were riding a shying horse with no saddle on. Their legs just moulded round the horse's sides like they were part of the same body, and their refined posture and superb strength reminded me of ballet dancers. I wondered if all the bareback riding, as well as the loose rein contact, had helped them to develop such incredible balance.

It's either that or they were just born that way, which hardly seems fair on the rest of us.

After a couple of fantastic days of learning all we could from Davendra, we were invited to stay with the mysterious 'Bonnie'. Throughout our stay with Davendra, Bonnie's name came up regularly, and it was clearly a name that was held in the highest esteem. We thought we had peaked in terms of accommodation experience at Davendra's palace, but as we approached Bonnie's fort at the centre of the desert town, we had to think again. It was just like a medieval castle, but made of biscuit-coloured sandstone, with crumbling walls and flaking painted murals. Instead of stairs, behind carved archways were sloping passageways big enough for servants to lug a sedan chair up, in fact there was an old one just visible through the long grass in the overgrown courtyard.

Our room had shutters set into the thick walls instead of glass windows, and a few yellow and black photographs of aristocratic children pouting solemnly in turbans. We followed a corridor that led to a mezzanine level balcony around the top of a parlour below. Pink and yellow silk hangings floated between cobwebs, and then beside a mound of dusty trophies and a tumbling stack of paperwork, sat four smiling Labrador dogs and Bonnie. Bonnie was a tall gentleman, with a magnificent curling moustache, absolutely in keeping with the Maharajah image. He had the voice of a master of ceremonies, and a contagious, deep laugh, which erupted in bubbles from the depths of his belly to the tips of his ears. He was renowned for his work as the head of the Indigenous Horse Society of India, lobbying the government over welfare points, protecting the breed and raising its profile.

We were collected from our room in the evening for dinner, and led into a different wing of the castle by an Indian boy who avoided eye contact and bobbed his head almost continuously in our presence. He showed us to a dining room that contained a dark wooden table long enough to sit twenty-five people, with two places set for us right at one end. The boy began to bring food out – steaming bowls of creamy dahl, and all sorts of curries and pickles and spiced vegetables that smelt of cumin and garlic and coriander. And a towering pile of chapattis – there must have been forty at least. While we couldn't remember if it was polite to eat everything or to leave something on the plate – we knew it would be rude to at least not make some sort of dent in this colossal feast, especially since we could occasionally see the chef peeking eagerly through the kitchen window. By the time we were both stuffed full there were still mountains left to eat, but our saviour came in the shape of a Labrador, who appeared optimistically at our feet, as though summoned telepathically by the potential food going to waste. Look, I know it's not great dog training, but needs must; we smuggled him a couple of chapattis under the table, giggling at his happily thumping tail.

The following morning, during a tour of Bonnie's extensive equine facilities my ears pricked up when I heard about their biggest problem – a seven-year-old mare called Mahek (which means 'sweet scent'). She had so far evaded being settled and would not tolerate a rider at all; she just kept throwing the boys off as soon as they got on, if they were lucky enough to get that far. I asked if I could work with her, and Bonnie decided to give me a shot, and sent me to the stables, with some of the boys to watch. We were also accompanied by another cousin, Diggy, a keen polo player who lived in America and who was willing to watch and serve as translator between the boys and us. Diggy made a fantastic translator, other than his tendency to add a colourful array of expletives in his Texan accent.

Mahek was a 14.2 liver chestnut mare, the colour of burnt ochre. She had little pony-like ears, and small, bright, wary eyes like wet pebbles. A lanky boy led her over to me on a long rope, and she kept a nervous distance, shuffling around to keep her handler well away from her left-hand side. I had seen how well the boys here could ride, so I knew this wasn't simply a problem of riding better or staying on longer. I didn't really fancy my chances compared to those lads, nor did I fancy exploring Indian healthcare in the desert. As I looked at the worry in her eyes when I approached her, I could see that the first step would be to get Mahek happier about being handled all over. I thought this would probably be a big challenge, but hoped that I could make at least a little progress for her.

I began by walking her in circles. After a few turns, I reached the back of my hand out toward Mahek's shoulder and saw her ear swivel toward my hand and her body lean away in fear. I waited a second without touching her and then walked away again, and she followed. The next time she let me touch her, and before long I was stroking her all over that left-hand side, walking away to give her a break occasionally rather than pushing things too far. At first, her coat felt taut and quivering under my fingers, and her tail swished cautiously, but as she began to relax, her muscles started to soften, she sighed deeply and her breathing returned to normal.

We have a game at home called Buckaroo. It involves a model of a donkey and players each have to put another piece of kit onto the donkey's pack. Eventually, something snaps and the donkey bucks the whole lot off. This toy is a brilliant demonstration that this is not a good way to train horses. The main point I was trying to emphasise to the boys through Diggy, was the importance of doing things in little steps and then reinforcing the right behaviour with big releases of pressure by moving away. The best time to stop is when it is going well, before the horse reaches a point where it cannot cope. I think this is what had gone wrong with Mahek, leaving her afraid of the whole concept of being ridden.

Each time I backed away from Mahek it gave her a chance to realise she was all right, and that accepting all this was working out to be a safe choice for her. The boys can probably get away with doing things quite quickly with most of the horses because they are good enough riders to hang in there if it goes wrong, but some horses, like Mahek, need a bit more strategy. I continued to build things incrementally in this way, and soon had her tacked up and getting quite brave about me leaning over her back. We were progressing better than I expected, and Mahek seemed to be a really quick learner.

Next I taught her to long-line so I knew that we would have some steering established if I did manage to ride her, and then finally, I found an old bucket to stand on and I began to work on the idea of getting on her back. I didn't have any intention of trying to ride through the problem, I just kept gently progressing and looking for where the very beginning of the problem was.

I alternated between getting her used to me up above her on the bucket, and short-reining – where I steered her from the ground, walking along next to the saddle. Each time I got back on the bucket I pushed things a little bit further, by leaning over more, or moving about more in that sensitive place she could not see on her own back. I slowed down my rate of progress if there was any sign of a problem and released the pressure regularly when things were going well. Before long I was fully leaning over her and she seemed really calm. I raised my upper body higher above the saddle and she seemed unfazed. I used my arm to simulate putting my leg astride – no problem there. So, I smoothly swung my leg over her quarters and found my stirrup, keeping my body low to her neck. I gave a deep breath out in the hope Mahek might feel my relaxation, then I gently sat up in the saddle, my fingers clasped around a chunk of her mane in case I was about to need something to hang on to. Mahek flipped one ear round to watch me, but stayed still.

At this point, I think the boys were impressed – they got their phones out to film – but I'm pretty sure they were hoping for a YouTube moment if it all went wrong. Of course the first thing I did was to get off again and walk away, and Mahek followed me without me needing to hold the reins – a good sign that we were working within her comfort zone and building a good rapport. We came back to the bucket and I got on again, and this time turned her head left and right and then moved her a step or two before getting off. Within a few minutes I was riding her around the corral with nothing but a headcollar on her head and with no sign of a buck or a worry. I was thrilled that one of the boys asked Diggy to translate many questions about what I had done and why, and what I would do with her next. He shook my hand and smiled at me as I left, and I was so proud that I had been able to share a way of working that they hadn't yet tried with Mahek.

This is when I recognised the second message of optimism: even fantastic riders do not have the training solution to every problem. This gave me faith in the value of the knowledge and ideas that I could offer to others during our travels.

The final part of this leg of our adventure involved a little bit of treasure. A couple of days later and we were back in the city; we had been invited to visit Davendra's cousin, Durga Singh, in Jaipur. We were sitting in a tiled courtyard outside a beautiful villa, drinking aromatic chai tea and I was trying to ignore the three or four biting ants that had got between my toes and my sandals. We were going to see a family heirloom that I had been hearing about all week at Davendra's, and I was pretty excited. It was a 250-year-old manuscript, an encyclopaedia of horsemanship, passed from father to son. Each ancestral horsey family kept a unique version, with remedies made of local ingredients and secret family tips, so this particular book was a genuine one-of-a-kind artefact. Durga was every bit as suave as his cousin, with a cosmopolitan air. Something told me he was perhaps more at home in his city dwelling than he would have been at the family's Marwari stables in Narwalgarh.

My heart skipped a beat as he carefully unfolded the lavender silk and revealed a leather-bound volume, about as thick as four dictionaries. With focused fingers, and without breathing on the tome, he opened the book on a random page. The thick pages were filled with handwritten passages and miniature paintings in faded colours. He had happened on a page that was explaining the different Marwari coat colourings along with their fabled links to temperament, or even luck. It was truly an honour to see this work, particularly since it was normally kept locked away in a temperature-controlled safe, and was brought out especially for our visit. The book contained information on feeding, hoof care, training equipment and practices of correct riding, though Durga said it had not been read thoroughly for decades and so nobody who was alive knew everything that was in it. It was so fragile and so important that it was stored out of the way, not used as a reference book for today's equestrian generation. Durga was hoping to find somebody to read and carefully translate each page, so that the information could be accessed without the book being handled. What a fascinating job that would be!

I wondered how much horsemanship had changed since the advice recorded in the book. For instance, I know that Davendra uses a modern adaption of an ancient worming recipe; his homemade pills contain kerosene, chilli pepper and molasses – which, just to be clear, definitely falls within the 'don't try this at home, folks' category. It's amazing how things evolve and change as they are passed down the generations, rather like the game I played as a child called Chinese whispers. Each player whispers a sentence to the next, and by the end of the line it is quite different to the initial utterance – though there will inevitably be something in the rhythm or rhyme that has remained intact.

Horse people in Britain can have pretty strong feelings about age-old horsemanship and traditional knowledge. Some feel that traditional horsemanship is the cause of all the bad training going on, and that what is needed are new ideas. Others feel an instinctive trust of techniques that have been tried and tested for years and distrust anything new and 'faddish'. The funny thing is, often the new methods that work, and the old methods that work really are similar, sometimes just expressed in different ways.

Mulling over Durga's book led me to the third message of our journey so far: to value old horse knowledge as something we should treasure and learn from, as part of equestrian heritage and a wealth of accumulated experience. But, this doesn't mean we should follow it without giving it a fresh evaluation every now and then from a new perspective. That magnificent book showed me that our travels could continue to present the ideal opportunity to evaluate our own, and others' traditional knowledge from a new viewpoint.

Finally it was time to bid farewell and thank you to Durga, and to head onwards with our journey. As we sat on our bags waiting for a train on the dusty Jaipur platform, we discussed our surreal experience in the Rajasthan desert, recalling it with disbelief. We had not known exactly what our travels were going to present us with when we left home but had been following a hunch that meeting horse people around the globe was going to be productive, although the few links we had made before setting off had fallen through within days of our arrival in the country.

When we stepped off the plane our only resource was our optimism. Our flights between countries were booked, but other than that we had very little idea where we would go, or who we would meet, and we sighed with relief as we admitted it was working out pretty brilliantly so far; after all we certainly hadn't imagined we would end up restarting a troubled Marwari horse in a desert fort.

The first three weeks of our trip had confirmed three things: that good lessons can come even from 'bad' horsemanship; that even the best riders can benefit from an outside perspective; and that even treasured old knowledge can profit from a fresh evaluation. But most importantly, it had shown us that maybe our optimism was not idealistic madness, that other people would be interested in meeting us, that the stories we were gathering would be worth telling, and that our quest was going to be worthwhile. So we boarded the train, slathered ourselves in after-sun lotion, then settled down in our tiny bunks for a swaying, noisy night as we journeyed towards Calcutta. On a roll from our Marwari experience, Hannah had felt it was worth a shot to email the Calcutta Turf Club and see if they, too, might be willing to give us a little of their time and share some horsemanship lessons from a very different field altogether. We were hopeful that our first chapter had set the tone for the standard of adventures to follow.

CHAPTER TWO

✦

MOTIVATION
In Calcutta, India

IT WAS THE TAIL end of monsoon season in Calcutta, which meant between the humidity and downpours I'd been wet for long enough to smell a little like an old PE kit. On top of that the bathing facilities at some of our hostels left you smelling worse on exit than on entry. And while hand washing some things in the bathtub, I had managed to muddle up the conditioner and laundry soap – leaving me with slippery socks and felt for hair. It was quite a challenge then, to pull off the 'English gentlewoman' image when we were invited by the Calcutta Turf Club for a day at the races. Luckily I wasn't only there to try and look pretty, and had more practical things on my mind than the dress code.

We had looked up India's oldest racing club in a small and sticky internet cafe, and sent an optimistic and carefully worded email. We'd explained that I was a horse trainer from England, travelling the world and learning more about horses in different cultures, and that I'd be fascinated to meet the racehorses of Calcutta. The reply that came back was certainly light in details: 'Give me a call when you reach Calcutta. Robin.' I must have read that sentence over twenty times on our long train journey to Calcutta from Jaipur. We just had no idea whether we were chasing a total red herring – but we were willing to give it a go.

Arriving in Calcutta it was certainly obvious that the town was a world apart from the sand dunes and camels of Rajasthan. Calcutta seemed to swarm around shiny slabs and clean lines of the grey Colonial buildings. Wide pavements reflected the heat of a heavy sky, framed by a horizon of lofty Londonesque Victorian buildings, cosmopolitan tower blocks and sprawling shantytowns. Down on the ground, Calcutta was an ants' nest under siege, everybody moving in patterns that we didn't understand. The streets changed tone as quickly as they do on a Monopoly board, every corner revealing a whole new side of town. The street-food street. The expensive-designer-shops street. The-stray-dogs-and-homeless-people street. The Indian-sweet-shops street. The banks street. The coffee-shop street where women in trouser suits chatted over lattes and croissants. The ominous-looking 'don't go down me' street.

It was dark by the time we reached our hostel room. We had bounced from hostel to hostel, trying to find somewhere suitable with space, and finally agreed on a good rate with a hostel manager named Shaun ('My name is Shaun and I am a Christian'). It unnerved us a little how many times he reinforced the fact we could trust him. In fact it began to have the effect of making us distinctly distrustful of him, as he ran his fingers through his well-oiled hair and smiled at us with narrow eyes. I wanted to check back over my shoulder to make sure he wasn't losing himself in a good old Disney-villain laugh as we disappeared down the corridor.

We then had to debate whether our 'Important Things' (passports, money, bank cards and computer) were safer locked in our room at Trustworthy Shaun's, or with us as we wandered the streets of Calcutta at night looking for a payphone to call Robin. We decided to split them, based on size, between our knickers and the room, which we locked three times before, on our way out, eyeing Shaun as he sat at reception drumming his fingers on the desk and looking generally cunning.

From a tiny phone booth I felt a little nervous excitement as I called Robin, who of course had entirely forgotten who I was. His accent was very English with no hint of Indian, and he seemed fairly short tempered and barked that I had better come to the track tomorrow early morning and ask for him. He didn't make it sound all that inviting.

As we left before dawn the following morning, we had to clamber over the bundles of bedding that contained the sleeping reception team. Carefully, we picked our way over the snoring lumps and stepped into the street. We were glad for some fresh air after a night in our window-less room, because we had washing hung from every possible place in the hope it might dry, but in fact it was sort of marinating.

On the long walk to the racecourse we came across some feral horses grazing on some unfenced parkland inches from the borders of the racetrack. They were thin and sorry-looking, with long feet. One in particular was old and pleased to have attention, so we spent a while visiting with him before continuing on our way. It was a reminder of the context of the world we were about to enter, and a contrast to the lives of the racehorses just a couple of minutes' walk away. We reached the racecourse and Robin's name seemed to work like a golden ticket with the gigantic security guard.

The racecourse seemed deserted, like a race-inspired section of an old, closed theme park. There were tall grandstands, a paddock, the odd betting slip blowing along the ground, and a large dusty saloon-type wooden building that seemed set up for crowds to gather and cheer and place bets. Something about the hot dust made it all look like it was from another time, an era of past glamour and spectacle.

Finally we found our way towards horses, in rows upon rows of stables. All the trainers stabled their horses directly at the track, rather than travelling them on race day as they do in England. We then found people, who directed us towards the office staff, who directed us towards Robin, who was much more hospitable in person (thank goodness) and our racetrack adventure really began.

Robin was a small man, probably in his fifties, with little hair, large glasses, and a small office that seemed to command fear and respect; he was head of the Calcutta Turf Club. An ex-jockey, his movement was stiffened perhaps both by old injuries and etiquette, his manner of speaking was plummy, but with a hint of the east, brisk and to the point. He was keen to meet us and talk about horse training issues at the track. He talked of his racing days as a golden age, and lamented the demise in horsemanship over more recent years. He seemed saddened that knowledge was not always passed on from trainer to apprentice in the way that it used to be. When asked for an example, he was on his feet and lungeing a make-believe horse around his little office, animated and alive as he demonstrated the body language involved in teaching a young horse to lunge. This type of subtlety, he asserted, dropping the make-believe lunge line and returning to mundane reality, just wasn't being taught to the lads who handled the racehorses. This problem was particularly visible, he felt, at the starting gate, where there was barely a race day without serious delays waiting for the horses to load. This was something Robin was interested in our opinion on, and so we were invited back to watch the horses training in the mornings and evenings in the company of one of the track's best trainers, leading up to the next race day, and then to watch the way the staff manage the horses at the gate on race day itself.

The following morning we were up before dawn and on the track as the sun rose. For a while, we were lost in a dream-world as the young Thoroughbreds galloped past, hooves drumming, breath misting, piston-like legs firing, silhouetted against a pink-grapefruit sunrise with the Calcutta skyline of temples and palaces as a backdrop. We made our way round to the trainers, a small group of men who stood studying the horses, with hands on their hips, or chins, or foreheads, as though quietly consumed by a riddle of utmost importance.

When they seemed a little less involved in their own thoughts, I began to chat with them, explaining who I was, and that I was interested in the way the horses loaded into the gates, and they all agreed it was a terrible problem. One man drew my attention to the other side of the track, where a few men were looking hopeless and desolate around the starting gates. I guessed whatever they were up to was not going too well. I scoured the area looking for a horse, before catching my breath when I suddenly spotted her lying on the ground, totally motionless, just a few yards from the gates. For a sickening moment I thought she was dead. But after a few silent seconds she heaved herself up, looking dizzy and dazed, and began to stagger about.

'Ha!' The trainer I was standing with exclaimed. 'She is ready for Bollywood, yes? She is just an actress!' and he turned away from the track, apparently unsurprised by the events and uninterested in what had occurred. I was totally speechless.

It must have been around this time that I first met Danny and Errol. Danny was one of the most successful trainers on the track, with seventy-five horses and some of the top owners in the country on his yard. We spent a lot of time with him over the following days. He was a friendly guy, with a good sense of humour, and he always seemed to be working on some clever plan, plotting away with wily eyes a little like a fox. He loved to be on top of the gossip at the racetrack, and though never on time, was also never in a rush. It seemed the world was happy to wait for Danny.

Errol, Danny's first in command, was a slender, suited, bespectacled sidekick who held Danny in the highest esteem. Errol was not a natural hands-on horse person, but he was a hard worker, efficient and loyal. He carried a clipboard most of the time and always seemed to know where Danny was supposed to be. Errol enjoyed what he referred to as Anglo-Indian culture, attending a gentleman's club that catered especially for Anglo-Indian interests, and he also had an endearing way of speaking with some traditional British dialect in his Indian accent, for example, always referring to other men as 'chaps'.

During our first morning with Errol, we were explaining a little more about our trip, and I was tactfully elucidating that sometimes I was learning new things and sometimes teaching the things I know. Errol really hadn't had the chance to get to know us yet and, as the only women on the track at the time, I think he assumed a certain (low) standard of horsemanship was likely.

'Well,' he piped up in a singsong voice with his delightful Indian accent 'Here I think you will be learning!' He smiled a genuine smile, the sort of encouraging smile you give a three-year-old for making it to the bottom of a slide, and proceeded to show us the feeding regime 'Now, have you heard of something that we like to call *colic* ...?'

Well, while I am open to learning from all sorts of avenues, I don't think it's going to be about basic digestive management from people who are feeding their horses almost 100 per cent straight cereals once a day. But I was touched by his warm welcome and willingness to share and got on amicably with Errol from this moment on.

Over the following few days, we watched the horses train every morning, and spoke with jockeys, trainers, lads, the head vet, the head starter, the course manager and commentator. Everybody was surprisingly open, welcoming and happy to talk to me and they all agreed there was a big problem with the gates. Too many horses and people were injured, too many races delayed. Too many good horses wasted if they couldn't get them loaded. But the fascinating thing for me was that everybody seemed to believe it was someone else's problem. The gate staff said the horses were not properly prepared by the trainers. The trainers said the lads who handle the horses daily were too rough, and too afraid of their charges, to be good for the horses. If the gate staff failed to get a horse in, they were blamed by the owner and trainer for not trying hard enough. The jockeys I spoke to seemed to know what the horses needed: time and a chance to move through the gates before being shut in, but it certainly wasn't their job to train each horse they ride to load. The lads who handled the horses daily had no facilities to practise loading, so perhaps responsibility lay with the track manager who handled the groundsmen and could create such facilities? Ultimately, the horse's behaviour at the starting stalls was causing everyone a problem, but was nobody's responsibility.

Race day came around. It became apparent that we were going to need dresses, and shoes, and more than a cold bucket wash, even though we were invited to be at the start gate where I had hoped smart horsewear would do. There are barely any ladies that go racing, near to none who go without their husbands, and absolutely *none* who go without wearing a dress. While I was gradually winning my way toward respect among the men of the track, I got the distinct feeling the dress code was non-negotiable, so Han and I had found ourselves some nice Indian dresses and some cheap but clean flat fabric-topped shoes and did our best with our hair given the facilities at Trustworthy Shaun's.

The transformation of the track on race day was incredible; it was as though it had been resuscitated from a coma. Like a stock exchange, the main betting area was loud, masculine, and full of consuming hope and fear – with jolts of realisation, glorious or desperate depending on their luck, coursing through the crowds as each race concluded. In the members area we were introduced to elegant people, whose excitement was filtered through a layer of classy nonchalance; they didn't need to win anyway. While there was some traditional Indian dress, most of the clothes were similar to retro British high fashion and, again, something about the style of the food (tea and cucumber sandwiches), decoration, the atmosphere and clothes, made us feel like we had time-warped back to a bygone age.

We spent our day between the grandstand and the starting gate. It was so exhilarating to wait for the head starter to nod in our direction and then race down from the grandstand and into the Jeep to get to the starting gate and watch the horses load. The loading itself was chaotic, dangerous and stressful by British standards, with horses throwing themselves about and their handlers working desperately hard to cram them into the gates in any way they could. There was a lot of shouting and huffing and puffing, and each time a horse was loaded it looked as though they were trying to stuff a cat through a cat flap. The horses were anxious, angry and, in some cases, very dangerous. My heart went out to them and I was committed to find some way to help.

So what was I going to do? The next day I retreated to the city's planetarium; it was air-conditioned, dark, hypnotically calm and quiet and was the only place to get any respite from the sticky heat and crowded streets in order to think through my plans. As the room turned dark, the first constellations began to twinkle, and the petite lecturer lost her temper with the number of people who had their mobile phones turned on. Despite having the shouting astronomer to contend with, it was still the most peaceful, cool place we had been for days and so, as her frantic ranting in Bengali melted into the background, Han fell fast sleep and I mulled over the starting-stalls problems.

The most tempting thing from my point of view was to explore the methods I might use to get one of their real problem horses to go in the gates, but I've had a good mentor in Kelly Marks and have been taught to look at the bigger picture. Kelly encourages students to think about their 'true north': to discover what it is they are really aiming for; what it is that acts as their driving force.

Looking at it holistically, it was no good me just telling these guys how I would fix their most problematic loader. In the grand scheme of things this would change nothing, since nobody would put the time into learning the skills, or repeating the unavoidably timely process with another problem horse. Instead I needed to find a solution that could fit within their current routine, current responsibilities and, most importantly, synchronise with their own driving force. Everybody wanted an easier time at the gates, but at the moment I couldn't think of one person who wanted it enough to actually do something about it and make a change. How would I convince them that they were capable of changing the gate problem, and that it was worth their while to try?

I thought about coming from an ethical angle, arguing for the welfare of the horses, or a safety angle that emphasised the reduced injuries to horses and handlers when horses are calm. Then I thought about putting forward the economic advantages, I thought about finding a sponsor for some sort of prize for the trainer with the best loaders, I wondered about using the increased professionalism and profile of having happily loading horses. As I tested the water on each of these arguments with the various members of race staff, they would nod in vague agreement, but nothing really seemed to make them bite. Finally the bait I needed came from an email from Kelly – a former European champion jockey herself – reminding me that horses who are stressed in the stalls are often slower to jump off than those who are standing relaxed and ready, with four feet on the ground. This struck home with me because we witnessed this exact phenomenon on race day ourselves, and we had video evidence of it. One of the horses had been difficult to load, and was worrying and stressing in the stalls, pawing the ground, mini rearing. When the gates opened, he came out at least two strides late, because he had been mid-rear and missed the moment to jump off.

Now if there's one thing trainers really care about, enough to actually make some changes, then it's the driving force that the horse has when it comes out the gates, because they can link that directly to his chances of winning. The increased driving force of a relaxed, prepared horse could well prove to create the increased driving force in the trainer's attitude towards gate training! I explained the theory, with the video footage, to Danny, who I thought would just love to develop a little secret advantage over the other trainers, and I saw his eyes light up. Having got to know Danny a little, I believe part of what makes him such a successful trainer is his resourcefulness. He is always on the lookout for a good idea or a useful piece of information – and he was willing to give some young girl from England a little bit of time.

So, I had him on board. Now I needed to give them a feasible plan! I came up with a three-point programme.

1. Better preparation

The young horses were literally unprepared for the gates. Not only were there no preparatory exercises completed (narrow spaces to walk through or leading exercises), but also most were not even walked through the gates at all! I asked one trainer how often they practise loading them and the answer was *never*; only, it seemed, if they were a real problem at the gates. Generally, the young horses were first loaded at a mock race. Talk about in at the deep end!

One of the fascinating things I found in Calcutta was the way that economics affected horsemanship. Each horse had his own stable lad. That lad was employed from 5am to 10am, and again from 3pm to 7pm, to do nothing but care for one horse! They groomed him, strapped him (a dying art in Britain, of stimulating the muscles through strong grooming strokes), walked him in hand, stood waiting with him any time when we might tie a horse up, brought him out for his rider, watched him ridden and took him away again, fed and watered him, and, of course, mucked him out relentlessly! While some of these lads were afraid of, or unmoved by their horses, from my observations the majority developed a real affection for their own horses. The head lad told us, 'they are not horses, they are all children, and each lad is a parent!'

Every day, the horses were hand walked in circles for at least forty-five minutes. I spoke with Danny about putting this forty-five-minute walk to good use. The track employs 200 groundsmen; it shouldn't be too much trouble to have a funnel system built to make a fake gate for the babies to practise with. I showed him a design that involves two halves built separately, so that when they are moved closer the funnel can be made narrower. This way, when he had a new batch of two-year-olds in, they can walk through the funnel forty-five times in just one day, without any extra effort or time from anyone! The horses would then get to encounter the narrow space with the lad they feel most comfortable with, in a low adrenaline environment, rather than in the race-day pressure cooker.

What is more, the stables here have wide, open doorways with gates across, but no doors. In winter, they have curtains which hang from ceiling to floor, I advised that they do not open the curtains fully but allow the young horses to find their way out of the narrow space every day. On top of this, if he really wanted to make a difference, each young horse should be led through the actual race gates several times, on several different occasions, before they ever jump out of them. There's definitely a case for the more effort that goes in, the more results Danny will see, but with such manpower, even with just a little tactical thinking and very little extra time, I believe fewer young horses will develop problems.

2. Managing the problems on race day

Since they dealt with such regular problems, the staff actually had some elements of a good system for simply getting the horses in – which is of course a very different task from training them to want to go in next time. The head starter had a notebook scribbled with notes from previous attempts to load each horse: this one must be loaded riderless, this one needed a blindfold, this one would get fractious once loaded, so must go in last, etc. Most of the tricky loaders were blindfolded, and a piece of canvas or rubber was used behind the horse to pull him in. Realistically, I can't expect all the gate handlers to be thinking like trainers; their aim is simply to get them in quickly.

Many of the horses were sticky to load, but the starters were under considerable pressure. If they didn't get one loaded, the owner and trainer complained. Consequently, they gave each problem horse much more time (and more of a struggle) before giving up, than I have seen in England. However, this meant that other trainers and owners complained about their horses waiting in the gates for too long, getting stressed. The result is a sort of mayhem or activity, with lots of starters trying very hard to cram lots of tricky horses in at once. The main thing missing in this situation was mindfulness. In the rush and high adrenaline, people lost awareness of their own body positioning and that of the horses around them. I saw one poor horse blindfolded, and then walked by a handler straight into a post, hitting his head square on. Unsurprisingly he wasn't so willing to walk forward after that! Another mare, waiting in the stalls, kicked out at one chap who hurried past frighteningly close behind her, I had barely breathed a sigh of relief at the close miss, when he was followed by the vet who did get kicked square in the knee and limped off stoically for first aid.

These starter lads were obviously used to a bit of roughness, they were padded up better than ice-hockey goalkeepers! The padding was there with good reason; out of the six races we watched, thirteen horses had to be held from within the stalls by a handler to prevent them throwing themselves around too much. I have always thought that starting stalls look small for the size of a horse – I've never thought there's much room for company in there. As you can imagine, the attempts to 'calm' the stressed horses from within the stalls are somewhat frantic.

My advice regarding the management of the starting gates therefore mainly took the form of an appeal to Robin to provide some training for the gate handlers, mainly in safety, body language and mindfulness. A better understanding of horse's minds and bodies (and how to get on the right side of both), would seriously reduce the number of crash helmets dented and vets ice packed, and would also lower the stress levels for the horses involved. I also emphasised that in my opinion the biggest improvement to the whole environment at the starting gate would be made by a change in the rules. Horses should not be allowed to race if they cannot load fairly quickly and calmly. If fewer loading problems were tolerated at the gate, then the pressure would be taken off both horses and handlers on race day itself, and the pressure would be on to prepare them better.

3. Curing problem loaders

Part three of the programme involved working with the horses who have already developed a problem; curing problems is so much harder than preventing them in the first place! Danny had seemed interested in all of my ideas about loading, and had heard me explain how I'd do it, but he hadn't actually asked me to have a go. I don't know if he didn't want to hurt me, or insult me, or respected me too much to let me get my hands dirty, or if it was the opposite and he simply didn't trust me to do a good job. It may well be that it had something to do with my gender, as it had felt as though we were challenging gender expectations from the very beginning. While everybody had been welcoming and pleasant to us, most had initially wanted to treat us like 'ladies', fetch us tea and a chair in the shade. It might well be that Danny simply didn't think it very gentlemanly to ask. Whatever the reason, he left it right until the last minute before suddenly asking, in a boyish way as though half-heartedly asking me to the prom, if maybe I'd like to take a look at Rocketball before I left. I'd heard all about Rocketball during our talks. He was Danny's biggest problem, with plenty of potential, but some serious behavioural issues.

Rocketball was apparently aggressive to handle, having bitten his groom only that morning, very difficult to load, and not jumping out of the gates well either – he would either cat leap in the air or try to turn backwards in the gates. As I approached the gates there were a couple of horses being ridden around the gate area. I could guess which was Rocketball: a lithe, bay horse, who already looked stressed, grinding his teeth, jogging sideways, wringing his tail and sweating foam. Danny had asked for a couple of other horses to come along to keep him company, one a lovely chestnut filly who could be a bit anxious in the gate. When she didn't seem to want to load initially, and I knew she was our option for a lead horse, I began to worry about how bad Rocketball might be. The jockey, a lovely chap (all the jockeys we met were incredibly friendly and well mannered), named Imran, told me that the starters had been very tough on him, and Rocketball told me that too. As soon as he was faced at the gate his back legs kicked out like pistons, he was keen to keep anyone away from the back end; a typical reaction from a horse who has been whipped.

To get him in on race day, among other things, they had tried a blindfold and four men with bands behind him pulling, this hadn't worked. I watched them begin to try to load him for a little while. They tried coaxing him with grass, they tried being gentle and talking to him, they tried pushing him with their shoulders, they tried backing him in from the front.

I asked if I could have a go. I had no Dually, a training halter which is an essential part of my kit back home, no mesh panels to create a wall beside or behind the gates, no facilities to create a wider funnel to practise in, no narrow spaces to walk through, no way to 'close the back door', not even a well-fitting headcollar (since the horses were all led in bridles). I had a stressed horse in a bridle, an open-minded trainer, and a small audience of very doubtful spectators, the challenge was on and I hoped I hadn't bitten off more than I could chew! It goes without saying that I would never even begin to train such a severe problem horse without the proper equipment and preparation in England, but what are you going to do? If I was going to make any sort of difference during my travels, then I was going to have to do the best I could with what I'd got. In this case, I seriously doubted that what I had would prove enough to significantly change Rocketball that morning but I hoped that I could at least help him to take a step in the right direction, communicate the techniques and inspire Danny enough to begin acquiring the right equipment.

The first change I made was to open up the fronts of the starting gates so that he could see he would not be trapped. I asked them to allow the chestnut mare to walk out the front of her gate, and bring her round again, so that she kept walking through alongside him, rather than leaving her shut up and worrying. I also got the jockey to dismount so that Rocketball only had one person to think about at once.

I took the rope from Danny and at first I tried clipping it to the back of the noseband so that I could use some pressure without pulling him in the mouth and causing him to raise his head, when this proved too loose so that it slipped over the horse's chin, I tried making a rope halter with the rope, but the rope was coarse and it didn't release as well as a Dually, so it was certainly second rate as far as pressure halters go. I tried to emphasise to the onlookers the importance of an elastic feel on the line, and the timing of releasing the pressure whenever the horse tries to come forward; even a tiny bit. After one or two repetitions of pressure and release, through moving Rocketball forwards and backwards, he took a big step forward and then licked and chewed, a great sign that learning is sinking in. I remember distinctly that moment of relief: he was getting it – perhaps we were going to succeed!

However, a few minutes later, and I was in the same place, trying to convince him to find his way through the corridor and out the front door. He had developed such a habit of fighting that he was really struggling to soften and give it a try. I could see Danny beginning to look unsure and he said, 'The problem is he is getting spoiled now, he has never had it so easy here. Let's give him one more minute and then pick up the pressure a bit'. Oh dear, I thought! It had only been seven minutes at that point and I was in no rush at all – every tiny movement forwards, even a thought forwards, was a massive leap forwards for Rocketball, who was only trying to keep himself safe – and we needed time to help him find his own bravery. Rushing him in that moment would have been awful! I could have been tempted to become a victim to pressure myself, but I explained to Danny that getting him in quickly, and training him to be good to load in the future are two different things, and that a little patience today would really pay off in the long run. I mentioned that the horse couldn't think, learn and remember when he is too stressed, that we needed to keep him relaxed, that we needed to train him to *think* of going in the gates before we could train him to *try* going in the gates.

As I said these things, I heard myself saying them as well, and found a renewed sense of patience. Rocketball obviously felt the pressure lift, and began to change his expression, he started to look forwards, sniff the gate, prick his ears and look right through the gate, daring himself to try it. Finally, after fifteen minutes from beginning the session, I saw him prepare himself and so I gave him plenty of room by getting myself right out the other end, and he came on through with me (albeit it a little fast like the Rocketball he is!) I praised him as though he was a champion and, for me, at that moment, he was! What a generous little horse for trying even though he was so scared.

When he'd been in once, he was worried about going straight back in, which is not uncommon in lorry loading and travelling problems too, sometimes the second time is harder than the first. It's often a sign for a trainer that something about the experience was too stressful for the horse. Once he did begin to come back through again, I could see what the problem was. He was so tickly about the solid ledges where the jockey's feet rest. He twitched and squirmed to get away from them, sometimes pushing more into the pressure and leaning towards them; horses will respond this way to some physical pressures when their adrenaline is high. This is exactly the type of problem that Monty Roberts' starter blanket was designed for, and I told Danny about it, but even a normal blanket to protect his sides during training would help him a little.

After coming through in a stop-start fashion a few times, things were improving but at one stage I needed just a little body language or movement from behind Rocketball to get him to try moving forwards again. There are sometimes moments where the right pressure from behind is more effective then pressure from in front on the rope. I didn't want him shouted at or whipped or chased but Danny produced the perfect stimulus by throwing a sponge at him! It was just enough stimulus and worked a treat. Although perhaps not textbook-perfect practice, if the starting-gate handlers are going to go from whipping to sponge throwing, that's fine with me! As the training progressed and Rocketball began to impress, Danny joked that it was the sponge that was lucky and needed to be framed! I think he was joking, but I wouldn't be that surprised to see it on the wall with a 'lucky loading sponge' plaque if I revisit. Rocketball was a quick learner and as we kept him walking through, and through, and through, he began to pause less on entrance and rush less on exit.

I don't think the gathering audience quite understood why I repeated the same stage so many times when it was 'fine', but I tried to explain that we weren't just getting him in, we were trying to install a new habit, and so until he had loaded *perfectly* with no hesitation or stress, at least five times, we weren't ready to move on (the entire follow-up to Rocketball's first rush through took forty-five minutes). Danny was keen to have a go too, so I handed back to him, and he did a great job of bringing him through the gate calmly.

Pretty soon it was time to put the jockey up, which only caused a momentary relapse as Rocketball's memories of race-day battles were re-awoken. Soon he was walking right through the gates with the jockey up and no leader at all! I hadn't expected to get so far given the severity of the problem and the lack of facilities, and I was so grateful that Danny had given me the chance and had the patience to let me show him how I work. Finally, we began to introduce closing him up in the gates. The timing here is critical, and it surprised me that some of the helpers on the gates had very little sense of timing, I made sure Danny was really aware of the importance of giving Rocketball an exit plan before closing him in.

This meant that he was led towards the gate with the front closed up but, as he approached, the front doors opened and he was allowed straight through. He got braver about approaching the closed gate, knowing it would open eventually, and so would tolerate walking right up to it, or standing in it, before it was opened – as long as he was con- tinually brought forward and the gates were ready to be opened when he needed it to keep him thinking that forwards was the way out, not backwards. I had to shout 'Open! Open! Make them open it!' a few times when the timing was slow, and we nearly had him stopping again a couple of times. It showed me just how vulnerable a horse is at this fresh stage of retraining. Everything must be done to strengthen the good, forward habit and not recreate the problem.

Then we began to close the back door, with the front gate open at first, so that he wouldn't come backwards and sit on it as it was being closed, if he panicked about the small space, he would go forwards rather than backwards to escape. But he was fine.

The next step was to load him with the front shut, close the back doors, wait patiently, open the front and walk him out. Finally it was time to put it all together and do a 'real' run through. Imagine the key change in a Westlife song if you will: he was ridden in by the jockey with no help from the ground, on a relaxed rein into a locked starting gate, the back was closed up, he waited patiently while I whispered sweet nothings in his ear from the next-door stall, the gate was released and he jumped out on a perfect stride!

There was a real feeling of celebration from everyone around. As Rocketball was walked through one last time to ensure the session did not finish on the high-adrenaline note of the jump-out and ruin all that good work, even the jockey said, 'Ma'am, I really like your methods'. Danny certainly seemed grateful and I really hope he will be using some of the techniques in future. To be honest I was as thrilled as anyone because I hadn't expected Rocketball to come quite so far quite so quickly, especially without all the right equipment, and I still don't really understand why he did. I was pleased with the work I did, and of course I believe in the methods I'd used, but I glanced up at Hannah, who was filming from on top of the starting gates, and we shared a 'Thank goodness for that' sort of look. It was only we and Rocketball who shared the secret that there had been a pretty good chunk of luck, and a huge chunk of generosity from the horse, that made me look so good that day.

The real change that needed to be made at Calcutta was not one of techniques or specific methods, it was simply getting someone to decide to try to change the behaviour rather than live with it.

It's easy to sit on the outside looking in, and spot places where horse people seem to have just accepted problems and lost their driving force to attempt to make any changes. We could get smug about the way we would have dealt with the problem much sooner, particularly when there is something obvious that could be done, like preparing the babies better by walking them through the gates before race day. The truth is, though, that all of us have become accustomed to some problems, whether it is foot handling or fly spraying our horses, and have somehow forgotten to ever confront them. On every yard there is a sort of culture that naturally seems to cure some problems and create others. No Thoroughbred in Calcutta had any issue with standing still thanks to the boys who stood around with them so much. None were scared of traffic, since the track was by a main road. None were scared of motors (the noise that causes so many clipping issues in the UK) since they all had electric fans pointing at their faces to keep them cool all day! So some issues are naturally addressed and others can be left to fester unless you find the driving force to sit up and make some changes.

It's all too easy to fall into the habit of thinking of the final furlong and forgetting the foundations. How many times have you scrambled aboard a moving target during mounting, or dodged gnashing teeth to get the girth done up? When were you thinking of paying attention to those behaviours? What driving force might get your attention? It's not my place to lecture (once my own horse Harvey is an absolute model citizen I might consider taking the moral high ground!) but that week in Calcutta had made me very aware that there are often issues we learn to live with that an outside eye could see as obviously changeable. Perhaps this chapter will provide you with the driving force to get on and deal with that fly-spray issue or whatever it is, because Calcutta showed me that the horses are just waiting for us to wake up, change our approach, and show them what to do.

CHAPTER THREE

✦

COMPANY

In Java and Bali, Indonesia

W HEN WE ARRIVED at Jakarta airport on the island of Java we
worked out, from the airport internet facilities, that we could
complete our journey to Arthayasa Stables in South Jakarta using public
transport. Jakarta is one of the most congested and crowded cities on the
planet. In fact we heard speculation that the city was soon going to be
frozen in total gridlock. Still, nothing gives Hannah more of a thrill than
making her way independently across a foreign city *sans* taxi, and the
route we had researched certainly looked plausible, if a little complex,
judging from the tidy version of reality available online.

Down on the ground things were different. I would say it was a
rat race, but there was actually so much human and motor traffic that
nothing could move anywhere fast at all, which created a slow-motion
chaos, as if all the people were bugs, frantically stuck in glue. Everybody
was fussing and buzzing, but nobody was getting anywhere fast. Signs
were hard to locate among the crowds, and none of the buses seemed to
be going where or when they were supposed to be.

A couple of bus rides into the journey and we had made it to a train
station, just as a plug in the sky was released, and warm rain began to fall

in cascades, battering every metal surface and creating instant rivers at our feet. Inside the small station was a portly woman sitting in a rickety shack selling soggy paper tickets, which stuck to our wet fingers. She point blank refused to sell us a ticket on the cheapest train fare, laughing at us and insisting we took the next price up. With a queue building up behind us, and a difference of a few pence, we let it go and bought the pricier tickets, then huddled under the drumming tin shelter on the platform with hordes of regular commuters.

Within a second or two I began to notice one or two people twitching in a peculiar manner, lifting a leg and hopping once or twice before returning to the dull gaze of people on public transport. Then the woman next to me wriggled a leg and brushed it with her hand – knocking an oily, black, writhing cockroach to the ground. It righted itself and then shot off to climb up a gentleman's trouser leg. Now that I started to look, they were everywhere, climbing out of the flooding drains at alarming speed and looking for higher ground. Most were scrabbling up parts of the building, but many were aiming for human legs and climbing urgently to escape the ankle-deep floodwater that was bubbling up from the drains.

A train pulled into the station, and the sign on the front indicated that it was the cheaper fare. The sign could only actually be seen when the eight or so men who were clinging on to the front of the train dismounted and before the next few brave train-clingers leapt on. Every carriage of the train was crammed so full of people that they were pressed up against the windows and splurging out of the doorways – the doors themselves non-existent. The roof of the train was heaving with people, who grabbed the arms of others wanting to board and lifted them up like a human crane, tossing their bags up ahead of them. Hannah and I looked at each other and our bulging heavy backpacks, and considered going back to thank the ticket lady for our narrow escape.

As soon as the train was out of the station, another arrived, and this one was ours. There was not as much difference as I had hoped, though this one was mostly full of women, and there was nobody on the actual roof. This train also did have doors, and it was amazing to see how the whole carriage of travelling ladies worked together to help anybody who wanted to board to squeeze within the confines of the doors and make it on to the train before it departed. You just extended an arm from the platform and it would be clasped by those on the train, who would suck you into the sea of bodies, the way a starfish eats a meal. With most of the passengers being Indonesian, we stood out like tall, white, bedraggled sore thumbs – all eyes were on us, and we smiled politely back. As the train swung around the bends in the track, the whole carriage of ladies swayed into one another, moving as one and crushing the unfortunate few who were near the wall. We were all pressed right against one another, and with our clinging wet clothing and sweaty skin, the air was humid and warm. I felt incredibly guilty about my backpack, which was surely causing someone discomfort behind me, but there was no way I could move.

'Where you going?' asked one lady with a friendly round face, her shiny dark hair tied up in a bun.

'Arthayasa Stables,' I replied 'Do you know it?'

'No.' She looked confused.

Then someone down the carriage shouted 'Where they going?'

'Stables,' was shouted back.

'Oh, I don't know,' came the reply.

After a few moments of dialogue, the ladies understood where it was we wanted to get to and looked very concerned at our current plan. Like a Mexican wave of information and helpful intent, questions and answers were ping-ponged up and down the carriage as the ladies squabbled over our logistical problems and came up with a solution.

'Tell them get off at next stop and go back.'

'No, tell them three stops then taxi; my brother lives near there.'

'No, taxi too much money. Tell them get other train line then bus.'

Finally a consensus was reached, and when we arrived at the stop they had in mind, we were manhandled to the doorway and then grabbed by people on the platform, who helped pull us out of the carriage like a champagne cork. We gulped in the slightly fresher air on the platform, then looked around, bewildered but touched by the kindness of strangers. We were now well off our internet plan and trying to work out where on earth we were.

Eventually we reached Arthayasa well after sunset, four hours after leaving the airport. After the smog and sweat of the city, it was an absolute oasis. The founders, Rafiq Hakim Radinal and his Russian-born wife Alla, were putting us up in one of the cottages on site. It was a beautiful Indonesian hut, with a roof that touched the ground on each side and an outdoor tiled bathroom, complete with palm tree and wonderfully welcome cool shower. When we woke in the morning, there were exotic flowers and large-leaved trees outside the window; and just a few yards away was a riding arena, covered with a thatched roof and with open sides that looked onto the tropical greenery. It would be easy to believe that we had been transported out of the city, but we knew from our journey the day before that we were still in the thick of it. Just beyond the confines of the equestrian centre were traffic and shops and businesses and honking horns. The equestrian centre was the last green place left for miles around.

Staying with Alla and Rafiq was a lesson in how to cultivate the sort of company you want to keep. While it might be very populated with people, until the development of Arthayasa, Java had been desolate in terms of equestrian activity. Against all the odds Alla and Rafiq had not only managed to build a successful equine business and first-class facilities, they had also created an entire network of horse people, who each acted as client, colleague, mentor or employee for one another, and so they were able to support this isolated pocket of equestrianism. Now there were saddlers, feed merchants, instructors, horse dealers, competitors and judges, all centred around this hub in the most unlikely of settings.

I wish I'd known about Arthayasa during heated discussions with my careers adviser. Arthayasa seemed to have adopted the *Field of Dreams* approach to speculative economics. For those of you who haven't seen it, *Field of Dreams* is a 90s film in which a guy hears an ominous voice telling him 'If you build it, they will come.' He rather obediently and optimistically constructs a full-sized baseball pitch in his backyard, and, low and behold, the ghosts of famous baseball players come back from the dead to play on his pitch and attract crowds of hundreds. Let's not focus on the reality of the ghosts' part; it's the optimism and the happy ending that are the moral to the story here.

It seems Rafiq did not wait for the equine scene in Jakarta to be large enough to demand a world-class centre. He got on with creating one, bit by bit, and the equine scene grew with it. At first it was just a few stables and imported Warmbloods. But Rafiq was an ambitious guy, and with each new ambition, new facilities were required. By the time we visited, the centre boasted two indoor arenas, an outdoor arena, a showjumping field, two lunge pens, a full international standard cross-country course, seventy permanent stables, quarantine boxes, vets' and farriers' facilities, shower boxes, tack shop, guest houses, and a hoard of fantastically skilled riders and instructors on site 24/7. The centre had hosted a number of prestigious competitions including the FEI Jumping World Cup Sea League, and both Rafiq and Alla had been successful on the international showjumping circuit in south-east Asia. This was a vocational business that had grown slowly and thrived, rather than the hobby of a wealthy funder.

What inspired me most was the courage to aim high, despite such a hostile environment. And this approach was not just adopted for building the facilities; they built on their own skill sets too. Whether travelling abroad for training, or inviting foreign trainers to visit them, the feeling of motivation to excel was palpable, and contagious, so that all of the riding club members also seemed driven to ride at the very top of their ability. The momentum that Rafiq had started spread through his clients, who eventually had clients of their own, and created a whole culture of support and improvement.

We only had a couple of days available to watch the lessons, talk with the riders and instructors, and walk the facilities, and by the second day, I was itching to ride. I jumped at the chance to ride Enya, a TB x WB mare. Enya was a sharp little thing, light bay, with spindly legs and darting eyes, and she felt as though she could get tense, spooky and agitated very quickly. On the flat I really enjoyed getting to know what made her tick and how to help her soften and relax. As is often the case, once she was straight through her body and softer and longer in her neck, the spookiness melted away.

Over jumps, it seemed that both Enya and I had no problem whatsoever with motivation. While the style felt good (if a little eager) on approach and while airborne, Enya seemed to find another gear on landing. She would take off for the jump like a spring lamb, but land like a jumbo jet hurtling down a runway.

Rafiq was on hand, so I asked his advice. He suggested keeping more of a contact down the reins in the air rather than throwing my hands forward over the fence. I do have a habit of throwing my hands forward, perhaps more than is needed, and Rafiq thought this was geeing her on a bit in the air. His advice certainly helped and we finished on a better note – though both of us sweatier than is ladylike. Enya went off for a sponge bath, lucky thing, while I didn't even have time to take my chaps off since the lift to the bus station was waiting.

At the bus station, the queues were like colossal migratory herds of people, and Hannah was starting to turn a rather strange, greasy shade of grey. We had known that illness was likely at some point while travelling, but the timing was not ideal; while Hannah seemed to be deteriorating quickly, the buses seemed to be coming very slowly. There came a point where it was clear Hannah needed to sit down before she fell down, so we gave up our places in the queue and I left her near a stray kitten to keep her relaxed while I went looking for another transport solution.

After a long conversation with a man in a high-vis jacket about the lack of taxis, he suddenly came up with a novel idea and wondered if perhaps I would like to hire a private bus. Apparently, it would cost just double the negligible normal bus fare, and take us wherever we wanted to go, and it would come very quickly. I looked over at Hannah who had stopped even noticing the kitten. Yes, I said, this is definitely what I wanted. Within about three minutes, a full-sized public bus pulled up playing the Vengaboys' song 'The Party Bus' and a smiling conductor beckoned us out of the crowds and onto air-conditioned salvation. We boarded the bus as the only passengers and were whisked away to the train station. This was incredibly surreal to the point of unbelievable, but on reflection, I am ninety-nine per cent sure I have not invented the scenario. Hannah can't be relied on as an accurate witness as her condition had worsened to the point of delirium.

Eight hours later we arrived in Yogyakarta, 270 miles from Jakarta. After settling Han into bed I began thinking about my jumping session with Enya. While it is easy to think speed means enthusiasm when it comes to jumping, it is often a sign of stress, fear, confusion or pain, so it is definitely a behaviour I would want to get to the bottom of rather than manage long term. I thought about the things I might try to improve Enya's rushing after the fence and I realised how my approach would incorporate a whole network of people, from physiotherapists, to Western trainers, gridwork specialists, eventers and riding coaches. I am so lucky to be able to draw on input and advice from a great many talented people when I am devising a training programme.

My ideal approach would have begun with my feet on the ground, teaching Enya to relax and slow down around poles, for instance asking her to stop and stand with two feet in front of a pole and two feet behind. Long-lining her over poles and jumps would help her to develop rhythm and relaxation without having to worry about the burden of a rider. Once riding, I could have worked Enya in a serpentine, curving around a line of jumps rather than going over them. Eventually, I could have begun to incorporate the fences, while continuing to work on the softness and the bend. Another applicable exercise would involve placing a pole a few strides from the corner in an arena, riding over the pole and then coming to a halt in front of the wall. The height of the fence could be raised incrementally, the distance from the corner could be increased, and similar jumps could be set up in every corner so that the horse repeatedly jumps and halts, jumps and halts, into different corners, hopefully breaking the rushing pattern.

I thought of these things as I fetched a wet flannel to mop Hannah's brow. Han was sweating, shivering and struggling to keep water down. As I tried to make her more comfortable, and realised how much we relied on each other while travelling, I knew that the strength in anything we do comes from the people around us. From the helpful strangers on the train, to the network that Rafiq and Alla had cultivated, to the people who have influenced my horsemanship over the years, success in life is not possible on our own.

Nowadays it seems that horse people are organised into loyal colonies. The scientists, the 'natural' horse people, the traditionalists, the eventers, and the showing crew – on and on it goes. Of course, as with all labelling of people, in reality there is more variety of people within groups than between them, and almost nobody is happy with the label assigned to them by others.

The new wave of alternative horsemanship devotees get called horse huggers, with their gimmicky gurus who are out for fame and fortune. The traditionalists are stereotyped as fossilised old relics, regimentally maintaining out-dated methods as stoically as they defend the class system. The dressage crew look down their noses at everyone – and so do their horses since they are trained to carry their heads between their forelegs for the sake of appealing to some odd fashionable aesthetic. The eventers jump first and think later, leaving horse psychology to those who don't realise there are walls that need jumping and ditches to throw oneself into; they don't see why it needs complicating beyond the two rules of horsemanship: 1) Kick on, 2) Stay on.

I'm sure I've offended nearly all my readers, but these stereotypes are unlikely to be unfamiliar to you – and this is just the tip of the iceberg. At times it can feel like exclusive playground cliques, and I used to think I was above it all. You see, like most horse people, I never set out to be affiliated to anyone or anything, preferring to remain free to pick and choose my methods for each horse and owner, and aiming to learn from and teach both traditional and alternative spheres. I found my 'home' at IH, which seemed to give me the absolute freedom to do this, as long as I used methods that a) actually worked and b) didn't hurt the horse or upset the owner. Seeing as this pretty much summed up my aims anyway, I felt as free as a bird to wander in and out of the different cliques without entering into tribal relations. Or so I thought.

After a few days nursing Han and visiting temples in Yogyakarta, I received an email from Parelli student Naomi, the owner of a tourist riding facility on the beach in Bali, asking for some help for some seriously troubled horses.

I'm going to be honest – the Parelli link nearly put me off.

You see, to me, the Parelli tribe seemed a fairly exotic one. It was all the stick twirling and circus tricks, not to mention the baffling jargon and the marketing machine. I didn't doubt that Pat Parelli could get some real training results; I had seen his horses standing on podiums, lying down on command, and loose jumping over barrels. I could see that many of the key principles that Parelli promotes, such as good timing and consistency, supported a lot of people in getting along better with their horses. It's just that my first exposure to Parelli left me with the assumption that it was not for me. I prejudged it as more about the show than the substance.

I was considering turning down Naomi's request, when, with horror, I acknowledged the fact that I had become part of hostile tribal relations myself. I was isolating myself from this particular opportunity to exchange ideas with a group of horse people who were training fanatics, and no doubt contained many talented individuals as well as a multitude of different ways of explaining horses. Did I really think I had absolutely nothing at all in common with them, or nothing to share with them, or learn from them? When did this happen? What had become of my intention to connect with horse people regardless of their culture or clique?

I guess it's just human nature to make some judgments on gut feeling rather than searching objectively for the best from each approach. But now I'd recognised it, I was set to change. I wasn't going to let my distaste for the marketing get in the way of a good opportunity to learn, teach, or both. As Naomi lived nowhere near any Parelli trainers, her Parelli education had been mostly through books and DVDs. I was hopeful that my ability to recognise what the horse was learning and enhance a training programme would prove universally applicable. So after a few days in Yogyakarta while Hannah recovered, we travelled to the beaches of Bali.

For a small island, Bali is really diverse – from bustling cities with nightlife cultures, to ramshackle towns that have fallen into barren disrepair, to my favourite area around Ubud, which was beautiful. The wet, thriving green rice paddies were sculptured into the hillside like the tiers of a wedding cake. Pink, orange and indigo flowers and fruits were left out as religious offerings at temple sites dotted across the landscape, and we instantly fell in love with the sweet, saltiness of Balinese food. The stables we were visiting were off the main tourist track, where the architecture was more pragmatic than beautiful and the beach would have benefited from a bit of litter picking. I hoped that Naomi was open minded, and that we would be able to find a way of talking about horses together that made sense to us both.

Of course, I had nothing to worry about. Naomi was instantly welcoming. She was Australian by birth, with long blonde hair and almond tanned skin. She had thought she was living her dream when she had taken over the tourist riding facility, but the behaviour of her horses and her staff meant it was rapidly becoming a living nightmare. She had been enterprising enough to go looking for better ways to understand and train her horses, and found Parelli, which gave her not only a new way to structure her training, but also provided her with a network of people to talk to through internet forums. So, of course, she had also been open minded enough to look for answers to her daily handling problems from a travelling horse trainer with no Parelli credentials at all.

The stables housed about twenty-five horses, under a tall thatched roof. Each horse had his own small stable, which was made of concrete up to the height of the horse's shoulders. There was almost one staff member per horse, which could have led to an incredibly close bond as well as plenty of time for extra training to iron out any issues. This certainly didn't happen. It was difficult to find experienced or interested equestrian staff on the island, and most of Naomi's workforce was made up of men who needed work and would have taken any physical labour going. It just so happened they had fallen into equestrian work, but it could just as easily have been anything else. They were, for the most part, not in the least bit interested in the horses and many were afraid of them – with pretty good reason.

I tend to find on average about one out of every fifteen horses puts its ears back over the stable door on most working yard environments in the UK. At Naomi's yard, that ratio was well out. Every single horse was angry, scowling, and willing to viciously defend his or her space. The worst of the issues arose during saddling and mounting, when the horses seemed to be in a state of absolute fury, and bit and kicked with chilling intent.

It was clear from observing the horses for a while that they were reacting defensively, rather than out of pure aggression; they were protecting their space through fear of human contact. The staff admitted to Naomi that they had managed the situation using harsh methods. They hit the horses, including around the head, in order to try to frighten them out of their attacks. Since Naomi was actually fairly new to horses herself, she found it very difficult to have any influence over the way the staff managed the horses. She was afraid to sack the worst offenders, who desperately needed the work and might well react in anger; she mentioned reports of stables being burned down in similar situations. So she was determined to work with the staff she had, but they simply had no incentive to change since, from their perspective, to be 'softer' on the horses would put them in danger. In one way, sadly, they were right: once horses have reached this level of violent defensiveness, simply being lovely and gentle towards them is not going to fix anything overnight and could very well get you hurt. I learned this hard lesson when I was about fourteen and tried to cure an aggressive stallion through love, kindness and soft stroking. He very nearly ate me alive.

I took a look at three of the worst culprits. First I saw Solomon, a pitch-black ex-racehorse gelding, about seven years old and about 15.2hh. Solomon's groom, Tono, led him out and handed him to me. On the end of the lead rope he looked pretty, in beautiful condition, far better than any of the other tourist working horses I had seen so far on my travels. I didn't have time to contemplate the lustre of his coat before I had a close-up view of the condition of his tonsils. He jumped at me from the end of the lead rope, ears flat back and teeth clamping shut just inches from my face. I had only a Parelli rope halter and lead line to work with, which was not the kit I am used to. I needed to get the feel of it pretty quick or else lose part of my newly tanned flesh to the jaws of the wild snapping beastie. I jumped back to avoid his bite, and I knew this was a bad move in the long run – he would be chasing me round the yard in no time at all. I needed to find a way to get Solomon to back out of my space so that I could keep that personal space sacred and correct him when he leapt forward to bite me.

On the Dually halter, which I usually use, the line attaches to the side of the head, which gives you significant power for quite little physical strength if a horse tries to run off, but also means the line and clip is not jangling under the chin, as on the Parelli halter, which seemed to encourage Solomon to want to mouth and play with it a lot as it fell right by his bottom lip. In order to back a horse up, both Parelli and IH prefer the horse to respond to body language first but then, if a clearer explanation or reinforcement is needed, the type of pressure used to reinforce the aid is different in the two camps. The technique I am most practised at in the Dually halter is the method of softly pushing the line away from you, creating a fairly steady, elastic pressure on the front of the horse's nose. Once you get the hang of it, this allows you to receive feedback from the horse, as you can literally feel him resisting or softening in your hand. The pressure feels like a sort of tactful conversation where you can raise or lower the amount of pressure spontaneously depending on the feedback you get and, crucially, release it at the split second it feels 'right', when the horse is beginning to step back away from the pressure. You can't do this so well in the rope halter because the fit and the position of the rope attachment just isn't designed for that purpose.

In the rope halter, Naomi had been taught to apply pressure by wiggling the rope. If he didn't respond, Naomi had been advised to wiggle the rope harder. Since the clip is really quite heavy, it clunked Solomon in the jaw and caused him to raise his head and blink his eyes. If he still didn't move his feet back, Naomi used the 'carrot stick' (a piece of Parelli kit, this orange-coloured stick is used as an extension of the trainer's arm) to tap on the horse's chest. When she had tried this, she had run into trouble because the horses would sometimes strike out with their front legs, bite the stick, or even charge forward at her past the stick. The advice Naomi had received on a forum (the advisor's credentials were not known) was to 'see it through' and use the stick harder, but she was concerned about how hard she would need to tap to get the horses to yield in the correct direction, and whether this would just cause them to fight back more. I want to be really clear that these problems are not problems with the Parelli method in general, since Naomi was still only three months into her learning with Parelli and had no access to direct teaching from an instructor at all – so these are just the difficulties she was finding day to day. It is so hard to learn the best way to use any tools without face-to-face training.

I also can't say that taking up a feel on the line as I described worked very well either. Even in a Dually halter Solomon would have been incredibly challenging; he simply did not back up at all. Going anywhere near his space to try to move him back seemed to enter into a physical challenge with him and he became threatening. I could quickly see that one advantage of the line-wiggling approach was that I didn't need to go into the horse's space at all, so with a biting horse like Solomon I can see how the line wiggling could actually aggravate the proximity problem less and keep the handler a little safer at more of a distance.

The problem was what to do when gentle line wiggling didn't work at all – how could we set up a situation where Solomon really yielded backward and yet didn't feel he needed to defend himself? The last thing I wanted was to find myself trying to be tougher than him. I didn't even know if I was capable of finding enough tug or shake on the line and enough abrasive-looking body language to drive him back. And if I could find it, I wasn't sure I was ethically OK with the level I would need to go to. I felt like I would actually have to roar at him like a bear to make him move back, which didn't feel much like the most intelligent approach. I wasn't even sure that it would not just be providing another short-term fix that would aggravate the long-term problem further, because Solomon already had so much tension and expectation of discomfort, which I didn't want to add to at all.

I was managing to get the odd shuffle back, but then again Solomon was able to get the odd shuffle back from me too. He was so angry, braced and challenging it felt like a battle, not a successful training strategy. I took a break on the backing up altogether, clipped a second line on the halter and gave one rope to Naomi, while I kept hold of the other. At least this way we could keep each other safe, since if Solomon went for Naomi I could pull him off before he made contact and vice versa. This worked an absolute treat, since when he lunged at one person the correction didn't come from that person at all, but from the other side of his head. We kept our body language fairly neutral, and our emotion steady and relaxed, and simply reset the rules of the world that if he tried to go for either person, he was magically stopped in his tracks from somewhere else. I knew we were on to a better tactic here, because pretty quickly we got to a place where he was relaxed and able to stand calmly between the two of us, contemplating his proximity with people in a slightly new light. But Solomon still didn't want to be handled; there was certainly no way that a stroke would be rewarding. In fact, when I tried to find a pleasant place to scratch him, you could almost see his skin creeping with disgust, his nostrils wrinkled and lips pursed.

The next step was to find a way to help Solomon accept human touch again. For this I needed an arm extension – not only because I value mine just the shape they are, but also because it would clearly be too much to expect Solomon to be able to deal with the proximity and touch of people at the same time. Using something to make my arms longer meant I could deal with touch from a distance first and make the process less stressful for us both. At home, we use a bamboo cane with a glove and a fake sleeve. I needed something makeshift that would do the same job. What could I find that was light and flexible and about a metre long? Well, I never thought I'd hear myself saying, 'Can you pass me the carrot stick, please?' but I did!

Solomon didn't seem to mind the stick moving around him or right near him, but when it first touched his withers he was beside himself. Biting at the stick savagely, jumping toward it. I made sure to release the touch only when he showed a moment of relaxation, and still used two lines to make sure we were both safe, preventing Solomon from repeating his destructive behavioural pattern of defence/attack. Naomi pointed out that this was similar to an exercise Parelli calls 'The friendly game', which she has been doing with her own horse. Soon, he was standing still with the lines loose, accepting the touch of the stick on his withers, but he was still very stressed, showing displacement stress signs like throwing his head, grinding his teeth, popping his lip, pawing the ground, and still occasionally reverting to snatching at the stick with his teeth or throwing his shoulder into it. I tried making the releases in pressure much bigger by coming further away from him frequently and staying away for longer, but this only slightly improved things. Although we were seeing some good results in terms of the frequency of biting, it was pretty heart-breaking to watch how desperate this guy was feeling. I wasn't entirely happy that we had found the ideal method for him yet, but wasn't quite sure how to improve the strategy.

Thinking perhaps he just needed longer at this simple level for it to really sink in, I left two staff members working with him in this manner while I met my second student, Pongo. Pongo had a much happier expression; he looked less tormented than Solomon, and more of a Jack the Lad, though there was also a degree of head-shyness that told me he too had seen rough times. Pongo was not led like a normal horse, it was more a case of him herding his handler about from behind, biting whenever they went too slowly. I was warned, 'If he bites you, he won't let go; he bites down hard and hangs on tight!'

Pongo's big problem was saddling and mounting, when the manners issue became really very dangerous. I started with some basic ground-work, getting better control of his feet, while setting up a nice big personal space boundary, which he was not welcome to come within. Pongo was easier to move about than Solomon, but when I struggled to get him backing up as softly as I'd like, I decided to try an audio stimulus.

I went for the bottle of pebbles, and it worked an absolute treat!

I was really worried that, as there was a serious language barrier between the staff and me, they would simply misinterpret this training method as scaring him into submission with the noise. I really tried to enforce the importance of the timing, using a good dose of mime, like equine training charades! Pongo was given a soft aid with body language to move backward first, followed by a few short, sharp shakes of the bottle if he didn't move back. This noise had to be stopped the moment he shifted backward at all, and couldn't be done with malice or in punishment. I tried to emphasise that the noise was only there to create the correct reaction, so that Pongo could pair that reaction with our chosen aid. It was there as an explanation for him and a way to set him up to succeed in giving us the right behaviour. I only needed it three times; after which Pongo backed up softly and calmly without any biting or resistance at all. Fantastic! The biting for Pongo had been as much about confusion and frustration, not sure what really was required of him, and what the boundaries were. He'd found he could explore and investigate the relationship as well as control the people he was unsure about through challenging behaviour. The clearer the boundaries were, the happier Pongo looked.

Knowing that tacking up was one of the worst problems, I began work with a saddle pad. As soon as he saw it he began to fidget, and as it was lifted onto him he flinched as though it was burning his skin. Once it was on his back he dug at the floor, gnashed his teeth, began tooth grinding and tail swishing, and actually turned and bit at his own shoulders, aiming a good few swipes at me as well. I decided to start smaller and folded it into a little ball, hoping the shape was unrecognisable to him, and rubbing it on his neck rather than back and, as always, releasing the pressure of course by taking it away any time his reaction was positive or accepting, and building up the level of stimulus in very small increments. There was a great improvement and after a few minutes we put him away to think about it. Over the next few sessions he made incredible progress.

During this initial time with Pongo, Solomon had very seriously tried to attack his groom, launching himself and biting his head – this had happened when he tried to get Solomon to back up, which wasn't what I meant him to be doing at all. I assumed he had used the stick on Solomon's chest, or some pretty 'hearty' body language and Solomon had felt threatened and reverted to acting defensively. Luckily Tono was not too badly hurt, and they had put Solomon away for me to have another go with later.

I needed to rethink. Why was it that all these horses were so aggressive? Most were ex-racehorses and clearly they had been subjected to some appalling treatment in their previous careers as well as to some tough handling by the staff since their arrival here. But the vast majority of abused horses become nervous and flighty; protecting themselves instinctively usually involves getting away from danger at all costs. Why did all these horses turn so quickly to their 'fists' first and look to fight instead of flight?

I asked Naomi and her answer was enlightening. Partly, she felt, it was because the horses are all stabled 24/7 so the stress and frustration level is naturally high. She also filled us in on some of the specific methods the staff used to reprimand the horses, which we found shocking. The horses were cross-tied, which meant tying their head still with two ropes, one on each side, and then they were hit about the head. That means they didn't even have room to turn their head away when struck, let alone to run away from the pain and fear. With no option to exercise their flight response, I could only assume the horses had tried out their other options, and the last resort of reacting violently had obviously bought them some control over their environment and paid off enough times to become a coping mechanism.

When I asked Naomi where the staff had learnt to treat horses that way, she replied that some had worked in racing stables on Java. This meant, I guessed, that this treatment might be used there as well, and explained why the horses arrived with some of these anger issues straight from the track.

I generally have very little trouble making connections with all sorts of horse people including those who have different ethical boundaries to me. I've worked successfully with owners and trainers who are tougher on horses, or softer on horses, than I am. I've tried never to judge others on their ethical boundaries since we are all trying to figure out the murky waters of what is and isn't ethically acceptable. I've simply tried to help where I can and learn what I can. For a few moments though, when the realisation of the extent to which these horses had been systematically abused dawned on me, I felt sick. To deliberately and regularly take the flight response away from the horse and then beat him, and also to confine him to the point that he can't even turn his head away and flinch, was such an awful, unnecessary trauma for a species that is really very trainable and generous given half the chance.

There was, however, no time to ponder my sympathy for the horses and my own feeling of responsibility to put right the awful abuse that humans had caused them. I certainly didn't want to make Naomi feel any worse than she already did about the treatment of the horses – she had only recently been able to acquire the knowledge about what was happening behind closed doors, had obviously banned the practice of hitting the horses at all, but was still desperately struggling to gain enough control over her staff to stop it continuing. We needed to get on with doing what we could to find proactive plans for change in the time available.

No wonder it had been so hard to get the horses to back up; the cross tying had taught them that they couldn't back away from human aggression and pain, they had to stand and take it or fight back. I realised that a key to helping the horses move on was in getting their feet moving again, showing them that they weren't trapped and that, if they needed to, they had the right to walk away from a situation that was scary for them. This isn't something that I often allow horses to do when teaching them manners, but I had a gut feeling that freeing up the horses' feet might help them reconnect with their instinct to move away from, rather than fight, the things they found challenging. This would be a much healthier evasion for them to show and an easier one to deal with. I also was so pleased with the effect of shaking the bottle of pebbles for Pongo that I decided to use it with Solomon, hoping that the audio stimulus would get his feet loosened up to moving backward, without having to use any physically uncomfortable encouragement.

The combination of allowing Solomon to move away from touch, and backing him up with the pebble noise if he came into my space, worked an absolute treat. During the next session Solomon improved so much that I could touch him all over with the stick without needing a second handler to keep me safe, and by the end of the session I was able to softly stroke him on the neck, with him standing still and looking, for brief moments, pretty darn relaxed. My heart absolutely sang when after a minute or two of tolerating touch he gently stepped away into his own space and sighed. OK so he still wasn't choosing human contact for long periods of time, but he had a much healthier way of telling me when he needed to get away.

The third horse I met had now been taken off work altogether since she was just too dangerous. During saddling and mounting she was so vicious in her behaviour that the only management technique that had worked to get tourists on her back was to get a good hold on her tongue out the side of her mouth, and several handlers to contain her. Remarkably, she had only been used for novice riders, since they were led, and she was too dangerous to be ridden off the lead line. Leading work was treacherous for the handler, who was bitten and pulled about throughout the ride. Her name was Gabby.

Gabby was a dark bay mare of about 15hh who had small ears and piercing eyes. She looked like she might have been part Arab because of her deep jaw and tiny muzzle. Poor Gabby was simply terrified, and very well understood how to control the people she was so afraid of. When you opened her stable door, she didn't flinch to the back of the box in terror, she met you head on, teeth bared, ears back, and protecting her space. Getting her halter on would be a suitable sport for an adrenaline junkie.

I absolutely congratulate Naomi on the differences she had already made to Gabby. I fully believed her accounts that by working on personal space boundaries, and practising lots of ways to control her feet through the Parelli exercises, Gabby's aggressive tendencies had subsided. Naomi was only three months into working with Gabby and was finding a few things challenging. Gabby would 'explode' very quickly with no warning, suddenly spooking, bucking, rearing, kicking out and trying to run. Naomi found this behaviour unpredictable, though she knew certain things that would definitely trigger it, backing Gabby up on the way back home for instance. There had also been a recent increase in the amount of biting and Naomi couldn't put her finger on why, given the progress she had initially made through Parelli.

In the first session I watched the Parelli exercises Naomi had been working on at the beach and then we worked through some ground-work. In the second session I felt it would be wise to establish some better foundations in and around the yard as Gabby seemed calmer and less stressed in familiar surroundings. In the third session, as I really got to know Gabby, I thought it was most appropriate to work on really changing the session from the very start, beginning with just standing near Gabby, putting the halter on, and leading her out the box without stress. With this approach, we began to change her attitude rather than simply manage it.

Everything for Gabby was about slowing things down, allowing her to relax, and being super consistent so that she could rely on your behaviour. She seemed to need a reliable set of rules that would keep her safe from human violence, and we could give her exactly that. In every way possible, it was about reinforcing the timing of pressure and release, and not entering into any sort of fight mode. It also made a big difference to her once we taught her to yield her front end and move her shoulders away, since throwing her shoulders into your space and biting was her weapon of choice.

During our sessions, Naomi learned to spot the very early signs that Gabby was starting to take control, or starting to become stressed. If she reacted early enough, before things had spiralled, Naomi was able to correct Gabby clearly but very subtly. It was wonderful to watch the two of them tiptoe slowly in and out of the barn, calm and relaxed. By the end of our last session, Naomi could approach Gabby in the stable and put the halter on quietly without any sign of stress or resistance, and while I had shown her a few techniques to help, mostly this had been achieved by just slowing down and doing very little. The real lesson for Naomi was that things with Gabby could be subtle, slow and gentle, and in fact needed to be, if she was going to avoid the epic battles that the mare was capable of. This didn't mean being soft on her – if anything, it meant being more of a stickler for perfection and more consistent in corrections; it was just all happening a good few notches down on the stress/adrenaline level.

In true collaborative style, it was actually a conversation with Hannah after the first session that inspired me to take things so very slowly and thoroughly on the subsequent ones. It was Hannah, too, who noticed the only interested member of staff, Tono, practising with Pongo in his own time, and she gave me the heads up to spend some time working on his timing. Training always ends up a sort of collage, a creation of all the people present who bounce ideas off each other, the books we've read, the demos we've seen, the lessons we've had, the horses who have challenged us in the past and taught us something new, the physical spaces available to work in and the equipment on hand. Training is never a solitary achievement.

The most interesting thing for me was that helping Naomi to find some ways to improve her horses' training did not involve convincing her to move away from Parelli. It had given her a network and a training mentality that she was committed to, and that was clearly going to be a big part of Naomi's future success. While I was able to add in some new and different ideas that aren't on the Parelli DVDs, I know Naomi will be using them in conjunction with the Parelli 'games', levels (of pressure), zones (of the horse's body) and 'horseanalities' in which she finds a useful structure and language. I hope I helped her to better read and relate to the horse in front of her in a way that would be hard to communicate through a DVD alone, so that she could choose which 'game' was appropriate at which time; and I also tried to encourage her to find her own innovative way of thinking so that she could adapt games or invent her own in order to help whichever issues were presenting themselves. While she found the structure of Parelli useful, I tried to give her the confidence not to feel bound to it and to feel able to be a little spontaneous in the way it was applied.

As we left Naomi my heart went out to the lonely job she had, trying to turn things around. She was the lone, shipwrecked trainer, with no other trainers to ask for help, no demos, no friends to bounce ideas off, and she was reaching out and making connections wherever she could. She was warm, welcoming, and sincere in her wishes to improve the lives of her horses. In trying to help Naomi's horses to break down some of their boundaries and begin to welcome outsiders into their worlds again, and in observing the solitary task Naomi had of fighting the one-woman battle to change the handling customs, I couldn't fail to recognise the value of company and connections.

Every horse person has a story to tell and may become a student, teacher, or friend as we all continue to negotiate the ups and downs of horsey life. The thing that was imprinted upon me through this experience was the importance of looking past the image, the discipline, the language and culture, and spotting a good teacher, a good student, a good horse person, or a good friend. In finding someone to learn from, the knack is to look around you for somebody whose horses are happy and successful, and get on with figuring out which bits of his or her programme are relevant to you. With demos, riding clubs, livery yards, and instructors from all sorts of disciplines and attitudes, let alone with the crazy world of the internet, there is now no need for us to be lonely. I thought back to the supportive, conscientious environment at Arthayasa, and to the list of people I would have chatted to about Enya if I were at home. I realised the crucial importance of the right team. It is as vital to your training as your choice of tack; to choose and cultivate the sort of company that is going to be supportive, kind and helpful to you in your horsemanship.

So the moral of this chapter is to take a *Field of Dreams* approach, and immediately begin building the culture and company that you want to be part of in the future. Surround yourself with people who share your priorities and values when it comes to horsemanship, or at least who respect any differences you may have and genuinely want you to succeed with your horse in the ways that are meaningful to you. Remember, if you build it, they will come. There's no guarantee on the ghosts but it's the sure-fire way to the happy ending.

CHAPTER FOUR

✦

WORDS

In Queensland, Australia

DURING OUR FIRST FEW DAYS in Australia it was such a welcome relief to get properly clean, calm and in control again after the relentlessness of pace and regular discomfort in India and Indonesia. I felt like the woman in a particular chocolate advert on TV; everything seemed soft, warm, silky and luxurious just because it was clean and safe. The trains came on time and we didn't feel the need for a shoehorn to get on them. All the signs were written in English and the washing machines worked really well. For a day or two we stayed with a relative in Sydney, Hannah's aunt Sally, and tried to eat our way through the patisserie she owns.

When it was time to hit the road again, we realised that all the comforts of travelling Down Under came with a price tag, and it was one that stretched our backpacker budget to bursting point. Han and I had signed up to something called HelpX. It's a system for travellers whereby hosts who need help, and travellers who need food and beds, can get in touch with one another. We had made a link that looked promising and were hopeful that the sustainable building project on a rainforest commune, near Australia's alternative mecca of Nimbin, wouldn't involve too many moonlit naked ceremonies.

Nimbin is a village in the Northern Rivers area of New South Wales; a small town with lovely views, nestled between hills that were green with either arable land or dense rainforest. It was November, which was local spring, so many of the trees were full of vibrant purple blossom; but nothing was quite as vivid as Nimbin itself. The town had hosted the Aquarius music and counter-culture festival in 1973, in which 10,000 hippies poured into the area to 'peace out'. I think some of them had never left, because forty years later, the festival spirit was still going strong. Every wall, door, or surface was painted with rainbows and flowers in lively colours. The shops sold tie-dyed clothes, herbal remedies and compost toilets, and the tourist bus pulled over on the way into town so the driver could remind its passengers that despite what they had heard, the laws on drugs applied just as much in Nimbin as they did in the rest of Australia. This was slightly hard to believe when the Nimbin museum boasted a beautifully painted sign that read 'Please, no dealing drugs *inside* the museum'.

Luckily, Vicki Thrower, our host, turned out to be really down to earth, and we got down to earth too and could be found for most of the week knee-deep in mud, building a cob wall. Vicki was slight, fun-loving, outdoorsy and strong, with greying blonde hair she wore loose to her shoulders, and a weathered tan. The only sign of her almost total deafness was that she was always shadowed by her beautiful hearing dog, Izzie, a black and white Kelpie cross. Vicki had retired to the commune where she had enough land to grow most of her own fruit and vegetables, and was in this area for the sustainable lifestyle rather than the 'medicinal' attractions. In fact, Vicki didn't take sugar in any form – let alone drugs or alcohol – so we felt fully cleansed after a few days of a sugar-free diet.

Vicki lived in a timber yurt just a short walk from an enchanting forest waterfall, and we stayed in her little caravan at the bottom of the garden. It was a cosy little den, which afforded us a space of our own in a way we hadn't experienced in months. We soon got used to the unbelievably gigantic spider that had expired and dried between two panes of glass in the window. We were visited by a few snakes and spiders during the week, but managed to give them all enough space to enable them to keep their venom to themselves.

Our host's knowledge of the rainforest wildlife was second to none – as was her bravery. She often ran in for show-and-tell with some sort of poisonous ant/rare wasp/thirsty leech clinging to the top of her proudly presented index finger shouting 'Girls, come and see this!' Once she even poked that index finger down a hole, wondering if it might house a venomous funnel spider and, one can only assume, hoping to discover the answer by using her finger as bait.

Other than the cob wall, our jobs included a good dose of tack cleaning, horse feeding, and me spending time with the two 27-year-old mares in the rainforest to stretch their legs and keep them ticking over. I love spotting wildlife when I'm riding, so I was pretty excited when one of the mares spooked a little at a rustling bush. I assumed it had been a pigeon or something but on closer examination it turned out she had shied at a wallaby!

One afternoon, while inadvertently covering ourselves in wood pre-servative more thoroughly than the fence we were trying to paint, Vicki and I got talking about horses, and she mentioned a trainer named John Chatterton, whose clinic she had attended and enjoyed. That evening I watched a little of his DVD, and was impressed enough to want to find out more. Vicki offered to make the three-hour drive to Queensland, and John kindly agreed to let us tag along with his training visits for the day to find out more about his methods.

We found John out by the barn with a little black pony and he looked up and gave us a nod of welcome as he continued to work with her. John seemed, from the outset, a thoughtful, wise horseman. He was calm and slow moving, as though he had tree roots that kept him grounded. He wore blue jeans, a black cowboy hat and a check shirt, and he walked as though he spent more time on a horse than off one.

Miss Muffet was a ten-year-old Dartmoor pony who had been a good broodmare and was now being started under saddle ready for a little girl to ride. It was really calming to watch John prepare her so thoroughly. She was not just learning to be ridden, she was learning to be wormed, shod, to have every part of her handled, to stand patiently for hours of fussing, to get used to all sorts of spooky objects and movement – in short, he was ensuring she was ready to behave like a child's best friend. I especially liked the way that John taught her to flex and soften her neck from the ground. This is an exercise that many trainers, particularly Western trainers, tend to run through with a young horse before starting, but I have rarely seen it completed so carefully and conscientiously.

When John teaches the horse to flex his neck, he picks the tail up in one hand and brings the nose towards him with the other. This is repeated often enough that the horse really knows the game, and when he lays his hand on the tail, the nose comes round to find him and gets a lovely soft stroke. It sounds like a somewhat strange signal, but I have to say it appeared to work really well. I'm not quite sure what the root cause is, but I know that if you can get the horse's jaw and neck to soften and relax then the horse's mind follows suit, so this seemed like a worthwhile area to spend so much time on.

I also really liked the way that John introduced the long-lines. We watched Miss Muffet's second day with the lines, and all that John required from her was that she took a few steps forward when he clicked his tongue. He wasn't bothered about in which direction she went, and if she worried a little and came to a stop he didn't hassle her. He was very clear that he was introducing only one step at a time. He explained his catch phrase: 'Aim for one per cent – the rest will follow'. That's the starting point. Miss Muffet bumbled about the little yard, in and out of her stable, with the lines quite passive – no steering or stopping from them at all. When I introduce long-lines, I will often teach steering and have a trot on the first day, so it was interesting for me to see long-lining introduced more incrementally. I could really see the little mare begin to understand the aid to walk on and offer more and more steps with each attempt.

The whole training session served as a good reminder to me to find enough time to train my young horses diligently to a level of excellence and absolute softness with even simple foundational exercises. It's so easy to pay lip service to the basics and move on to more exciting training once the horse is 'good enough'. John's work with Miss Muffet showed the value in not settling for 'good', but repeating and retraining until even simple tasks can be completed in a wonderfully competent, proficient way. Nothing that John said or did was really a surprise to me or anything altogether new; it mostly focussed on getting the groundwork right, using pressure and release, and building learning progressively.

But what was a surprise was the way he described his methods and distinguished them from everybody else's. I had my first sign of this when I was complimenting him on his work with Miss Muffet. Unfortunately I gave him a compliment that backfired. 'Thank you so much for letting us watch. That was a really wonderful session. It's great to see how much time you are putting into her foundational education. Would you say it's the thoroughness of your approach that sets your methods apart from other natural horsemanship trainers?'

John had been standing with his thumbs hooked in his belt loops, and as he heard the words 'natural horsemanship', he clenched his jaw and stared at the floor. Ali, his female student, piped up quickly, 'Umm ... no, John's not a natural horsemanship trainer at all.'

I don't even know why I had used the phrase – it's not the clearest of terms to use – but now that I had seen his reaction I was curious as to why he was so unhappy about being associated with natural horsemanship. So I apologised for my mistake and asked how he differentiated himself from NH.

'Well,' John said 'I don't believe in hunting a horse about and upsetting him for no reason, that's for sure.' He went on to adamantly stress that his training was absolutely nothing like natural horsemanship in any way, shape or form. This was a bit awkward, as he obviously hadn't realised yet that I had some links with the NH world myself.

To me, he looked like a NH practitioner – he had the outfit, the entourage, the guru-like mellow attitude. He sounded like a NH practitioner, and he obviously used many of the same principles of pressure and release, groundwork, and incremental training. I bet if you took a chunk out of his black cowboy hat it would even taste like a NH trainer, but he was very careful to distinguish himself from NH as he recognised it. This is because, sadly, John had seen many horses ruined by what had been described as NH training.

The natural-horsemanship label has always seemed a bit odd to me too; after all, the *most* natural horsemanship possible probably involves not getting on horses at all and watching them graze in groups from a distance through binoculars. I have also seen some really good horsemanship make use of the horse's natural traits, even if it looks more mainstream and doesn't call itself 'natural'. So when people say 'natural horsemanship' what is it they really mean, and why did John want nothing to do with it?

Well, as I said earlier, for some people it means 'horse huggers', as a lot of the people attracted to NH are looking for a kinder way to interact with their horse. For some people NH refers to trainers from a Western-riding background who have contributed ideas to English horsemanship. For some it refers to the big theatre-style demonstrations and performances that some clinicians put on. For others it means a certain type of language, talking about things in a way that often refers back to the relationship between horse and human – and often emphasises the importance of being trusted and respected by the horse. Many NH clinicians will often talk of the horse seeing you as the leader of the herd.

It was the last point in particular that really riled John. The way he saw it, the quest to become your horse's 'herd leader' was a red herring, encouraging people to do all sorts of daft and sometimes cruel things in order to get their horses to submit and yield to their 'proper place' in the hierarchy. They wasted time working on this hierarchy, sometimes confusing the horse in the process, instead of targeting the training towards more practical aims. He argued that the 'relationship' stuff was overcomplicating things for our own emotional needs, and it was resulting in people feeling like they needed to dominate their horses more than they actually just needed to train them.

Even though ninety per cent of my client base back home probably call me because they would like a better relationship with their horse in one way or another, I could see how John was talking some sense. Sometimes people seem very ready to see things in terms of dominance when there is often a simpler explanation for the horse's behaviour. It might be, for instance, that the horse has just never been taught the advantages of showing more desirable behaviour, or it might be that bad behaviour is linked to pain, fear or confusion rather than a resistance against the human's 'leadership'.

I know many people dislike the old-fashioned advice to 'show your horse who is boss'. In some ways the new fashion for 'leadership' can develop this same idea of achieving 'dominant' status over your horse, and putting most behavioural problems down to the horse's lack of respect: 'he won't go through water because he doesn't trust me'; 'he won't be clipped because he doesn't respect me'; 'he won't go in the trailer because he doesn't obey me'. John feels that maybe he is simply afraid of the water or the clippers (or whatever), and focusing on getting him over that fear would be more productive than pining over his 'faulty' feelings towards you.

Typical human beings; we love it to be all about us – what the horse thinks about us, and how we fit into the picture. The truth is it doesn't make us feel all special and warm inside when the horse doesn't do what we want, so this makes it hard for us to be objective. Maybe John has a point, and sometimes it isn't about our relationship at all, it is simply about systematically training the horse to behave in the correct manner. After all, if you visit another country and inadvertently break the rules, is it because you don't respect the authority of the foreign police or is it just that you don't understand the rules and systems yet? John insisted that rather than describe undesirable behaviour as a product of an unhealthy relationship, it would be better to talk about it as incomplete training. If the horse doesn't lead well, it is because no one has taught him to yet; it has nothing to do with how he feels about you.

I listened to everything John had to say about his training being nothing to do with bond, but as I watched him with Miss Muffet I was convinced that something emotional and social was going on in the way she followed him about like a doe-eyed puppy dog.

We piled into the car to make the journey to John's first appointment. There was Hannah, Vicky, me, John, and two of his students (Ali and Chad), who clearly held John in the highest regard and were keen that I recognised his superior skills and knowledge. During the drive, John and I tried to work each other out. John had initially been quite adversarial about other trainers, and I think it was slightly confounding him that I had some links to NH and yet was not the marketing-obsessed cult member he expected. I was openly complimentary about the work I had seen with Miss Muffet, and when I did challenge his wording or thinking, it was in the name of good, balanced debate rather than trying to humiliate him or get him to back down. I asked him a few awkward questions to encourage him to explore and explain his position on horse human interaction, or his insistence that he used no body language at all in his work, and while some of my questions made him pause and frown for a few seconds, I listened to his answers attentively and respectfully. I think he was not at all sure what to make of me and whether we were going to be great friends or terrible enemies. I almost tipped that balance the wrong way at one point when I put my foot in my mouth.

As John was showing me his own design of halter, I piped up, 'Yes, and I bet your halter doesn't come with a ridiculous price tag either!' I suppose I hoped it would help us to bond with each other if I said something anti-NH. This was a really bad idea. It's always a bad idea to try to bond with people through being negative about others, and karma gave me a kick in the teeth when Ali looked away awkwardly and John muttered 'Actually it's $77.' Cringe. Slow-motion silence. The car felt suddenly very small. 'Oh, but it *is* very well made,' I offered as an olive branch. I thought to myself: look, this guy even has his own loyal followers and a pricey gimmick – how much more NH can you get?!

On the remainder of the journey John continued to clarify why his training was unique, with Ali and Chad occasionally chipping in like backing singers. John emphasised that he didn't do any of what he called 'hunting about' or chasing; he didn't agree with 'getting up in the horse's face' to challenge him, or in pushing and pulling him about. The language he used about the techniques he disliked was pretty emotive but not that pragmatically descriptive – chasing a horse, or hunting a horse, or dominating a horse – what *exactly* was it that he thought was unethical? I have to agree that I don't think a horse should be dominated, unless, of course, you consider controlling your horse to be dominating him. Would lungeing a horse count as chasing? It would be hard to listen to John talk and not be won over by his standpoint against NH. But while it was clear that he didn't agree with a horse being terrorised round a pen and chased until it was foaming in sweat, I wasn't sure that John was really distinguishing his own actions from other *good* trainers, so much as distinguishing himself from simply awful training under a NH banner.

Fundamentally, it seemed his approach was practically very similar, but conceptually, he chose a totally different route to describe it.

One clear difference with John's method was that he did not like to back a horse up. He saw it as challenging the horse unnecessarily. I wondered how on earth he coped without backing a horse up. It's such a valuable tool in teaching any horse to lead, and to stand, at a comfortable distance from the handler. It's often pretty quick and easy to teach, and can really transform the attitudes and habits of many nippy or bargy horses. I wondered what John *did* do to maintain his own space and, if he did nothing, what affect did this have on the horse's behaviour?

And while I sound like I'm the expert on backing up – let me tell you I haven't got it all filed away and finalised happily in my head either. Having recently come away from the aggressive horses in Bali, I was all too aware that backing up is not always easy. It seems to me that with the horses for whom it is perhaps most essential, it also presents the biggest ethical dilemma. With the very rare horses who are really going to throw themselves over the top of you, who are very aggressive (usually defensive – but just as dangerous), or what I would describe as 'fighty', backing up seems the best way to keep yourself safe. It can help the horse to relax in his own space and prevent the battle between horse and handler continuing. However, getting those first few steps backward with that type of horse can be really tough! I'm always on the lookout for the least fractious way to inspire the horse to move back and maintain my own personal space boundary.

This is not easy, and the couple of times that I have come home from work wondering if I might have been too tough on a horse have both been when teaching 'fighty' horses to back up. Could it be that John had a way of working with these horses that gets them onside, relaxed and willing without needing to back them up at all? I could hardly believe it, but I certainly hoped so, and I hoped I'd get to see it, learn it, and take it back home.

Having talked through all of this in the car, we were pretty ready for some fresh air and thinking space by the time we arrived at the first client's place. We were in a flat, green landscape with empty roads (not unlike Norfolk) and the property we pulled up at consisted of a series of small paddocks, each about half an acre with a field shelter in one corner. John was going to work with Icey, a 14hh Cremello yearling with blue eyes – but Icey was nervous and shy, and she wasn't sure she wanted to work with John yet.

She was proving a little tricky to catch. John used a form of negative reinforcement that he calls 'face-up'. During this process, if the horse runs away, John swings his rope in order to put the horse under pressure. If the horse turns to look at him or steps towards him, he drops the pressure, lets the rope hang still, and backs up a pace or two. The idea is that the horse will learn that coming towards the human is the most comfortable option.

So, as John walked toward Icey, she looked, spooked, turned and ran away, and he then began to swing the rope in large circles. Seeing this, at first, she sped up further away from him, ears straining backwards to keep an eye on the rope. She fled to the furthest corner of the paddock. John continued to walk toward Icey and she turned her head away from him, ducked back on herself and ran skittishly to the other end. Things continued like this for quite a while before Icey turned to look at John and he stopped swinging the rope and stepped back.

This process has some similarities with one called 'advance and retreat' that I was taught by Kelly Marks and continue to explore with the other IH tutors. Both methods are ways of catching a tricky horse. However, in advance and retreat, the level of pressure is much lower – I'd suggest it's almost negligible, as the focus isn't so much on making it uncomfortable for the horse to do the wrong thing, as it is on inspiring the horse to come with you. To do that, the way you use your body is really important, the angle that you move towards the horse and away from him, the timing of when you wait and when you walk, the direction you walk, the amount of eye contact to use, all make a difference to how likely it is that you will draw the horse to you. It is a totally addictive art to keep working on these skills and to become one of those people who can 'feel' how to draw a horse nearer. In simple terms, you move towards the horse and, as soon as you have his attention on you – before he moves off – you turn and walk away. There is no driving or extra pressure involved.

Sometimes the horse will follow, but almost always, he will let you a little nearer the next time. If the horse does walk off, you follow him, but with a nervy horse I wouldn't personally add any more pressure or encouragement for the horse to move away at all, especially not in a large field, and especially not with a horse who looks worried; you might just end up driving them away and reinforcing their fear. It would be like trying to teach someone to open their eye by poking them in the eye until they did – the pressure/release logic makes sense but the choice of stimulus would be working against you.

Icey spent about twenty minutes running about the paddock in a worry about the rope swinging. I can see how the rope swinging might work really well for a horse who is just a bit clever about being caught and doesn't fancy coming in because he is enjoying the spring grass, but for one who has some fear, like Icey, I think a more passive system like advance and retreat would have worked better. I have to say, though, that John's timing was incredibly consistent. He remained calm and patient and took all the time in the world when Icey did think of coming to him.

Eventually, his diligence paid off. And what he did then was fantastic, rather than catch her up and get on with his own agenda, he gave her a rub and left the paddock with her watching him, curious about where he had gone. Her owner was then able to enter the paddock and repeat the process and catch her within a few minutes. Many trainers would think the real training was only just about to begin with whatever else they had planned, but John's choice, to end the lesson on that good note, impressed me, and was another insight into the benefits of John's approach.

At the next yard we called at, our subject was called Jelly's Baby – or JB. Another youngster, this time a little younger and still with mum. JB was still covered in babyish chestnut fuzz, but was lithe and handsome, already made of muscle, full of youthful energy and boyish confidence and desperate for someone to rough play with.

John initially used the same process as with Icey to encourage JB to stand with him rather than run away. After this he was very careful in preparing JB thoroughly for his first halter. He was clear that JB should be happy to be handled all over the head before the halter went on. He did this using some smooth, slow movements of his hands over JB's eyes, ears, and poll, and one particular movement that surprised me involving JB's muzzle.

I've generally understood this area of the horse to be very sensitive and also fairly personal – horses don't go around being tactile with each other's muzzles and faces as a dog or cat might. They tend to scratch each other on the neck or back and rarely have nose to nose contact. When they do touch noses it is often not a low adrenaline, relaxing situation, but a first meeting or a play fight. Generally, I have given a polite and respectful distance to the horse and refrained from fussing or rubbing the nose and muzzle, preferring to go to stroke the neck; it seems less likely to invite nibbling, mugging or pushing, and they simply seem to enjoy it more.

I was totally surprised by the affect that John had when he placed his whole hand gently under the muzzle and cupped it. In fact we saw him do this with every horse that day, and although it took them a moment to understand how to relax into the feel of it (he used pressure and release, taking his hand away once they relaxed) all of the horses seemed to really soften into his hand and even gently seek out the chance to rest their muzzle in his palm; no nibbling or fussing, just gentle relaxation. It was very nice to watch, I can't quite believe that it wasn't just fluke, but you can't ignore four flukes in a row!

I was then able to see a little of John's approach to nibbling with JB. When JB nipped, John would immediately swing the rope towards his back end – sometimes catching him over the rump two or three times, and JB would rush off. John would then keep swinging the rope until JB turned to face him, at which point he would go back to the exercise he had been working on before the nip. I was a little concerned that this might encourage JB to kick out at John as he scuttled past, or to develop a 'hit and run' habit of biting and dashing off, but while it took a good few repetitions, JB did seem to drop his playful streak and become a little more sedate and less likely to nip.

What was really interesting to me was that John did not see this as 'sending him away' or as 'moving his feet' or as 'maintaining his own personal space' or as 'driving him off'; he wasn't happy with any of this wording to describe his actions. He was adamant that all he was doing was making the wrong thing uncomfortable for JB and the right thing comfortable.

It really highlighted to me the importance of language; what one man might describe in one way, doesn't work at all for another. I didn't personally feel that John's approach was any more ethical than moving JB back into his own space, and I was interested in John's argument that pushing him back is more confrontational and so he doesn't like to do it.

We all know we want to avoid too much confrontation, for our own enjoyment and safety as well as any ethical issue, but how on earth can we confidently define confrontation? Couldn't swinging the rope over his quarters be seen as confrontation too? I was just getting more confused. John didn't like to be associated with any sort of 'hunting' or 'chasing', yet he had encouraged the first horse to run about the paddock for several minutes. He didn't believe in confrontation, yet he was fine with the rope spanking the colt for nibbling. It was not his ethics that bothered me, and I don't think either horse suffered, it was just the explanations of his ethics that I found muddling. He was able to use wordplay to make his own approach sound much more ethical than anyone else's, yet in practice, the horse's experience during training was certainly not in a new realm of pleasant, painless, fearless training, beyond and above any NH or other technique that I had seen.

On the way to the next appointment, I asked John more about how he would deal with a very bargy or aggressive horse, and he talked me through his 'pull and release' method – whereby you step backwards, further away from the horse, and give a pull on the halter. This is similar to the technique Naomi and I had used with two lines attached to Solomon. But with only one handler pulling the horse towards them, I worried that John's technique would bring the horse further on top of the handler, which could allow things to escalate or become dangerous. I hoped I would be able to see this 'pull and release' technique in action – but unfortunately I was only able to see it used once, in a much more familiar scenario. It was with the next horse, a Warmblood colt who had been roughly handled by a vet. John was visiting to teach the youngster to load onto a trailer. When the colt went to run past John as they came through a gateway, John let him run a little bit on the long rope before giving his 'pull and release' technique. It worked a treat and did bring the colt to a stop. But in this situation, where the horse is trying to leave your space, the pull and release seems perfect, obvious even – it's a shame I didn't get to see it with a horse that is trying to move *you* out of *his* space.

One thing that did seem entirely original (from my experience at least) was John's halter set-up. It was very interesting to hear that John had been through the process of previously using a halter with pressure over the poll, and had found that in inexperienced hands this was likely to cause horses to rear. So he had redesigned his current halter to apply pressure further down on the head, in a less sensitive area. This is exactly the process that Monty Roberts went through in designing his Dually halter, but unlike the Dually, John's halter uses pressure that comes under the chin and cheek.

John told us that he felt the nose is too sensitive an area for pressure, and that the jaw is less likely to cause pain. I wish there was a way we really could know exactly what horses do feel, because I am happy to use a Dually precisely because I'm confident that it doesn't work on an overly sensitive area of the face! But how could I possibly say that with total confidence without having a horse face myself (no comments please)? In my experience, and having looked closely at diagrams of the nervous system of the horse's face, I had no reason to believe that using pressure over the nose is particularly painful. So, yet again, John and I found ourselves singing from the same hymn sheet but coming to different conclusions. His wording when arguing for his halter was almost identical to the way I would have argued for mine, but the logic had manifested itself in quite different pieces of equipment.

All we can do is keep trying different types of halters and watching horses' reactions to them. Pressure halters are described in all sorts of ways and sometimes marketed as though they will somehow instantly imbue their wearer with love and respect for the humans around him. The naked truth is that with any pressure halter, there is going to be some degree of discomfort when it is used. If it was totally comfortable, there would be no motivation for the horse to work out how to release it. Ideally, we need to find a type of pressure that is uncomfortable, rather than painful. I was keen to see how John's halter worked in real life.

John went ahead and loaded the colt very successfully. Rather than grip the rope with a closed knuckle, he used open hands, an elastic feel on the line, and clever angles, to encourage the colt to try a step forward onto the ramp. He then released the pressure, praised the colt, and backed him off the ramp to repeat the process. We saw the colt learn how to release the pressure on the line – which at times was just fingertip light – and begin to develop bravery about the strange ramp, and eventually the small trailer space. Within about fifteen minutes he loaded and looked very settled in the trailer.

John was clearly a thinking horseman. He'd even designed his own trailer to prevent horses scrabbling and falling when travelling. The idea came to him when he was walking around showgrounds and noticed the scratch marks where horses' legs hit the walls. It's quite alarming if you look out for them; almost every trailer has a good dose of these marks, especially where the back legs go. John noticed that the marks were worse on the nearside of the trailer, which he deduced must be from the camber of the road. That meant that horses on the inside were travelling better which, in turn, suggested to him that travelling could be improved by the angle at which the trailer wall hits the floor. His trailer is designed to skirt out and give the horses more room around their legs, so that they can spread their feet but not be encouraged to lean into the wall. I'm not sure if anything similar is made in the UK but I do know plenty of horses travel better when given the whole trailer rather than only one partition space, and so it seems likely to me that a design like this might help those horses to be able to travel more comfortably in company.

The last horse that we saw was an absolutely gorgeous teddy bear of a coloured cob foal. He was no trouble at all for John to handle and worm for his owner. Coloured cobs are rare in Australia, so this little baby was precious to his owner who clearly adored him already. After the session, as the sun went down across the green valley, Hannah stood in the barn and scratched the mare, and the mare scratched the foal, and the foal reached his long nose up and scratched Hannah, and it was lovely for a little while to have a total break from spoken language and just be quiet. It gave me a chance to reflect on the day.

Is backing a horse up challenging him, or is it moving his feet, or is it asserting one's leadership, or teaching him something new? Is swinging a rope at a horse chasing him, dominating him, or making the wrong thing uncomfortable? Is natural horsemanship obsessed with dominance, or is it an escape from traditional methods that are dominance-obsessed? The same actions can be given quite a different spin by the descriptions offered.

John tried to describe his methods in a way that had nothing to do with horse-human relationships since he had come across problems caused by that type of language. But I didn't think John's system of explaining behaviour told the full story either. There is some value in referring to the horse's behaviour as part of a relationship. For one thing, I have seen the remarkable effect it can have on the horse when the handler starts acting in a more confident, authoritative manner. If you tell someone they have to earn the respect of their horse, it can inspire them to become more clear, consistent, emotionally grounded and so practically better at training their horse than they were when they thought his behaviour was nothing to do with their own.

Just like in a job interview, horses can get rubbed up the wrong way by some people and can be totally won over by others. On top of that, over time, horses learn what to expect of you, how much they will enjoy their sessions, and how you are likely to react. However objectively you look at it, I think that could be described as building a relationship, since the horses are developing a bank of memories and lessons about your likely behaviour. What's more, it's not just getting them over their fears that we want to achieve, it is teaching them a new way to react if they are ever afraid by something new in the future. Ideally, the horse has learned to be obedient to you in any situation, which could be described as trusting you to make that decision. Whether you call it a relationship or not, the way you act around the horse has a direct effect on the way they act around you, in that moment, and in the future.

I don't believe horses literally think that we are other (very ugly, two-legged) horses that have been promoted to managerial levels, but I do think there is something innate in them that does respond better to some people, especially people who are comfortable being in control and making confident decisions.

It might be that partly, the 'leadership' language is more useful to people – in getting us to act in a way that horses respond well to – than it is necessarily accurate as a complete way to describe every behavioural interaction that occurs.

If, in some scenarios, the 'leadership' language is actually encouraging people to act with power-crazed paranoia – as can sometimes happen with that whole 'show them who is boss' thing, then I second John Chatterton's point that in those instances it is probably doing more harm than good. It's no good someone talking about love and leadership while they confuse the horse and bash it about hoping that it will eventually 'yield' to their control – which is exactly what John wanted to distance himself from.

Thankfully what matters to the horse is not how we describe things, but how we do things. The experience they get rests on the way we use our bodies and tools to interact with them. The way we use our words has more of an effect on other people. But words are powerful, and for anyone who teaches others, it's important to remember that the language we choose has all sorts of consequences when it is interpreted and passed on by others. The best advice I have, in this tongue-tied tangle of words and abstract concepts, is to avoid falling in love with the theories that sound good, and to keep evaluating the training experiences the horse is actually getting. There could be all sorts of different learning mechanisms, emotional or social processes going on when the horse is learning good or bad behaviour, and it is easy to get confused about which system of language is most accurate and whose systems of description make the most sense. I remain a little bit sceptical about the ability of any wording system to get it 100 per cent accurate all of the time, so I think it is best to keep looking at the horse and recognising his experience. If he looks very scared, confused, in pain, or distressed, someone is doing something wrong whatever they say about leadership, or love, or learning theory. If, like Miss Muffet, he seems calm, willing and clever – something is going well even if you don't quite relate to the system of chatter the trainer chooses.

CHAPTER FIVE

FREEDOM

In Bellingen, Australia

THE SILVER BRUMBY (a brumby is an Australian wild horse) is the star of a series of children's books that had me absolutely hooked as a child. I spent far too much time, up to an embarrassing age, being 'Thowra' – the equine hero of the stories – in the garden. Our Labrador was scripted into various roles: a stallion encroaching on my territory, a snake, a foal ... any non-speaking role really. Occasionally I let him be Thowra so that I could do better justice to the foal's part. Mostly I would just gallop around jumping over things and snorting, and the dog would bounce about being hopelessly canine. To me, and many other children reading the tales, Thowra's adventures in the Australian outback represented freedom. Fifteen years on, Hannah and I were feeling pretty darn free ourselves as we shrugged off our heavy backpacks and made ourselves comfortable on the bus to Bellingen, a small New South Wales town about 300 miles north of Sydney, where we were heading in search of brumbies.

The weather was bright, and we smelled of sweat and sun cream. We sat near the front of the bus and watched the world go by – beautiful purple-blossomed jacaranda trees, green rolling hills. The bus driver –

a skinny, bearded man, whose uniform made him look like an adult boy scout – really seemed to be enjoying his job. He must have caught me looking at him, because he stopped humming to himself and asked where we were headed. We explained that we were off to Bellingen as we had received an invitation to visit the Save the Brumbies centre and learn more about how they tame the brumbies ready for rehoming. We told him a little about the nature of our equine adventures so far. Suddenly, an idea hit him as though he had been slapped round the face with a wet flannel, and his jaw dropped open. 'Well, you gals just gotta meet Buffalo!' he exclaimed with excitement. He became increasingly animated as he told us that Buffalo was a 'mountain man' who lived up in the hills and tamed wild brumbies. 'Now just wait there a jiffy and I'll see what I can do.'

With that he pulled the bus over to the side of the road, hopped out and made himself busy on his mobile phone – tracking down a way to contact this Buffalo fellow. Before long he was grinning and nodding and giving us the thumbs-up gesture – something of a plan was afoot. He had left a message with 'Janine' who would let Buffalo know that two girls from Britain were staying at the local youth hostel and wanted to meet him to learn about his methods of horse training. Hopefully, if Buffalo felt like it, he would find a way to contact us – we had no phone at the time. We thanked Rob profusely when he dropped us off – I'd been quite amazed by how willing he was to go out of his way to help us out, and he waved us off with one final warning: 'Hey gals ... that Buffalo ... he's a bit of a rough diamond. But you'll be OK because you're together. You won't hear from him after 6pm, and if you do, best to wait and respond in the morning – he likes a beer in the evening. But you'll be fine in the daytime. You'll be fine. Good luck, gals!'

And then we were standing on the side of the quiet road, watching the bus disappear and feeling bemused. Still, there was nothing to do but wait and see how it all panned out, so we heaved our bags onto our shoulders and set off in search of the youth hostel. Bunks bagsied and tea consumed, we were ready to track down the Save the Brumby group in this area. Only problem, they were not within walking or cycling distance from the town itself, or our accommodation, or any public transport. But where there's a will there's a way, and if nothing else I'm a woman who knows the power of a good chocolate cake – so with a little eyelash fluttering and offering of baked goods, we were able to borrow the youth hostel's radically painted minibus. After nearly three months of public transport, we had our own graffiti-clad wheels for the first time. We remembered how to drive, then chugged off up into the mountains, feeling as wild and free as the brumbies we were hoping to meet.

We found the wooden gateway to the brumby centre halfway up a steep mountain-forest road and, as we proceeded along the driveway, the fields opened up in front of us and I began to spot brumbies grazing. We parked the minivan by the wooden stable block and were welcomed in by Jan Carter (Save the Brumbies founder), Megan Hyde (who is usually based at their Armidale site, New South Wales) and Lilly (Megan's ten-year-old daughter). Jan had a soft smile and her long hair was done up in a bun, and Megan's demeanour was as bouncy as her short curly hair. Jan and Megan were tirelessly devoted to the breed and every individual of it. They filled us in on the basics of the brumbies' predicament.

Brumbies are descended from horses who were brought into Australia by human settlers and escaped captivity, and so are not native to the country. They are considered a feral pest as their numbers are increasing (I believe that estimations are near a million now). Save the Brumbies aims to provide an alternative to culling as a control on the population; they trap the brumbies, tame and train them, and find them suitable homes. These are not feral horses like ours in the UK, which are routinely rounded up, wormed and medicated, these guys are totally unhandled and will never, up to this point, have had their movements restricted or directed by man.

The brumbies are trapped using salt licks, hay and water as bait. The traps are erected, the bait is set and the brumbies are then given time to get used to the semi-permanent corrals/traps, which are shaped like a clover leaf. As the horses come and go, they become increasingly relaxed in the traps and, once they are acclimatised to the space, a remote-control gate is operated to shut the brumbies in. The clover-leaf corral becomes an ideal environment to divide the group into smaller family groups ready for transport to the centres in Armidale or Bellingen, where they will be rehomed onto private land as a breeding group, or tamed and trained and found homes as domestic riding horses.

The alternatives were bleak – debates still raged about the future of the breed. In their current numbers they had an impact on the environment that was deemed damaging: from soil compaction caused by their hooves, to tree damage, trampling of native vegetation and spread of disease to domestic horses. There was also apparently a widespread assumption that they were weak and diseased animals with high levels of inbreeding. Save the Brumbies disputed this, pointing out that in their area DNA testing had shown less inbreeding than in the modern Thoroughbred industry. Much of their work also aimed to show off the quality and strength of the breed and raise their profile. One thing was clear, the brumbies were a man-made problem, but man was struggling to find an ethical, humane, cost-effective, environmentally efficient, long-lasting solution.

Discussions were still divided with many claiming fertility control is not cost-effective and mustering is over stressful and so culling remains the main solution. Jan and Megan insisted that there was a real market for brumbies, who should be given more credit as a heritage breed and brought increasingly into domestication as a competition, work and leisure horse. There was also an argument for leaving a well-managed population wild on specifically allocated areas of land, valued as an iconic image of Australian freedom.

I was particularly interested in how the wild brumbies are initially handled, since I teach the handling of feral horses on courses in England and I'm always on the lookout for other tricks of the trade. The system that Jan and Megan use to initially handle the horses involves a chute or crush. Theirs is a wooden construction that is not much bigger than the size of a horse, with gaps between the wooden boards to make human/ horse contact possible for worming, management or training. I've seen different ways for a chute to be used. At its worst, it can be used to confine a terrified animal and force it to accept handling. This is not only a dangerous experience for horse and handler (they can kick through bars, climb walls, flip over backwards, pin arms and more) but it can also be such a traumatic experience that it leaves long-lasting mental scars.

However, any tool is only as good as the people who use it, and as Jan and Megan talked me through their use of the equipment I could see it was a well thought out and considered approach. The underlying ethos is to use the small space to show the horse that touch does not hurt after all, and that human contact isn't scary, in order to get the first halter on without prolonging or imbedding the fear of it. I could certainly see the sense in this.

Although one would imagine that bigger spaces with an easier option to run away would create more stress-free training, many horse people across the globe have found this simply isn't the case. When horses run away from something, the fear of it is reinforced. Allowing horses to run away from something is not a great welfare decision and can ingrain a fearful habit. Behavioural scientists and practical horse trainers alike have found the same phenomenon to be true: setting up a scenario that does not allow a major flight response to happen keeps the horse calmer and allows training to progress more quickly.

When I was about eighteen years old I attended, as a student, the course I now teach and I remember that the first exercise was to try to get as close as possible to a wild horse in a sixty-foot round pen. In this size of space, it was easy for the horse to move away, so, despite my very best efforts at using body language and timing, I was nowhere near putting a halter on that horse. The idea of the exercise is to show students the value of having the right type of space to work in, and the contrast in results and stress levels between the smaller space in which the horse has become relaxed and the greater space in which the horse has more freedom.

We tend to use an open corral about the size of a foaling box. In this size space, the horse is more confined and, I reiterate, you would think this would mean he is more stressed, but in fact this is not the case. As long as you progress with small incremental steps, horses very quickly

Australia

overcome their fear and begin to enjoy the handling. While they have room to move a little, the full-on flight response is not an option, and the physical boundaries encourage them to explore new behaviours.

This is not the same thing as simply grabbing a wild horse and trying to force him to accept handling. It is not a matter of either free choice on the one hand, or confinement and forced acceptance on the other. There is a middle ground, where the environment sets the horse up to try the right behaviour and the clever trainer makes sure the experience is as stress-free as possible. Over time, while teaching on this course, I have noticed that horses given the most choice and freedom of movement during this first exercise are always a bit trickier to train through the rest of the course than the ones who are started in the smaller space from the beginning.

At eighteen I found it hard to reconcile and accept the idea that cheating the horse out of the option to run could be in his favour. But now I find examples of the same lesson in all sorts of places – and there is a big difference between controlling the horse's available choices and 'forcing' the horse. The difference, I think, is that forcing involves struggle, resistance, stress, whereas controlling the horse's choices in a clever manner should do precisely the opposite.

With this all in mind, I was willing to believe that Megan and Jan could use the chute to train the wild horses in a way that was not cruel or forceful and the outcome of the brumbies' training was lovely, if the ones we met were anything to go by. Each horse wandered up happily to say 'hi' when we entered their paddocks, and were very polite company while we gave them a rub.

Brumbies in the flesh are everything I hoped they would be: 14–15hh, a little broader than the average New Forest pony, with straight sturdy legs, good sloping shoulders, a deep girth and strong back. Their faces vary, you can see traits of their mixed heritage in each one: a noble Thoroughbred nose, deep Quarter Horse cheeks, wide Arab eyes, or ponyish ears, which means they all have their own character, but nothing overstated or flashy. I really enjoyed riding the little star of the centre, Kelly. She was a strong-looking liver chestnut who had been out winning in the show ring against Warmbloods in hunter classes. She was even having a darn good stab at dressage, with an ideal trainer in Megan, who before her brumby days worked in Thoroughbred racing and competed in dressage to Grand Prix level.

We had a lovely morning riding. We all rode, swapping horses between us and getting new ones out to play. I loved the real feeling of collaboration with Megan as we discussed various exercises to try out in order to improve each horse's way of going. Before I wanted to leave, it was time to go, and it was only when Hannah and I were back in the van that I learned the real gravity of the brumbies' predicament.

While I had been playing ponies and talking training with Megan, Hannah had been learning Jan's story and that of the brumbies' history and future too. I had assumed that the brumbies were being dealt with in a similar way to the USA's management of mustangs, but things had been quite different here. In 2000, 600 brumbies in Guy Fawkes National Park were shot from helicopters with many badly wounded and left to die a slow painful death. Jan joined the mass uproar when the news found its way into the media. She was a professional harpist and in the wake of the shootings she wrote an album that reflected the different periods of a brumby's life and dedicated herself and her profits to starting the Save the Brumbies organisation. I couldn't believe it when I heard that there was a strong argument in government to eradicate the wild brumbies entirely within five years. It was sickening to hear that whilst some states, largely thanks to people like Jan and Megan, were considering and exploring alternatives, others continued to march forward with their 'management' schemes of mass culling from the air. I had been so naive, living in my childish brumby daydream for the afternoon. I had foolishly assumed that there would always be some brumbies living wild amongst the Australian mountains. I had thought Jan and Megan were doing a good job in trying to find homes for surplus wild brumbies but hadn't realised that they were fighting against a plan of eradication for the entire population. The scale of the past and potential future cullings left me sincerely shaken.

We drove back quietly absorbing the morning's experience, returned the minibus and discovered that Buffalo had left a message with staff. Apparently he would be calling in for us in due course. The response of the local staff only left us more perplexed and intrigued. They were very confused as to why the local mountain man would be leaving messages at the youth hostel for the British girls. They raised their eyebrows and sucked their teeth. Buffalo was described as 'quite a character' with a 'bit of a reputation', and more often than not 'rough diamond' was the term people settled on. 'Rough diamond,' I thought, 'what does that even mean...and is the emphasis on rough, or on diamond?'

I was expecting to see a children's book character who looked like a pirate on horseback, but wearing one of those Australian hats with corks on strings, and brandishing a boomerang. I silently hoped he'd greet us with a growled, 'Arrgghh, g'day' and a wink of his glass eye.

Buffalo's arrival didn't disappoint. He did indeed turn up on horseback, with one in tow for me to ride, but (thank goodness) he was not half as scary as I was expecting. I think the beard was the rough bit and the toothy smile was the diamond. Though missing the pirate wooden leg, he did have one arm in plaster – a bad break from a horse-related injury – but this didn't seem to give him any reason to alter his usual routine of riding and training the brumbies or driving his truck.

He asked Hannah to drive his truck and trailer to a meeting point and she set about getting it out of the lay-by ditch in which it was stuck in first gear.

Buffalo's horse, a fairly legendary brumby stallion in this part of the world, was called 'Me Mate'. His gigantic, bear-sized slobbery dog was called 'Big Dog' or 'B.D'. It took me a while to get used to the names. Every time Buffalo spoke about his horse – 'So, do you like Me Mate?' or 'Watch out for Me Mate' – I was looking around to identify the person he was referring to. I also wasn't quite sure how an outsider should refer to the stallion. Was the etiquette to call him 'Your-mate?' or was he 'Me-Mate' to everyone?

I was given a bright bay horse, the lovely Kaysan, to ride. Buffalo (real name Dave) and I chatted about horses while we rode, and then we loaded the horses into the trailer and headed out to one of his fields in a town called Dorrigo, to meet some of his youngsters. As with many journeys in Australia this involved a surprising lurch into spectacular scenery as we crawled up a steep road, through the rainforest and alongside thundering waterfalls to Dorrigo.

I'd been preparing myself to see some pretty rough-and-ready horsemanship – I mean, men from the mountains aren't always known for their gentle approach – but I was ready to learn what I could and find the positive about anything he was willing to share with me. We pulled up at a gateway to a fifteen-acre field that had once comprised several separated paddocks but whose fencing had fallen down and gorse-type bushes had taken over much of the grassland. To our surprise Buffalo took a box of apples into the field, balanced precariously on his plastered arm, and began to call, 'Come on, me babies. Buffalo's here. Come on, come on, me babies,' in a high-pitched voice. The herd galloped over as a group and the bravest of them began to plunder the apples at speed, while Buffalo cooed at the mob of gobbling brumbies, giggling when they got a bit rowdy like he'd been tickled by a feather. The brumbies pinned back their ears at each other, and at Buffalo, and chased one another off the booty. None was well handled or easy to catch; this was a semi-feral gang of entire colts, mares and foals behaving like badly organised armed bank robbers in a vault.

Buffalo was evidently a guy who loved his horses, and he couldn't stop smiling as he dodged the odd charge and threw more apples at their feet. Eventually, there was nothing to be done but abandon the box entirely and retreat haplessly to join us at the gate and watch the feeding frenzy. If Buffalo's story was to be made into a film (and by God it should be) then this scene would have to be played by Bill Bailey. My prejudices and expectations about Buffalo's tough mountain-man approach to training dissolved into giggles of surprise and relief. He was as much in love with his horses as every little girl in England, and I had no problem relating to that.

We had returned to our youth hostel that evening and the following morning, just as Han and I were polishing up our thumbs ready to hitchhike up to Buffalo's nearest town, his friend, the lovely Michelle, who we'd met the day before, turned up at the hostel to give us a lift. Apparently Buffalo had been online and seen our blog from the rest of our trip. He had decided that he was going to impress us with his horse training and feature in the blog. The thing is, I had been thinking about the broken arm. It had apparently happened when Buffalo had planned to serve a mare with a particular stallion and then realised he didn't want that stallion on that mare after all. He decided to intervene and abort the planned encounter much to the resentment of both the amorous stallion and the willing mare. This and the apple-riot had left me wondering where this was all going; he seemed like a nice chap, but was I going to have anything to learn from this guy? I pondered these things on the way to his place, which was more than a little out the way in the middle of nowhere found by turning left at the dead kangaroo and following the 4 x 4 flattened path through the undergrowth.

The first job of the morning was to teach two-year-old Cedar to load. Most of Buffalo's brumbies take their names from Australian plants. Cedar was quite tall for a brumby, and rangy. He was greying out but looked like he was probably born a bay, and was in that lovely in-between stage that looks like bonfire smoke. It quickly transpired that Cedar had previously had very little lead training at all, and didn't seem to have a basic grasp of the relationship between the pulling sensation on his head, and the movement required of his feet. Nonetheless, Buffalo cheerfully managed to wobble him over toward the trailer, which was in the middle of quite a big field full of grass and other horses. This situation was giving Cedar a whole lot of freedom to make the wrong choice, ignore the bearded pulling man, stay in the big grassy space and refuse to get into the small dark cave on wheels.

Buffalo was willing to give anything a go. He tried a few different things to convince Cedar that the best choice was to get in the trailer.

After a bit of hanging around on the ramp and a few half-hearted attempts to see if Cedar wanted to load on his own, Buffalo tried using Kaysan as a good example. This was particularly interesting to me, since I once completed my own study into whether or not horses can learn by observing others, and I found that they possibly can but only in very specific situations, and with very specific tasks. Watching another horse is never going to replace the lessons they learn from their own experience. Buffalo asked me to hold Cedar while he loaded Kaysan a few times in front of him, but this didn't seem to make much difference when he tried Cedar again.

Next he tried to load Cedar with Kaysan still in the trailer. It wasn't really a big enough space for two – with no partition to divide the horses from one another. What is more, Cedar and Kaysan had not met before. Kaysan seemed to be in season and Cedar was of an age that meant he was beginning to work out what that means. With Kaysan loaded onto the trailer and Cedar hanging out indefinitely on the ramp just behind her, things took a distinctly romantic turn for a second or two. Cedar looked like he finally had a good reason to get in the trailer and get lucky. Then Kaysan changed her mind, squealed like a pig and kicked out at Cedar with both back legs, catching Buffalo square on somewhere between the knees and the navel. He bent over double, absorbing the shock with nothing more than a manly 'ooooooooooh' before regaining his composure remarkably quickly. Kaysan was promptly removed from the scene by a grumbling Buffalo, but he returned none the worse for wear and ready to try again. When Hannah asked if he was OK or injured, Buffalo replied, 'Oh I'm fine. It's just the way with horses; you get kicked all the time.' His bravery was admirable, but also telling. I hate to think of his insurance premiums.

Next Buffalo tried using food, but since it came quite readily and without too much of a pattern involved, Cedar continued with his previous tactics of standing firmly on the bottom of the ramp looking the other way – only now he was chewing greedily at the same time. Cedar was beginning to enjoy this not-loading business.

Then Buffalo tried a bit harder with pulls on the rope. The best way to use pressure on the line when loading is to make sure you release it every time the horse even thinks of moving forward; trouble was, Cedar wasn't going anywhere. He was named after a tree and had grown roots just like one. Buffalo tried for a while, and wasn't deterred, he then arranged a rope in a loop that fell over Cedar's hindquarters, with a long end that Buffalo could pull on to encourage Cedar to move. Finally a technique that was working well for Cedar, and he began to realise that he needed to move his feet in order to get rid of the pressure on his quarters. Progress was visible, but slow, so Buffalo decided it was (only now?!) worth cleaning the trailer out so that it wasn't slippy with the pile of other horses' droppings, so he left me with Cedar for ten minutes while he took the trailer to a nearby hose point.

Finally, when Buffalo returned, he went back to the pressure-and-release technique and before too long Cedar had loaded into the trailer. I was impressed with Cedar's good temper and Buffalo's tenacity. It takes some grit and determination to train horses this way, stay alive and keep trying. All jokes aside, what I really respected about Buffalo was his positive attitude and his willingness to try different things rather than lose his temper or blame the horse. He talked to us about where his training ideas came from, and like many others across the world he draws largely on a book called *The Jeffrey Method*. This method, along with those of the Dorrance brothers and other great old horsemen, are the ancestry from which many of our modern horse whisperers' and natural horsemanship techniques have grown. The main thing that Buffalo was missing was not technique or timing. It was that he was so brave he didn't really mind when things went wrong, so he didn't put a whole lot of effort into planning things so that they were likely to go right. He just jumped right in and gave it a go regardless of the chances of success. Losing teeth and breaking bones was part of the fun.

We stopped by another field where Buffalo grazes brumbies to meet Jarrad, the most beautiful brumby you could imagine. Surely there was something Iberian about his heritage, his thick wavy mane, grey-dun coat and large wide eyes made him look like a mini Andalusian. Buffalo was very proud of Jarrad and keen for me to see him ridden. As Buffalo tried to catch Jarrad he said he had forgotten how long it had been since he had last been caught, handled or ridden. Jarrad, it seems, thought it had perhaps been too long and had forgotten that he was ever a trained horse at all; he'd gone a bit 'free-range'. Eventually, with the help of food, Buffalo caught him and decided almost instantly to tie the lead rope to the halter like reins and jump on him bareback. Buffalo is a fairly sturdy chap, so rather than vault on like a gymnast, he jumped as high as he could then aimed to use his plaster cast as a sort of hook to lever himself up. With his right arm in plaster, this meant it dug into Jarrad's back just above his flank, and Jarrad lurched away in surprise. Buffalo landed on his feet and, to my amazement, he tried again two or three times, each upsetting Jarrad a little more, before turning apologetically to me and saying he didn't know what had got into him and that it must be the plaster cast.

I asked if perhaps Buffalo would like me to help since I didn't have a broken arm, and might be able to mount his feral brumby in the field with no tack, in a smoother fashion. I recognise now that this was ridiculous and there was no way I should have been getting on that horse. Maybe Buffalo's enthusiasm was infectious, maybe I just wanted to work rather than watch for a while, maybe it was that Jarrad reminded me so exactly of the way I had pictured Thowra. Whatever the reason, I decided to have a go. I also am not a gymnast so needed a prop to get on smoothly. I took him to an upturned bucket and spent some time leaning over and stroking him gently before getting on and off a few times and then finally staying on and riding around bareback for a bit. Some moments in life slow down and lodge in your memory like slow-motion film. Riding Jarrad bareback, in the sunshine, in Australia, that day felt timeless. My twelve-year-old self had gone to heaven.

We drove over to Buffalo's home place where he has the use of 300 acres to run brumbies and ride. When we arrived with Me Mate on the trailer, Buffalo unloaded him and left him in a well-fenced corral about the size of an outdoor arena. Me Mate started calling into the distance. 'He's singing for his ladies,' said Buffalo. 'Let's go for lunch and let him catch them for us.' Sure enough, when we got back from lunch, Me Mate was still in his enclosure but surrounded by a herd of about ten beautiful brumby mares. While they were keen on being near Me Mate, they weren't so happy to be caught, and it took Buffalo the best part of an hour to catch the mares we were going to ride. They darted away several times, often at the last moment just as the headcollar buckle was being fastened. 'You'll never get the wilderness out of a brumby,' Buffalo smiled. We saddled up Me Mate, Kaysan and Ginger Megs and set off for a ride across the bush.

Buffalo apparently got his name for throwing himself into things head first, and he certainly took a devil-may-care approach to trail riding – who needs bridleways when you're on a brumby? These little guys were like four-wheel drives, and we tried out their off-road ability through grass that came over our knees, deep tangled brush, streams and creeks. We even saw a red-bellied black snake, one of the most venomous snakes in Australia, scuttle across the path, but the brumbies were entirely unshakable (I may have squeaked just a little). The mares that Hannah and I rode were comfortable and surefooted, though neither was particularly soft or sensitive to rein control. Ginger Megs would throw her head about when Hannah tried to slow her or steer her, but luckily, Megs and Hannah reached a consensus on leaving each other alone as long as they followed the other horses, and this seemed like a workable compromise.

I was excited when Buffalo offered me a ride on Me Mate himself. Buffalo beamed like a proud parent as I tried him out. And he had good reason to be proud. While it had seemed that some of Buffalo's training was more about enthusiasm than refined technique, Me Mate's training was truly first class. Me Mate was impeccably mannered, with a great work ethic and a happy outlook on life that infused into the rider. His small pricked ears and strong thick neck made the best possible frame to the stunning scenery we rode through. He was comfy to ride, light to the aids, and incredibly easy to get along with. Apparently he's even starred in a few films now (including 'a futuristic Western with an eco-theme').

When we realised we had dropped our camera (blinkin' tourists; can't take us anywhere) Buffalo swapped back onto Me Mate to gallop back across the bush to look for it. Han and I waited amid the wildlife having settled the mares down after their main man raced off. We kept an eye out for snakes and spiders, and listened for movement in the under-growth. Suddenly we could hear hooves thumping and bush breaking and then Buffalo and Me Mate reappeared in a wildly disorganised manner, at speed, almost choosing separate sides of a tree but hanging together somehow. Puffing and grinning, and looking decidedly pleased with himself, Buffalo held the camera aloft like a winner's trophy.

As we made our way back through the dappled sunlight of the woodland, it was a breath-taking moment when we came across some feral brumbies, grazing in groups. They had spotted us before we saw them, and stood stock still, heads up, watching us from between the trees. Two of them had dun-coloured coats that looked almost mystical amid the fallen leaves and the columns of tree trunks. Here was a privileged view into the brumbies private world. They watched us with curiosity, as we silently pointed and gestured at them as we rode past.

As we rode between the free-ranging brumbies, on the domesticated ones, I realised that Buffalo was in a unique position to appreciate the value of the horses as friends and workmates, or as free beings. He didn't feel the need to tame and employ every horse that he owned. He showed us one heavily pregnant mare, who was incredibly fearful of people. He wasn't sure what had happened in her past to cause such a level of trauma, but I had a lot of respect for Buffalo's decision to let her live out her days on his place as wild as she was born, with the herd. She was strong, quick and beautiful, but he didn't need to ride or control her to appreciate that. Her value in the world was not dictated by her financial or practical value to mankind. She was her own being, important to her herd mates and her unborn foal, and we were entirely irrelevant to her. When we got back to camp and let our horses go, the stallion along with the mares, it felt wonderful to see them gallop away to join their friends, some tame, some wild, and enjoy the freedom of the bush until the next time Buffalo popped in.

The whole brumby experience had me pondering on the freedom our horses are allowed during training. It seems of particular importance to many horse owners in Britain at the moment that horses are 'free' to choose their own fate throughout their training. I think this concept comes in part from the human rights that are important to us, and in part from a cultural backlash against forceful and cruel methods that are no longer tolerated by most modern British horse people. The image of a horse choosing to follow a leader without a rope, to listen to aids without a bridle, or to take a rider into a jump willingly is one that we all pursue.

However, talking with Buffalo, Jan and Megan, I realised that this degree of freedom is the end point of training, and not the beginning. While early training should not be forceful, it also shouldn't be left down to the horse, or worse, to luck, that things go well. The trainer should be setting things up pretty carefully so that in all honesty, the horse's choices are already made for him. I think this sort of approach might involve less 'freedom' in the strictest sense of the word, but also less stress and confusion.

Take, for instance, teaching a young horse to jump. I had asked Buffalo while we were riding, what he found the most difficult element of training. 'Jumping' he replied. 'Brumbies are not good jumpers.' When I then asked him how he was working on that, he responded, 'There's a wall I want to jump. I gallop them at it pretty fast, and they just stop right in front of it. Sometimes I fall right over their heads and hit the wall. I guess Brumbies just don't wanna jump.'

Those of us from a culture that regularly teaches horses to jump will find this idea pretty laughable. How can you tell if a horse wants to jump or not when you set it up so badly? We know that really, what you need to do is to create a situation where the horse is bound to have a go – poles on the floor, perhaps with wings or guide poles, moving towards home, perhaps following a lead horse, perhaps on the lunge or loose first – all these things are altering his choice. When Buffalo gives his horses the 'choice' of jumping or not, without any pre-training, he is giving them little chance of choosing 'yes'.

'Freedom' is something that seems fundamentally important to us, but in our hearts we know the most free our horses could really be is at the other end of a pair of binoculars, innocent of human impact.

No, it's not really free horses we are after, it's freely compliant horses that we truly want; a state which is undoubtedly only achievable through conditioning and education. While we might always be aiming for that holy grail of freely compliant horses, in fact their choices are always somewhat predetermined to a degree by our previous training choices, and our management of the situation. The horse should never feel forced, but in fact his options are manipulated to suit our needs.

The concept of freedom also has a real market value, and is utilised to gain favour (and income) from audiences who pursue 'ethical' horsemanship. I think it is useful to think pragmatically about the freedom that is demonstrated to you in bridleless demonstrations or with trick horses. Start to ask yourself some questions when you see a horse choosing positive behaviour freely. How has that choice been prepared, how are the options limited, how is the situation set up so that while the horse, and audience, feel as though the choice is free and not forced, in fact it is predetermined and inevitable? There is more to learn about horse training from these tricks and demos than simply being inspired or impressed by the end point of a very careful and strategic system.

In some cases, I wonder whether the abstract notion of 'choice' is more of a human value than necessarily the horse's top concern. I can't help feeling that it's more important ethically to consider stress than to consider freedom of choice, particularly since it seems to me that horses are less concerned with 'fairness' than they are with 'safety'. I now try to choose the least stressful course of action rather than the one that gives the horse the most autonomy. This notion sits in tension with my own yearning for my horses to choose and want their lives and jobs with me. But I guess a horse who chooses to do what you want is the proof of good training, the outcome of a successful programme, rather than necessarily the starting point. Buffalo loved the free spirit of his brumbies, and prioritised leaving some freedom in their nature. Jan and Megan, took a much more structured, rigorous approach to training. While Buffalo's horses were perhaps more free to make up their own minds and resist or evade, Jan and Megan's were more compliant, and less resistant. The exception was Me Mate, who seemed to love Buffalo's wild side as much as Buffalo loved his, and who seemed to thrive under Buffalo's fun-loving training regime.

It's a difficult truth of horsemanship that we all must negotiate the level of freedom we allow our horses in their daily lives and choices, often balancing this against other priorities such as their stress levels, safety, and our own training agenda. It dawned on me, over the few days in Bellingen, that this mental process is so much easier when, in the back of my head, I know that somewhere out there, wild horses are living truly free, for better or for worse, negotiating the landscape with no knowledge of the way they feature in our politics, environmental plans and bedtime stories. It's hard to forge a logical path through such complex ethical issues as those surrounding freedom, but it's easy to know where my heart lies: while I know that my own Harvey sleeps happily in his stable on a cold winter's night, I desperately hope there will never be a day when there are no wild brumbies left to sleep out under the stars.

CHAPTER SIX

✦

SHOW TIME
At Equitana, Melbourne, Australia

IT WAS NEARLY MIDNIGHT and, though it had been hot all day, the temperature had dropped surprisingly low, and I was so cold I couldn't sleep. I pulled another sweatshirt on and buried deeper into the nest of blankets that we had made in the car, put my feet up onto the dashboard and tucked my hands into my armpits. We had hired a car so that we could travel along the spectacular coastline of Victoria's Great Ocean Road, in the south east of Australia. To make up for the cost of the car, it had to double up as our accommodation. We had found an empty car park, which served as access into the rainforest for walkers, and so while I tried to still my mind to sleep, it kept crawling and wriggling with images of all of the poisonous wildlife Australia is famous for. Much of the Great Ocean Road is covered with 'no sleeping here' signs, and we had found a spot that didn't actively seem to discourage it, but it's fair to say we weren't entirely confident we were on the right side of the law. I have never been very good at breaking rules, and so perhaps it was also my guilty conscience that was keeping me awake under the unfamiliar stars.

Suddenly, there was the noise of another car engine approaching, and then the gravel crunched under somebody's tyres; they had pulled up right next to our car. Hannah woke up and for a moment we were frozen in entirely illogical fear; perhaps we were going to be in trouble. What if we had stumbled onto some sort of midnight drug-trafficking spot or inadvertently parked in a space that was home to some other illicit night-time activity that we would not want to witness? Perhaps the driver of the strange car was an axe murderer! We stayed very still and waited to see what would happen. The other driver did the same. Moments passed, and then minutes, and we began to sneak more and more of a look through the window to ascertain what our grizzly end would be.

Finally, I realised that the driver of the other car was a woman, and all nervousness instantly evaporated, since in my sleep-deprived sexist logic, women are clearly absolutely legitimate in their night-time forest exploits. Pleased that we were not going to be axe-murdered after all, Han and I waved and got out the car, as did the young woman, who had curly hair and was wrapped sensibly in a big duvet-type coat.

She looked equally relieved at our gender and lack of axes, and we exchanged pleasantries. Juliette, an Australian, was also travelling down the east coast and had heard that a short walk from this car park was an ideal spot to see glow worms. She had come to see them, but now that she looked into the thick blackness of the undergrowth, she wasn't sure she was brave enough to go in on her own after all. Han and I liked the sound of glow worms, so remarkably quickly we satisfied ourselves that not only were we not in danger, but we were actually trusting enough to follow this lady into the forest with only one torch between us. We found the opening into the trees and began to creep forward together.

The undergrowth chirruped, scratched and rustled as the nocturnal food chain busied itself all around us. At least the path was well made enough that it seemed unlikely we would become lost, and even with the meagre light of the torch, the pale footing of the path could be followed. I held tightly on to Hannah's hand and walked with my head cowering below the leaves, ducking imaginary cobwebs and deadly snakes.

The tree cover became thicker and blocked out the light of the moon and stars. We turned off the torch and visibility was reduced so that all we could see were the vague blue-grey shapes of each other and the few leaves that were closest to our faces as we walked. After several minutes of tiptoeing through the blackness, there was movement in the bush just yards to the side of me. I turned round, squinting my eyes into the undergrowth to see what had caused the noise, but all that I could make out was that it was something the size of a small dog. It rushed across the ground and began to climb a tree, and by then Juliette had turned the torch on and put the spotlight onto the grey furry lump that was now clearly a possum, with her baby clinging onto her back. She seemed surprisingly unconcerned by our proximity and she watched us from halfway up her tree for a while before continuing upwards on her way. We turned the light off again and continued on our way too.

I began to wonder how much further we had to go; it had been about a forty-minute stumble so far. But then we could hear the sound of a waterfall, and saw a glimmering yellow light up ahead on the path. It glowed at about knee height and as we approached it, we could see four or five more.

We turned the corner onto the most enchanting sight I have ever seen. A clearing in the trees allowed the silver glow of the moon to illuminate our surroundings. A waterfall fell from above us into a small drop pool that reflected the glittering lights, and rising banks of earth and rock encircled the waterfall. Dotted into the rocks were hundreds of little glowing embers that, like a galaxy of stars, shone peacefully, softly gleaming and entrancing us entirely. Hannah put her arms around me, and the three of us stood breathing quietly, trying to absorb the beauty, and feeling privileged to be witness to this secret moonlit magic.

Eventually we turned away from this enchanted glade, tiptoed back to our cars and said our goodbyes. Juliette drove away and we nestled back down into the car. I sighed deeply, and then fell straight into a sound and peaceful sleep.

It was only when I next reached an internet connection that I discovered the ugly truth about these little dazzlers. They are not worms at all, but the larvae of a flying creature called a 'fungus gnat'. What is more, the glowing, which comes from their abdomen, serves a sinister purpose of attracting flying insects, which the glow worm then feeds on. Remembering our moonlit encounter, I felt a bit of a twerp. We had been standing there romantically twirling, having a 'Disney' moment, in the wondrous surroundings of … an infestation of fungus gnat larvae as they tricked, and then munched on, juicy little bugs.

As we got ready for Equitana, the biggest equestrian show in the southern hemisphere, I was thinking about the entertainment value of horse-training demonstrations, and wondering about the different worlds of the trainers, the horses and the audience members at such events. We were going to Equitana to watch the colt-starting competition, called Way of the Horse, and we were both really excited because we were going to be meeting friendly faces from home, Kelly Marks and Angela Hobbs.

By this point, Kelly had been a big part of my equestrian career for ten years, and while I am not normally made of 'fan' material – I rarely get star-struck and I often look at even the best trainers with a carefully critical eye – I have to admit I am absolutely a Kelly fan. From first seeing her in a demonstration, to helping behind the scenes, to eventually earning my stripes to ride in the demos and take part, I have seen her training from all sorts of perspectives. It is Kelly who taught me to watch other trainers objectively and to stay open-minded in order to learn new techniques or concepts, and she has always encouraged me to read books and take lessons from other practitioners. For those of you who want to know some behind-the-scenes gossip about Kelly Marks, let me tell you some things I have learned about her over the years.

1) She gives out boiled eggs for breakfast to anyone working for her who looks like they might not have started the day in a nutritionally appropriate manner.
2) If she hadn't become a horse trainer she would have been a fantastic librarian – she can smell out a bookshop anywhere she goes. She loves reading and recommending books to people, particularly social science and personal development books.

3) She believes there *is* a solution to any problem – equine or otherwise – and this stubborn dedication to optimism means she is able to sometimes create solutions that were never there before.
4) She believes in community and, a little like a Mafia mother, would do anything for someone 'in the faaamily' – which might include her staff, her friends, her neighbours, her students, certainly her cats and horses, and of course her actual relatives.
5) She loves fig jam so much she would rather eat it with her finger than give it up at airport customs.

Angela's role, as Kelly's best friend, is to keep us all sane; she provides an intelligent, but not horse-obsessed opinion, a level head, a very good laugh and an insatiably positive disposition. I couldn't think of anyone better to be with us, watching some training demos at Equitana, and Han and I were instantly comforted and cheered by Kelly and Angela's familiar presence.

Melbourne Equitana takes place across four days, with six different arenas showing world-class competitions, clinicians and equestrian displays as well as a whole heap of shopping. The Way of the Horse (WOTH) competition is the biggest crowd-puller of the show. Colt-starting competitions have come under heavy criticism in the past few years for putting young horses under too much pressure and, having seen some of the footage online of weak young horses panicking during training, it seemed the critics have a good point. However, WOTH was adamant on its website that this was not going to be the case here because the competition was not a race to the finish line but would be judged on the standard of horsemanship and quality of training. I was keen to see how this played out in real life as well as seeing what tools and tricks the world's best colt starters were using.

Thousands flocked to the area to watch the competition – astounded by the idea that it might be possible to take a horse who can't be led, and within three hours of training, be riding him round an obstacle course. Typically, owners will send horses away for at least six weeks to professional trainers to see the same standard achieved. So while I was watching, I found myself pondering on time; how much time does it really take for horses to learn? What are the consequences of rushing lessons through quickly within a show?

The venue was huge and the stadium-type seating vast, with the crowd murmuring expectantly as three untrained stock horses moved about their round pens. We were all trying to speculate: which horse looked like the best potential student, which competitor seemed to have a good bio in the leaflet, even which area in the arena might give the best advantage. It was surprisingly cold in the hanger-type venue, and we huddled together with a blanket over our knees, in the front row of seating, with notebooks at the ready to record the day's events.

As the seats continued to fill, the three youngsters in their pens alternated between standing still, staring intently at something in the arena, looking bewildered, sniffing the ground, and trotting about looking agitated. At times they paced up and down the edge of the pen looking at the horse next door, and occasionally called out. They were understandably unsettled, but not in frantic distress.

I have been amazed at the reaction of horses to crowds when I have worked in demonstrations myself. As I lead a young horse into the arena, his eyes are on stalks looking at all the people in the audience and he's trying to take in all the strange shapes, smells and sounds. But within seconds of entering the round pen, he will often seem to detach from what is going on outside the pen walls, and focus on the trainer who is in the pen with him. I don't know why that happens so well, but I have seen it first hand time and time again. Maybe there is a constant amount of visual stimulus that the horse just gets used to as 'white noise'. I know that a big sudden movement, for example someone taking a coat off, can snap them out of their apparent relaxation for a second. I also know that horses might be more afraid of *one* coat hung on the fence of an empty arena, than they are if that arena seating is entirely filled with people, coats and all. Things just look different to horses than they do to us, and of course they have no concept of the stage fright or shyness that might make us feel socially vulnerable in front of a big crowd. Perhaps the horse feels protected by the round-pen walls, because I have also noticed that things horses are supposed to be 'phobic' about often don't cause a reaction at all until you bring them inside the pen with the horse. There is something about working horses in a round pen that gives them quite a different experience to working in the same environment without it.

While some critics have argued that even attending these events is too stressful for young horses, I believe that it is the actions of the trainer that make the experience of appearing in a demo or training competition a positive or negative one from the horse's point of view. The show atmosphere itself seems less of a problem to them than you would expect.

After a few moments, the chattering audience became still as the commentator's voice boomed across the stadium, and the gigantic video screens came alive with shots of wild horses. The rules were explained: the trainers had one session per day over three days to train their horses. It was not a race, but the quality of the training would be assessed by a panel of judges. On that panel were Mary King (eventer), Kyra Kyrkland (dressage), Ali Al Amera (film horse trainer), Josh Lyons and Richard Winters (both Western riding/behavioural clinicians), so a great representation from the very top of various disciplines. The competitors were working towards a skills test on the final day. In this test, they would have the opportunity to demonstrate the progress of their training by riding the horse around various obstacles, including poles set out in certain shapes, a tarpaulin laid on the ground, cones, and a jump. Untrained horses are naturally very nervous about walking on strange surfaces, as they could prove dangerous. Walking over a tarpaulin might seem like an odd challenge, but it demonstrates the horse's bravery, obedience and trust in the rider. Even simple tasks show considerable amounts of learning have taken place, for instance, in trotting figures of eight, the horse has to learn how to respond to the rein aids, how to rebalance and maintain a rhythm, and how to deal with the sight of the rider first on one side of their vision and then on the other when they change direction.

On the first day the trainers had seventy-five minutes, including a compulsory ten-minute break, which they could use whenever they liked. The competitors were introduced. Just to confuse us, all three were wearing the 'uniform' outfit of blue jeans, a blue shirt and a dark cowboy hat. All the trainers were Australian. In the left-hand pen, and the darkest shade of shirt, we had Paul Clarkson. He looked young, lean and dynamic, and I had really enjoyed his clinic the day before. His bio in the literature explained his thirst for knowledge and his studious approach to learning the best techniques. I thought he looked as if he had a strong chance. In the middle pen was Naish Hogan, slightly stockier than Paul and in royal blue. I didn't know a lot about him yet, but he seemed to have a calm way about him and, since he worked with both Western and English horses at his ranch, I was interested to see how his approach brought these two worlds together. In the right-hand pen and in the palest, sky-blue shirt, we had Ken Faulkner, a regular clinician in Australia, the eldest of the competitors, complete with greying moustache. We had been particularly impressed by his five-year-old bridleless horse, Sundance, at his clinic the day before, and he certainly seemed to have the biggest (or at least noisiest) fan club.

As the three men entered their pens, Paul began with a clever rope trick that I have not seen before nor since. It involved fastening a rope to the side of the round pen, and stretching it across the pen so that it virtually cut the pen in half. His horse, Lilly, a dark liver chestnut with a blaze, stood in one half of the pen. (Although it is called a colt starting competition, in fact often the horses used are geldings or fillies.) Paul then moved towards Lilly, and as she walked away from him, she had no choice but to walk towards the rope. He held the rope at just the right height so that, as she walked into it, it came across the underside of her neck. She continued to move forward with the rope across her chest. Paul then released the rope end from the side of the pen, and, still working at a distance from Lilly, tied the rope to itself in such a manner that he could pull on the end and make the loop smaller and smaller until it was a ring around Lilly's neck. He had done all this without crowding or frightening her, and she had still not broken out of walk. A very cunning process indeed. She turned her head to one side and strained an ear towards her new appendage, but looked confused rather than panicked. While it's often simplest to assume that quick training is stressful, this seemed like a great example of how sometimes the easiest solution is the quickest, and also the least stressful for the horse. Paul's horse was caught within just a few moments of the session beginning, and it didn't seem to have caused her much worry. There was a gentle appreciative round of applause from the audience.

Naish and Ken began by using their body language to try to draw the horse to them. They would move toward the horse and then turn and move away when the horse looked at them. Ken's chestnut gelding, Ginkgo, and Naish's dark bay gelding, Action, both seemed interested in the trainers when they walked away, but the minutes past and neither seemed to really be getting any closer to putting a halter on, in fact Naish's horse seemed to be getting more worried by the whole process.

Ken moved on to his plan B after a little while, by which point Paul had already haltered and handled his horse and was working on some groundwork exercises. Ken's plan B is one that I certainly don't have in my tool kit – a lasso. I have been told off for calling it that, apparently those in the know simply call it a 'rope'.

I have only ever roped two things in my life. One was a chair about ten feet away, after quite a bit of practice, the other was a very tame goat, who was eating out of a bucket by my horse's feet at the time. So I wouldn't subject a horse to my efforts with a rope, but Ken made it look very smooth. First he allowed Ginkgo to get used to the movement of the rope swinging, and he used his body positioning to encourage Ginkgo to move forward at a consistent, steady speed of trot. Then he threw the swinging loop and it fell, as though it was magnetically sucked into the right place, around Ginkgo's head and onto his neck. Gingko shrank back in fear as it landed, but Ken did not pull on the line at all to start with, and so Gingko was able to realise that the rope wasn't hurting him and came to a stop in his own time.

Naish continued to work on 'advance and retreat' body language for the entire first session, and for the first half of the second session. His shoulders seemed rounded and he looked soft and calm, his movements were smooth and looked confident. To me, there was no hint of the pressure that he must have been feeling on the inside, as his fellow competitors caught, led, and then were even getting onto their horses backs, before he had even convinced his to be touched.

We heard some of the spectators praising Naish for being willing to go at the right speed for the horse, but I'm not quite sure that told the whole story. While the horses had seemed very similar when the three trainers first entered the pens, at the end of the first day, I'd say it was Naish's horse, Action, who looked the most worried. Action seemed to know the only way to make Naish go away was to look towards him, because Naish would walk toward Action until he looked in his direction, and then walk away. Sometimes Action just continued to walk away or to trot or canter away for some time, but occasionally he would allow Naish to get pretty close. But when Naish gingerly lifted his hand toward Action and tried to touch him, Action just couldn't bare it and reeled away in flight. Despite Naish's efforts to begin the relationship on Action's terms and with no ropes or restrictions involved, it looked as though Action's worry about being touched was actually becoming more ingrained.

On the second day, after repeating the same tactics for several more minutes with no improvement, Naish decided to use his plan B too, and set up a rope trick that was similar to Paul's. By this point Action was deeply suspicious of Naish and had begun to build a pattern of blasting away from Naish and avoiding touch, so even with the rope on, Action's progress was slow. It is so hard to say whether Action began as a more difficult horse than Lilly and Gingko, but it seemed to me that Naish's approach had been the most gentle from the audience's point of view, and yet the most stressful from the horse's.

It looked as though Paul's horse had the least stressful experience of being caught, even though he caught his horse the quickest. This isn't to say that fast lessons are *always* better, but simply that it is amazing how quickly horses can progress when the lesson is made simple for them. Sometimes, horses need more time, but sometimes trainers need a better idea.

As we certainly knew from our glow-worm experience, audiences can enjoy the spectacle that animals create without an understanding of the experience of those creatures. I have come across just about every different perspective that an audience member can possibly have when watching a training demo. For instance, if a young horse bucks with his first saddle, most of the audience will erupt into fits of giggles as he humps and jumps about. But a few audience members might turn away, upset by the image of a horse who is afraid or uncomfortable and trying to rid himself of his load. For many, in fact for most, it's the dramatic leaping, rearing, bolting horses that are their absolute favourites and provide the best opportunities to 'prove' the effectiveness of the training, since, if the trainer gets it right, they can show the biggest changes in short time frames. However, for some, these horses are under too much stress and they would rather see more subtle training. Some audience members have much higher expectations of ethics during a demonstration than they do of their own horses' training back home; they can be ready to criticise clinicians for the slightest stress yet are fine with all sorts of confusion that their own horses experience. Others are the exact opposite, and will tolerate much higher levels of stress during a demonstration with their favourite trainer than they would ever allow close up with their own horses on their own property.

The whole raison d'etre of training demonstrations rests precariously somewhere in between education and entertainment. One good thing about the colt-starting competition was that there were three different trainers to compare, and so I hoped this would encourage the audience to use some objectivity in analysing the training that was happening in front of them and learn from it. Still, changing people is a much slower process than changing horses, and some people are always going to see what they want to see, which might be why even though Naish's horse had achieved the least *and* was the most upset, whispers of congratulation for his gentle style were all around us.

Once the horses were caught, all three competitors went on to use pressure and release on the line around the neck to begin to teach the horses how to lead and to get close enough to get them used to touch. I always think that young horse training consists mostly of two types of lesson. Firstly, they need to learn which things to tolerate, ignore and accept, such as human handling, popping balloons, tight girths, riders losing stirrups and all the other potentially frightening or uncomfortable things that are going to be part of their life as a ridden horse. Secondly, they need to learn which things to respond to, and how to respond to them, such as lead-rope pressure, leg aids, rein aids, and voice commands. When you look at it like that, it is a pretty tricky job for them as we shape their natural instinctive behaviours towards either appropriate reactivity, or total lack of reactivity, to suit our needs.

There was no doubt, as we watched the final day's training, that Paul had covered the most ground with his horse in terms of preparation for the test. He had lunged his horse over a jump; steered her through cones, she was trotting smoothly in figures of eight while carrying him, he had picked up all four feet several times and had her very comfortable with the noise of his stock whip cracking – I think he had prepared this latter trick as an extra party piece to show how relaxed and accepting Lilly had become. Generally, Lilly had seemed like she was engaging well in the learning. I had been unsure what Paul was trying to achieve with some of his groundwork manoeuvres; for example, during one section of the second session, Lilly had looked confused, sweaty and stressed as he tried to move her around him on the lunge and he seemed to constantly correct her for mistakes that I couldn't spot. But by day three, he had subtle control of Lilly's feet on the lunge line, moving her shoulders away in either direction and yielding her hindquarters too. While I would have liked to see no stressful moments at all, I felt that, overall, Paul's preparation for the skills test was thorough, incremental, innovative and well thought out, and Lilly's training experience was much better than the average horse's training experience would be at amateur and professional training yards across the world behind closed doors and without the crowds.

In the next pen down, there were some differences in Ken's approach. Ken had covered less ground than Paul, but seemed to prioritise absolute softness in his approach. His horse had only seen the smallest tarp, but was entirely relaxed with it and had stopped noticing it. He hadn't practised steering through the cones, or trotting figures of eight, but his horse was turning at the walk with Ken on board in very smooth curves off a gentle open rein (held away from Gingko's neck). The difference between the two approaches was subtle, but perhaps most visible during early ridden work where Paul used a fair bit of leg to initiate some forward movement, and then kept Lilly on a tight circle with an inside bend. Many trainers use as small circle like this as the horse is less likely to buck when moving round than they are when on a straight line. Since he wanted her to continue stepping round, he needed quite a bit of hassling to get her moving, and quite a lot of rein corrections to keep her turning.

In Ken's pen it looked a little quieter, he seemed to prefer two soft steps to ten hurried or braced ones, and so he was opening the inside rein to get a step or two and then stopping and relaxing for a while before asking again. It wasn't all perfect in Ken's pen, however, as he had some issues bridling his horse who seemed poll/ear shy, and he still wasn't really 100 per cent happy about being mounted. He would walk off a few steps almost every time Ken got on, and fidget as Ken prepared to mount. I really believe mounting training should be done thoroughly, and I wondered whether this was less of a priority for Ken, or if the time scale of the competition was encouraging him to bypass the extra work that might be required. Still, Gingko had never really had a sweaty or overly stressed moment, and although it looked as though Ken would not be able to complete as much of the test as Paul, overall, what he did do might be more relaxed.

On the third day, we settled back into our familiar seats and were ready for the final skills test. I really wouldn't have known where to put my money between Ken and Paul. Paul's horse had looked pretty thoroughly prepared but Ken's horse had shown some moments of real softness. The horses were led out of the arena and the course was constructed.

When Ken entered the arena he started off by saddling his horse, who was a little tense about the process, fidgeting a bit. He took his time, and then led Ginkgo around the whole arena, moving nice and slowly but confidently, allowing the horse to check things out. He chose not to bridle his horse for the test, perhaps because when he had bridled him in training he had found Ginkgo was worried about his ears. Instead he rode in a rope halter. He then mounted up, circling a little to get on (i.e. he put Ginkgo on a small circle so that he could mount even while the horse kept moving). Gradually he made his circle bigger and walked off around the arena on a long rein. Now Ken was on board, Ginkgo looked much less babyish and raw than he was; he actually looked pretty grown up and relaxed. He walked, trotted and cantered around the arena. There seemed to be an element of letting the horse choose the gait, or at least taking inspiration from what the horse felt like doing, and going for trot when he offered it. This gave the appearance of a more thoroughly trained horse, but it also made things less stressful for Ginkgo, so it worked well for both of them.

I was certainly impressed with the balanced, loose and comfortable way that horse trotted around. Ginkgo's ears were flickering about to Ken and to his surroundings, but he looked pretty relaxed in his strides. Ken then worked his way around the obstacles, starting with the easiest ones: standing in a square of poles, walking over three trotting poles, steering round a chicane of poles; all were negotiated without drama and with just a few wobbles off track. Ginkgo had a little spooky look at the cones, since he'd never seen them before in training, but then moved on easily and his steering through them was nice and controlled. He circled the tarp once before being brave enough to walk across it, and then climbed straight over the tiny cross-pole jump at a walk without any problem (these cowboys don't seem so keen on the actual jumping part!).

Ken took a look at a bale-pulling exercise – where the rider holds a rope tied to a bale and rides forward to drag it along – but when Ginkgo seemed a little spooked by the obstacle he decided not to do it, preferring not to risk pushing it too far and upsetting his horse at this early stage. He jumped off and picked up all four feet, with Gingko leg waggling a little on the last one before settling with it. Overall, Ken's demeanour was steady, calm and secure, and this had a settling influence on both a twitchy audience and the young horse. He was calming and easy to watch, and I imagine, fairly calming and easy to work for.

When Paul came in things were looking good. His horse had little trouble with the obstacles in training, he had picked her feet up many times and he even had an extra trick prepared. Even though she'd seen everything in training, Paul started out really sensibly by leading her over the tarp, over the jump, around the cones and to look about the arena. Surely she was going to find this all easy now. She stood perfectly still to be mounted and it looked like Paul was going to clinch the prize. But the ridden work was not quite as soft and loose and relaxed as Ken's horse had been. She was a little bracier on the reins, she seemed more aware of where the gate was, and almost did a mini-nap on that corner at one point. Perhaps if Paul had ridden her in the halter rather than the bit she would have looked more relaxed in the jaw and neck, like Ken's horse. Mouthing may be one of those things that just takes longer than these competitions allow. The transitions seemed a bit stuffier and I'd say Paul looked as though he had to try a little harder with his aids. On reflection, this might be partly because Ken was very clever at asking for transitions when the horse felt like doing them anyway, whereas Paul seemed to decide where he wanted to change pace and then commit to it – a good example being that Paul asked his mare to canter on the corner where she had shown a slight nap – the transition didn't go very well and he lost all his straightness. The back up was not quite as soft as Ken's, and although he did a lovely job of all the obstacles, including having a go at pulling that bale, the overall picture was one of a little more bracing and evading than we saw in Ken's round.

Naish brought his horse in and worked him on the ground around the obstacles. There's no way of knowing for sure whether Action really was a tougher horse by nature, or whether something in his training did not bring out the best in him, but Naish's test round showed me that you can go more slowly, and yet the horse can still *feel* too rushed. Action appeared very tense and worried, and under very little control. When Naish approached the tarp to lunge him over it, it was too much of a challenge and Action scooted round it a few times nervously before Naish realised it was too tough and moved away.

Given the fact that Naish had taken things so slowly the day before, I couldn't understand why he didn't fold the tarp up and place it under a pole or, in fact, forget the tarp and work more on the poles, which Action had already seen during his training. Again, we heard people's whispers commending Naish on his decision to take the horse slowly and carefully. To me, this just shows how easy it is to assume that slow progression and careful training are always the same thing. At least he hadn't tried to force Action into anything or use fear to coerce him into accepting training through force. The good news for Naish was the audience didn't seem to judge him too critically, and were pleased to see a horseman who never got frustrated or hurried in his demeanour, and seemed to want to be on the horse's side.

When it came time to announce the winner I thought about how much respect I have for any trainer who has got to this stage and is brave enough to put his training in front of an audience to see how it measures up, no matter the outcome.

The whole stadium was quiet. The commentator had wound the crowd up and built anticipation, and now he was waiting for the excitement to peak in the silence before revealing the result. The trainers were standing together, looking at the ground and preparing themselves to react appropriately to the unknown outcome. Then, when Ken was announced the winner, the silence was shattered by a lot of foot stamping and whooping applause; clearly he was the audience's favourite! I think it was a pretty close call between him and Paul.

Ultimately, the softness of Ken's horse as he moved about with the rider on board is what clinched it for him, even though, in some ways, Paul's horse was better prepared for the challenge, and was certainly calmer with foot handling and mounting. Ken had done a beautiful job of preparing his horse for soft rein aids, and made the whole process look easy and pleasant.

We joined the huddle of people making their way to the exits, carrying our blankets and thick coats, and adopted the penguin-like waddle that seems necessary when masses of people are queuing to fit through the same small door. As we made our way out, we talked about ideal time scales for training. Had the timing of the competition made the trainers progress too fast? How long does it really take to make a good start to a horse's training? Well, I had to admit that Paul and Ken had certainly shown that horses can be started under saddle and become rideable very quickly. But when those horses were sent home, would their owners be able to catch them in a field of friends, lead them into the yard through the puddles, tie them up while they fetched the tack, tack up, mount from a block and then head out on a hack or ride in a big arena with other horses under full control? Watching the training and final skills test, I doubted it. And of course, they certainly were not physically prepared for full ridden life. It would take plenty of time for the core muscles to strengthen to allow them to carry a rider in proper balance and without harming their backs.

It seemed the horse's education had being advanced in a very narrow direction – towards that skills test – and it would take those horses some time to generalise the lessons they learned into more of a rounded, holistic education. Horses have the capacity to learn very quickly – after all it takes only one electric shock for most of them to get the hang of electric fencing. But lessons that involve overcoming instinctive reactions or piecing together more complex tasks are always going to take longer. Thinking back to the job that John Chatterton had done with Miss Muffet, the WOTH horses were given nowhere near as much time to perfect each lesson and to relax into multiple repetitions of each stage. On the other hand, had the horses seemed too stressed, the WOTH trainers would have had no hope of winning. It was in their interest to maximise the horse's learning ability, but to do so within the limits of what the horses could cope with without getting confused or stressed.

I liked a phrase I picked up from another clinician at Equitana, David Leverner: 'Horse's learn by doing'. I interpreted this to mean that horses remember the things they have actually practised, which is not always the lesson you think they ought to have learned. For instance, if you spend an hour riding your horse and pulling him hard in the mouth to teach him to be lighter on the reins, does he learn to be lighter the following day? No, because he spent an hour practising pulling.

This means the important question is not how long do things take, but how is the horse spending his time? How much of his time does he spend afraid, or uncomfortable, or confused? In that time, he is not practising the things he ought to be: being brave, clever, responsive and accepting. Thinking of it this way, it wouldn't matter if a trainer felt he needed to spend a very long time teaching a horse a certain lesson, or if other lessons could be learned quickly; what *would* matter is whether the horse was stressed, confused or uncomfortable during whatever time he was working through. Let's be honest, it's pretty hard to guarantee *no* stress for the horse. Critics who insist on this are probably being unrealistic. None of us are weightless objects to carry after all. And domestic horses need to learn appropriate ways to deal with worrying things. It just isn't possible to think that every experience the horse is going to have is going to be 100 per cent positive. But if the training can follow a system where the majority of the time is spent practising good behaviour and good attitudes, it is amazing how quickly they can learn and how little time, and stress, training can take. Looking at it like this, the fact Naish took a long time wasn't a problem but the fact his horse was stressed for most of it was.

I hope the judging continues to reflect the *quality of the time* the horses experience, rather than how little time the trainer needs to achieve certain aims. As long as we continue to look at what sort of experience the horse is having, rather than how much can be completed within a set time frame, then I think these competitions might well be a great thing for the development of horsemanship. WOTH will continue to put the top trainers under pressure to come up with new, clever ways of making training more effective and less stressful. Audiences have the opportunity to compare three different trainers, and to learn what is working and what isn't. I hope this will encourage audiences to become more critically evaluative in the training they watch, and so make them more thoughtful and informed when it comes to training their own horses. I desperately hope that it doesn't backfire and encourage novice horse people to think they can copy the techniques and start horses in three days themselves.

But we can't keep techniques behind closed doors in case they are abused by others. Training has to happen out in the open, so that people can learn from it, and scrutinise it, to keep the standard high.

The value of these training demonstrations rests on the learning that the horse and the audience obtain as a result. The worrying thing is that since audiences are not always great at looking at things objectively, the audience can have a fantastically exciting experience even if the horse has a terrible time. Of course, the horse can have a great experience and the audience can have a poor one if the demo is too boring or slow moving from the crowd's perspective. If the audience has a poor experience, the demonstrations will not continue; there has to be a happy paying audience to make the whole thing viable.

As we finally found ourselves free of the huge stampede of audience members, it struck me that this audience is a pretty powerful entity with a pretty big weight on its shoulders. Of the three parties involved in a demo; the horse, the trainer, and the audience, we might be forgiven for thinking the audience is the passive party; that their responsibility is simply to learn and absorb and appreciate. But in fact, the audience has a lot of the power to influence the way demonstrations are created in the future, particularly with Twitter, Facebook and other means of giving public feedback. Ultimately, trainers know that without paying audiences, demos won't take place.

In some ways, the public are the directors of these shows, which is why it is so important that the audiences, unlike us at the waterfall with our fungus gnats, know what on earth it is that they are looking at and don't become dazzled by the bright lights, the fairy-tale feeling, and the magic.

So I'd like to leave you with two lessons from this chapter. Firstly, be an objective, active, audience member; go to demonstrations that you would like to support; learn what you can from all sorts of clinicians, and do give feedback about what you are seeing. Secondly, when it comes to planning your own training time scales, remember 'horses learn by doing', so try to plan your sessions around the *quality of time* your horse

ABOVE *Durgha Singh shows us a family heirloom: a hand-painted horsemanship manual in Jaipur, Rajasthan.*

LEFT *This mare has been trained to dance for tourists and weddings in Nawalgarh, Rajasthan. The stress she seemed to be displaying was difficult to watch.*

At the Calcutta racetrack, jockeys walking horses back to the stables as the sun rises behind the Victoria Memorial in the background.

Chaos at the starting gates. The horse is blindfolded and has a strap behind his quarters. The jockeys wait in the stalls for their horses to be crammed in.

Me, working with unfamiliar kit in Bali as Solomon tries to take a chunk out of the stick. By this stage, his expression was softer and his level of aggression had largely subsided!

John Chatterton near Brisbane, teaching Miss Muffet to lower her head.

ABOVE *Shortly after meeting Buffalo in Nimbin. I am riding Kaysan and he is on Me Mate. I am looking at the plaster cast and wondering what it might tell me about Buffalo's training strategies.*

LEFT *Tourist ponies on Mount Bromo at dawn.*

is having and the attitudes and habits he is spending his time practising. There is no 'too fast' or 'too slow' as a general rule, but if your horse is practising fear, stress or confusion, the chances are you are going to be making very slow progress indeed, and you might need a new idea or two. And, as we keep on discovering, you never do know where the next new idea might come from!

CHAPTER SEVEN

✦

SCIENCE

At the Australian Equine Behaviour Centre, Clonbinane, Australia

IT WAS THREE IN THE MORNING, and my head was ringing with the screeches and whoops of a gaggle of teenage girls. It sounded like they were on a roller coaster. But they weren't, they were running up and down the corridors of the youth hostel we were staying in, having, one could only presume, a very exciting time. The hostel was exceptionally crowded, and Hannah and I had taken the last two bunks available. Our room, which we shared with about twelve other people, was really more of a corridor with no actual doors. None of the other beds was occupied yet, and the lights were neon bright and flickering, it was clearly not bedtime for the gap-year crew. Somehow, we had inadvertently found ourselves at a 'party hostel'. At about 11pm, I had found it sort of cheering to hear them having such a good time – I was reminded of my teenage sisters back home – but by 3am, I was just confused; what could they possibly be doing that had sustained this level of euphoria for so many hours? It was like they were at a Beatles concert, only without the Beatles. It was important to us to get some sleep because the following day we were going to be meeting another group of people that I sometimes struggled to fully understand: equine behavioural scientists.

The day after Equitana and our long sleepless night, we met the others, hired a car and set off to the Australian Equine Behaviour Centre in Clonbinane, about an hour and a half outside Melbourne. I was a little hesitant about the journey, let alone the day, since everyone else in the car was apt to suffer from car sickness. After a stare-out over who would get the front seat, we all piled in and hoped the air con would keep things at bay until we got there. There was Hannah in the driver's position; brave woman with four back-seat drivers – Kelly, Angela, Cara Kimber, an IHRA now based in Perth, and me – offering assistance and directions. We also had three maps that failed to reach a consensus regarding the Melbourne geography and a strong 'road trip' vibe. Since we were heading into the unknown Australian landscape, and beyond that into the maze of equine behavioural science, we all felt pretty adventurous.

The Australian Equine Behavioural Centre's founder, Dr Andrew McLean, has written widely influential articles and books investigating and explaining equine learning processes. I was excited to have the chance to meet him while we were in Australia, but a little daunted by his profile and academic acclaim and the fact that some of our thinking might be at odds. You see, I was a little ambiguous about the world of equine behavioural science.

When compared in particular to the glitz and glamour of shows like the Way of the Horse, science seemed to offer us the chance to cut through the advertising spiel and fashionable approach of the moment; to examine what really works and why. A scientific mind set could empower horse people to be able to analyse horses' behaviour and calculate the most appropriate responses.

In theory, science is defined as: 'the systematic study of the structure and behaviour of the physical and natural world through observation and experiment' which basically means looking at things sensibly, so that sounds pretty good. Being non-biased about observations and making conclusions that are supported by the evidence seems like a great idea for horsemanship, and for everything, actually. It's the sort of system that ought to stop us kidding ourselves into thinking our horses are substitute husbands and children and getting offended when they don't buy us Mother's Day cards or Valentine's gifts.

But I have been really surprised to find that science, as a system, can also come up with some pretty bizarre things. In some ways it seriously seems to have lost touch with reality. I can only fathom that this has happened because science is constrained, limited and even choked by a couple of strong leashes. The first one is money. Science needs lots of it. When I was a child, someone must have led me to believe that the quest for knowledge is pure and true and somehow beyond the limits of finances, like Father Christmas and the tooth fairy. This is not true. Beneath that mythical, wise, fuzzy grey beard of 'knowledge' is just some red-faced sweaty businessman who wants to see a return on his investment. That means the only investigations that get done are ones that are going to make money in one way or another. Money leads science on a merry dance or two around the bushes, in quite different directions than it would have wandered if left to its own devices.

Practically, this means we have a whole heap of science that explores how well racehorses can breathe and not a whole lot that tells you anything about your horse's airborne gymnastic behaviour at a sponsored ride.

The second restraint has to do with the scientific method of limiting variables. For a nice, clean, tidy experiment, scientists would really like only one thing (variable) to change with each trial. This would make it really easy to see the effect this variable had on the results. If I went about my normal business, exactly as I usually would, apart from this time wearing a bikini – it would be reasonable for me to assume that any differences in my day might well be down to my beachwear. This is a good and rational way to collect useful evidence from which to make conclusions.

The problem is, in reality, it just doesn't happen that way; multiple variables interact in a complex, messy way that can't really be summed up in a graph. The consequence is that many investigations into horse behaviour seem to me to be over-simplified, limited, or incredibly abstract. For instance, a study that aims to look into training methods might claim to start with 'twenty untrained female ponies' and might record the heart rates of these ponies from the very beginning of recorded training sessions. But I think, 'how did you find yourself twenty untrained female ponies ready fitted with heart-rate monitors in the right place at the right time?' Either that's a mighty handy coincidence, or some training has happened during catching, selecting, transporting, equipment fitting, etc. that the researchers are discounting because it doesn't fit into the tidy experiment design. It is also the limitations of the scientific method that means occasionally a new piece of research hits the media and has horse people laughing up and down the country because it has 'revealed' something that they have known for generations: that horse's can communicate with their ears, for instance.

Many experiments don't take any account of what happens in real life: the inclusion of a rider (who comes with a whole heap of variables), for example, makes an experiment all too messy; it becomes really hard to keep things clean, so most of the experiments into training methods take the rider out of the equation altogether. This means there have been many studies that look into whether positive reinforcement (e.g. getting food) or negative reinforcement (e.g. escaping discomfort) are better ways of teaching horses to touch certain targets with their noses. Even though the majority of horse trainers do use negative reinforcement for most of their real training, they would also tell you the best way to teach ponies to press buttons is with food. But that's just it: most of us don't need ponies who press buttons. We need ways to calm the darling beasties down when a peacock jumps out of a hedge, their friend turns tail and runs off and a rubbish truck is coming. This sort of thing just never happens in laboratory environments. So the scientific conclusion from the button-pushing test: that positive reinforcement which is the least stressful and most effective training method, can't always be readily applied to real-life riding; and it is frustrating as a horse trainer to read scientific evidence for the 'best' training methods, and to find it so far removed from real-life training needs.

I also can't help feeling that science doesn't do a great job of recognising the emotional aspects of horsemanship. Watching a good horse person feels more like watching an artist than a test in a laboratory. Horses are social animals and working successfully with them needs empathy, intuition and 'feel' – that mystic quality that words and paintings, let alone numbers and science, would struggle to define.

When I studied research, I felt that some equine behavioural scientists were working with a whole different species than the horses I have got to know. The horses in their research seemed like robots rather than sentient beings, so I wasn't yet convinced that science could provide all the answers to the questions that horse training creates. While I absolutely believed in taking a scientific attitude, I wasn't about to trust the scientific culture and system to give me the truth, the whole truth and nothing but the truth when it comes to making informed training decisions.

Equitation science is a new discipline that tries to rectify some of these problems by providing science that is relevant to real-life equitation (hence the cunning name!) This seemed like the type of project that would be right up my street. But I had read some of Dr McLean's work and I could identify at least three areas that could be pretty awkward if they came up for discussion. These included Kelly's and Dr McLean's very different approaches to human/horse relationships, whip training, and Join-Up.

I was familiar with Dr McLean's book (with Dr Paul McGreevy), *Equitation Science*. While I loved the way it made science really readable, easy to understand and applicable to everyday horsemanship, I had also found the book's approach to be pretty clinical; it seemed that everything could be reduced and simplified. It was all very black and white. If a horse bolted, it simply needed the stop response to be reinforced through the proper application of learning theory. If it reared, the go response might well need further conditioning. There was less concern about what the horses or riders might be feeling during these experiences, and the book read a little like a car mechanic's manual that instructs on where to find the throttle and brake and how to fit new ones.

There didn't seem much room at all in Dr McLean's book for the emotional, cultural, or personal elements of horsemanship. Training the horse seemed more like programming the right responses into a machine. I felt that the attitude of the book seemed to suggest that any training method that talked about the relationship between horse and rider was using the idea of 'bond' as a marketing tool, and obscuring the truth about how horses are *really* trained. Sometimes this felt like a dig at horse trainers for talking about the horse's emotional responses, as though in doing so we were either deliberately conning the public with our sentimentalism, or worse, we were bumbling idiots who didn't even understand the basics of stimulus-response learning mechanisms. This was pretty frustrating reading.

So, I just didn't know how much common ground we were going to find if we got on to talking about the way humans and horses relate to one another.

I had butterflies in my stomach as we parked the car, but it didn't take James Bond to ascertain quickly that this was no evil-scientist lair. It was a picturesque wooden stable block with views over a rolling valley, flowering shrubs and then – just to top it off – a wombat waddled across the road and into the blossomy bushes.

Dr McLean ('call me Andrew') was more softly spoken than I expected, very courteous and kind. He approached our group as we got out of the car and extended his hand for a warm handshake. He had grey hair and more smile lines than frown lines. For some unknown reason, I had expected someone stern and poised and maybe a little self-assured but in fact he was gentle and contemplative, and when he walked his footsteps were quiet and light.

You might recognise the feeling of having carefully prepared a polite, tactful, and hopefully educated way of wording an argument only to be met by your opponent looking at you sympathetically and saying, 'Yes, dear, we already know …' It was a bit like that when I met Andrew. Much to my surprise, he already seemed fascinated by the relationship between horse and rider that science has not yet started to chew on. He was also refreshingly open to new learning, and new questions, and I loved the number of times I heard him note to himself, 'Hmmm … that would make a good investigation.'

While I had previously had the impression that Andrew thought science had all the answers, in fact he came across as very aware of the gargantuan abyss that is not yet covered by science, and seemed excited about the chance to nip away at it however he could. It became clear that while he was a world expert in his field, he was not about to rest on his laurels. He was keen and ambitious to continue questioning, researching, and communicating his findings. Far from being dismissive of our ideas about horse-human relationships, he was interested in our opinions and experiences, listening in earnest to our training stories and contemplating the possible neurological processes at play. We had had to go right around the world to meet the man behind the book and realise that actually, since we were all obsessed with horse brains, we had a hell of a lot in common.

Although you can't get to know someone in a day, I was so pleased to find Andrew to be a thoughtful and thoroughly likeable guy. I loved watching him teach a riding class with utmost sincerity; every student and every principle seemed genuinely important to him, and I quickly became less daunted by his academic acclaim, and yet more respectful of him at the same time. Hannah too found this approach most soothing – so much so that she may have closed her eyes for just a second and nodded off – I am sure this has nothing at all to do with the quality of the lesson but perhaps more to do with the travelling schedule and sleeping arrangements. Still at least no one noticed.

After we had a tour around the facilities (imagine your ideal set-up, then double the roses), we had a look at examples of Andrew's approach to training through negative reinforcement. I'm going to take a moment to give you some background on my mind-set during this demo; I have some reservations about the way the term 'negative reinforcement' is applied by some horse people. Negative reinforcement is the learning process at the heart of most of our domestic horse's successful training. Some people hear the word 'negative' and worry that this training is cruel, but it needn't be so. 'Negative' in this context means anything the horse wants to get rid of, but not necessarily something painful or frightening, it could be a tickle, a nudge, an irritating noise. When you apply a negative stimulus (like putting your leg on when riding) and the horse responds in the desired way (like moving forward), you then take away the negative stimulus. The behaviour is reinforced, the horse got a 'pay-off' for doing it, and so the horse learns to do it again. It's an absolutely brilliant learning mechanism often referred to as pressure and release, and horses are great at learning things this way. When you get it right, it's like magic and they just soak things up like a sponge.

The problem that I have with negative reinforcement is that the phrase can give an air of scientific validity to some really bad horsemanship too. If, for instance, you put your leg on and the horse doesn't go forward, it can be tempting to drift into sheer stubbornness: 'I must keep my leg on until he moves forward'. Unfortunately, horses just don't work on a binary system as simple as this approach suggests. What if he gets increasingly stressed, runs backward, or rears, or plants forever and ignores you? Once the person is committed to the nice simple binary rule, it can be all too easy to make it the horse's problem to solve, and it can validate the trainer putting the horse through a fair amount of stress by maintaining, or even increasing, a pressure that the horse is just not properly prepared to respond to correctly.

Remembering the lessons from Equitana, it was still fresh in my head that horses 'learn by doing', so that while this rider may *think* he is using negative reinforcement to teach the horse to move forward, the thing the horse is actually learning is the thing he is practising: resisting, ignoring, evading the leg. Every minute that passes with the horse offering the wrong response is a minute that could strengthen the wrong habit, never mind be stressful or dangerous. It seems to me that the cleverest way to use negative reinforcement is to put a bit more thinking and creativity and, yes, that rather unscientific enigma, 'feel' behind any pressure that you put on the horse.

You need to be a little bit tactful. Let's say your partner is trying to change some habit of yours that they don't like but, for whatever reason, they aren't going to talk to you about it directly. This gives us a sort of training scenario similar to the one we face with horses. Let's imagine they are trying to get you to use the laundry basket. The worst thing they could do is choose to use a pressure that makes no sense to you at all and actually makes it hard for you to offer the right behaviour. They might, for instance, poke you in the eye until you show signs of moving toward the washing pile. This would clearly be a misdirected strategy despite its links to the science of learning.

On the other hand, they might put a different pressure on you by sulking and giving you the cold shoulder. But if you have no idea what on earth to do to get rid of this pressure, it's going to be a tricky time for your relationship. You might try buying flowers, you might try making a nice dinner. You might then try ignoring them back, or getting a bit grumpy yourself. You might eventually get stressed out and shout; finally, you might just give up and go out, maybe for good and never come back. You might never figure out the way to release that pressure, and your relationship might be damaged in the process.

Imagine now that your partner knows how to be tactful and she or he gives you some good little hints, like doing their own laundry in an overly animated way, leaving extra time for you to sort your washing before serving dinner, talking about the annoying laundry habits of other friends' partners and moving the laundry bin so that you have to trip over it to get into bed. This would make it really easy to figure out. If you want the horse to learn how to release the pressure, the best way to do this is to get really cunning, and to set him up to succeed.

Let's apply the same tactful tactics to the horse who doesn't move forward from the leg. Rather than simply maintaining pressure and waiting to see if he does get it right eventually or not, we could think about *why* he isn't moving off the leg, and what we could do to make *sure* he does. Is it because he doesn't understand or because he doesn't want to do it? What would motivate him to offer the correct response? What type of working space, what type of preparation, which way is he going? Is he comfortable moving? There is a lot to think about; there is a lot that goes into successful training.

We need a plan. What should we do if he *doesn't* move instantly forward from the leg? Get a leader to walk in front of him? Have someone behind him use body language to drive him on? Shake a bottle of pebbles? Use a bit of energy from a flick of the reins? Have another horse moving off? Which of these stimuli is *guaranteed* to get the response we want, both from his feet and his attitude? Having set it up to succeed, then we can put the pressure on, get the response we want, release the pressure and repeat the positive practice.

Getting it right for each individual horse is more like a craft than a science, so although the learning is based on the principles of negative reinforcement, there's imagination and creativity in its best application. Riders who take the term 'negative reinforcement' to justify a determined state of kicking/whipping until the horse submits are no more likely to create a forward-going horse than they are to get their partners into good laundry habits. Negative reinforcement should never be used as an excuse for being pig-headed about things.

Of course, the misuse or over simplification of 'negative reinforcement' as an idea is not Andrew's fault, any more than misuse of a double bridle is Carl Hester's. But since some of the worst applications of negative reinforcement that I have seen have been done under a 'scientific' justification, I was curious about what Andrew might do to ensure his students were receiving a more colourful, textured and individualised message.

We saw a brilliant slide show demonstration by one student that showed how 'overshadowing' and negative reinforcement can be used to help a needle-phobic horse. 'Overshadowing' is similar to what I know as distraction. The student, a vet from Edinburgh called Gemma Pearson, showed us photos and videos detailing how she had taught a bay Thoroughbred mare to back up and come forward using negative reinforcement, on the headcollar and with a whip tapping the legs, and then kept the horse moving backwards and forwards at the same time as getting the horse used to the syringe and covered needle by her neck. This worked because the horse prioritised her attention to the backing up and coming forward, and so the danger of the needle was less of an issue. The key was not to progress with the syringe too quickly. Gemma explained that you could tell when the horse was ready for the next stage when the backing up became soft and easy again. If the horse was difficult to back up, it was a sign that the handler had gone too far with the syringe and the overshadowing wasn't working any more.

There was certainly a large degree of individuality and feel involved in this process, which had stunning results on two different, fairly extreme cases, and I think Gemma did a great job. I've not worked with many needle-phobic horses professionally, but I do remember having to inject one daily when I was younger and the trauma it caused both of us in the process. I wish I had been thinking more like a trainer in those days.

By this point in the day, we had got through the horse-human inter-action disputes and found that we were on the same side, but we were now thoroughly into the realm of the second potentially problematic topic: whip-tapping. The advantage of whip-tapping is that you can reach parts of the horse that are too far away to touch with your hands, which might make some things much easier to teach. But, it has always seemed to me quite likely to make horses brace, or encourage them to kick. I suppose it is most likely that I will have come across horses in the past who it really hasn't worked for because the ones who it *did* work well for would not have needed to come looking for a new trainer. I am, therefore, bound to have a fairly skewed set of stories. I guess a few bad trainers have given the technique a bad name. I have seen some seem to lose their ability to think creatively and become drawn into the old problem of mindlessly tapping just a bit harder if things aren't going right, which eventually becomes a good old smack or even an out-and-out whipping tantrum.

I tried to keep an open mind when we had the chance to watch Gemma demonstrate whip training with a four-year-old chunky buckskin (named Buck) who had some loading problems. First she used the whip to tap his front legs to teach him to back up, releasing the pressure, i.e. stopping the tapping, when he stepped backwards. Buck seemed to understand this fairly quickly, and Gemma was able to use this then to teach him to 'park' or stand still on the end of the rope while she backed off a good distance away from him. She then taught him to move forward when the whip tapped his side, around the girth area, again by tapping there and then ceasing tapping when he took a step forward. We were watching with Andrew, who was happy to answer any of our questions while being supportive of Gemma as she showed us the techniques. Next she went to the trailer, tapping the girth area to ask him to come forward onto the ramp, and stopping the tapping when he did, often then backing him off the ramp by tapping the chest, before asking him to come further in. A few times, Buck responded to the tapping by flying backwards several steps, with his ears back and his neck braced, and Gemma had to move pretty quickly in order to remain in a suitable position to be able to keep up the tapping as he ran back.

I did wonder at this stage whether this might be difficult with a more challenging horse who rears up really high, since you need to try to keep yourself by the front legs in order to reach the girth spot for tapping. I thought it might even encourage some horses to try rearing or striking to get rid of you. I wondered if the tapping might escalate tension and fear in a horse that was more extremely evasive or phobic than Buck. But this was just speculation, since in Buck's case it didn't take too long at all before he loaded into the trailer. While it didn't convert me to using whip-tapping myself, I was pleased to have seen the method used well. The tapping was never so hard that I would call it hitting, and Gemma was skilful with her timing.

We had a fabulous lunch, piled around a gorgeous rustic wooden table, with views over a small lake, and ate a wonderful warm quiche with a crumbly pastry, which I still remember. There was also something soft and malty called lumberjack cake. The chatter was busy with ideas and comparisons, and the McLean and IH tribes found plenty of common ground. We also couldn't forget we were the other side of the world when we discussed the forest fire dangers and the previous year's fire damage and destruction. We are so lucky with our safe and comfortable climate in the UK.

So having found there was definitely some commonality on the human-horse relationships issue and having found some internal peace regarding the great whip-tapping debate, there was one more area of discussion to address, and that centred around Join-Up. Kelly and Buck demonstrated a Join-Up for Andrew and some of his students and colleagues and, as I watched, I wondered what Andrew was thinking, since scientific treatment of Join-Up is rare but varied.

It seems to me that some scientists have written papers about Join-Up without really learning what it is, and how it differs from other similar techniques. The way I see it, there are various ways to get the horse to follow you, and all sorts of different learning or emotional processes could be at play with these different types of following, not to mention when they are carried out at different speeds or in different settings.

Some scientists don't like the way Monty explains how Join-Up works. They insist that rather than talk about a social interaction between the human and horse, whereby the horse chooses the human as leader, Join-Up can be better explained by looking at it as a type of negative reinforcement. A recent experiment demonstrated that horses can even learn to follow a remote control car through negative reinforcement. The car moved after the horses until they turned to look at it, and then it stopped. The horses did not like being followed about by the car, and so eventually they learned they had to keep looking towards the car, or some even tried walking towards it, to keep it at bay. This is the same reinforcement process that John Chatterton used when swinging the rope to get face-up.

This type of explanation for the process of Join-Up has led some researchers to conclude that Join-Up is a bad idea, because horses have to learn to follow the very thing they are afraid of, which could be a really horrible experience for them. The ethics of this type of following-training would depend on how afraid the horse was of the stimulus, how long you made him run for, and how easy you make it for him to follow. After all, the horses were not totally terrified of the remote control car, but it was unnerving enough to motivate them to find out how to control it. But I'm sure that Join-Up is not quite the same as the John Chatterton face-up method or the remote control car experiment. There is something else going on besides negative reinforcement.

To illustrate the point, let me tell you about an experience Hannah and I endured when we were in India. We had been travelling to Keoladeo nature reserve, which was known for its rich and varied bird life, including trees that were heavily laden with hundreds of storks. The easiest way to get there was by bus, and the nearest stop was a tiny town in which we had booked a room at a hostel. We hadn't quite accounted for the fact that a flat tyre meant the bus dropped us off in the middle of the night, but the bus driver assured us our hostel was just across the road, and would be no problem to find.

Sadly, this wasn't the case, and after walking up and down the dark, empty town a few times we had attracted the attention of a few local lads. They were following us and shouting out compliments about parts of our anatomy that are frankly not open for public assessment. We decided to cross the two-lane highway and walk along in the wide grassy central reservation, that way we would always have two lanes of traffic between the boys and us. They followed at the first chance they got, and were getting closer, so we crossed again. As we dashed across the road for the third time, back into the central reservation, they were laughing and jeering, finding our discomfort hilarious and it was clear that retreating was only egging them on. We couldn't see anyone about in the deserted shadows of the tiny town to ask for help.

This time, on the dark, bumpy grass and litter, I tripped up towards the traffic, and my heavy backpack prevented me from righting myself; it fell forward over my shoulders and pinned me to the ground. Hannah heaved me up by the shoulder straps before a lorry roared past, my knee was bleeding and my skirt was torn, and by now the boys had nearly caught us up. There was no way of knowing whether this was just banter or whether we were really in trouble here, but they were so close now that running away was no longer a possibility. My heart was thudding in my throat, and there was absolutely no option left but to be brave. I spun round toward the loudest perpetrator, who was so close he could have grabbed me. I was brandishing a water bottle, which I had coldly decided I might poke right into his eye if needed. 'Go away!' I shouted. 'Go right away, turn around and walk away right *now!*'

Surprisingly, this actually had the desired effect and he even apologised for scaring us. We later learned that this is a local custom – 'eve teasing' – and we were probably not in too much danger at all. But the relevance of the story is that we had experienced being relentlessly pursued to a point where turning to face the perpetrator seemed the only option. The only way to release the pressure was to confront it. This is not a pleasant experience, and not one I would wish on any horse.

However, I am sure this is not the best way to describe the phenomenon of Join-Up. I don't think this is the process that is occurring at all. While there is no way we know for sure what's going on in their heads when they follow, I think we would be better off looking to horses' hardwired herding instincts to discover what is occurring. Having watched hundreds of people learn Join-Up, with very variable success in their early attempts, it is clear that the specific body language that the handler uses is incredibly important to the success he is likely to get in follow-up. The person's manner of moving away from the horse (we call it 'invitation') is a fundamental part of their success in getting the horse to follow – i.e. the angle at which you move off, the way you are breathing, the speed, direction and focus with which you walk away. The horse is not pursued to a point of desperation; in fact he completes only about fifteen circuits of the round-pen and does not need to be travelling at speed. A successful invitation feels much more like a successful pick-up in a bar; the right eye contact, the right body language, then walk away confidently and the object of your admiration might well follow. The successful pick-up scenario is nothing like our experience in India, and ways of getting horses to follow people are just as diverse.

We don't fully scientifically understand the way mammals can relate to the body language of other species yet, but it's a clear fact that they do. Quite 'naturally' and without training, most dogs, cats and, of course, horses, will instinctively relate to your body language and emotion. It doesn't mean they literally think you are a horse. I believe Join-Up uses the horse's tendency to be drawn towards certain ways of moving and pushed away from other ways of moving, just like fish-ticklers know how to move their hands to draw fish out from under rocks. There's probably an element of negative reinforcement in the process since the horse finds peace and quiet when they come and join the handler, but it is body language that initially inspires the horse to take steps towards you; you do not wait for the horse to turn in towards you *before* releasing the pressure. This small distinction of timing is really important if we are going to get scientific about it.

It has to be said that I have found there are also many horses who will simply follow the handler without being 'sent away' first at all, particularly when they are in an unknown place or in a restricted area and, again, more likely if the handler can walk in a confident, smooth manner, ideally in arcs and circles rather than straight lines. I believe this keys in to their herd instinct, to feel more comfortable in company, and to synchronise with the movements of the group. Whether or not scientists agree with Monty's way of explaining Join-Up as social, I think they could have plenty to learn from Monty's use of body language and the effect it has on the horse's behaviour.

I hope Join-Up has more time in the scientific spotlight. We not only need to investigate what is happening in the horse's mind when it works, and why it works, but also to look at any changes in the horse's attitude brought about by Join-Up. In that way we could begin to scientifically comprehend how Join-Up works, how the horse experiences it, and how it might be useful in training. While I certainly don't think Join-Up has had a full and fair testing yet, I'm glad there are scientists like Andrew curious and motivated enough to consider putting it through the mill until it is understood better. I just hope they continue to 'join-up' with the trainers and horse people who have plenty of experience with really using Join-Up, so that they can tailor their investigations using the practical knowledge that we have built up.

Unsurprisingly, Kelly demonstrated her Join-Up beautifully. Kelly is always so positive towards the horses she works with and, in return, they always seem to bring out their best side for her. Andrew's training steers away from ever creating the flight response in the horse, and as such, he doesn't use anything that 'sends the horse away', so the section where the horse is moved ahead of the trainer round the pen was probably as hard for him to watch as the whip-tapping had been for me. But I hope he enjoyed seeing that the send-away section of Join-Up could be quite gentle, as Kelly moved Buck about in a gentle trot each way before inviting him in. When Kelly dropped her eye contact away from Buck and walked to the other side of the pen, Buck seemed to move as though he was part of the same shoal, connected by an invisible thread. He walked up behind Kelly's shoulder and reached out his lovely dun nose to meet her. This was great for showing Andrew that the success of Join-Up did not rest on the horse being tired or afraid, and he seemed respectful and interested as he watched.

My own attempt to show another Join-Up wasn't quite so picture-perfect. I worked with a 16hh chestnut mare called Melody. I moved Melody around the pen and she looked quite frustrated at being moved away and as though she clearly wanted to come in. I invited her and she came right to me. She was paying attention and I read her expression as trying to please – her large ears full on me, a lovely soft eye and a relaxed droopy lip – so off I walked, and did she follow? Not an inch. She was looking at me pleasantly, interested, but not even a hair of a step towards me. No problem, I tried plan B. I moved round her in an arc. Plan C, I walked at her and away in a little V shape movement. Plan D, a stroke between the eyes and then walk off. Nothing, nada, no follow-up at all.

I looked up at Kelly and Andrew, somewhat blankly, and her owner exclaimed 'Oh, she's been trained to park – that means not to move off with the handler unless she feels the rope give the signal.' It was explained to us that this is quite a specific stage of the training that Andrew's horses learn. They don't mirror body language and follow handlers forward unless specifically cued to do so with a light pull on the lead rope. The reasoning is that it is supposed to be less confusing for the horse when you tie them or want to leave them somewhere, since they know not to come with you until asked. 'Would the park-training have an effect?' the owner asked, and I confirmed that it definitely would! I was quite relieved that it wasn't that I had just lost my touch at the very least opportune moment possible, and I gave her a nudge on the halter to let her know she was allowed to follow.

Discussions continued in the car on the way home, in between map-reading disagreements, and well into our last supper with Kelly and Angela before they went home. We talked about the training we had seen, and the way horse trainers and scientists really could benefit from collaborating more often. Hannah and I walked Kelly and Angela back to their hotel, and when it was finally time to say goodbye and head back to the party hostel we felt suddenly sad and lonely to be losing our company. Kelly and Angela had come with stories from home, had joked with us, listened to our travel stories, and helped us make sense of the horsemanship we had encountered, not to mention looked after us well and treated us to lovely dinners *and* puddings beyond our travelling budget.

Now we were going back on the road and we wouldn't be seeing anyone else we knew for months. When we got back to our hostel room, we noticed a new foot-sized hole in the wall next to our bunks, we saw all the sleeping, nocturnal teenagers beginning to wake up for the night's activities, and we felt a little desolate. But in just a few days we were flying to Fiji and then on to New Zealand, and Hannah had found that we could block out the noise by listening to Desert Island Discs through our earphones. We settled down to sleep and looked forward to the next adventure.

As I lay in bed waiting for sleep to find me under the flickering light, I reflected on the lessons of the day. The first was that I had vastly underestimated Andrew and his commitment to sharing important information about the horse's brain. The way he sees it, people are far too often likely to over-complicate the horse's behaviour and see it in human terms, and by sharing the nuts and bolts of learning mechanisms, and the way they can be applied to horsemanship, he can save a lot of horses and owners a huge amount of stress and confusion. That's a pretty cool aim, and I should have been more generous in the way I had read his book and the image of him that I had created from it.

The second point I mulled over was the question, is horsemanship a science or an art? I guess I'd still argue that it is an art, but that good science can help us to understand the properties of our canvas and materials. The best trainers, like the best artists, might well not understand the physics and chemistry behind what makes their art beautiful, and the best scientists might not develop the feel and creativity required in cultivating a perfect picture of training. That's why I believe trainers and scientists need one another, and normal horse people need both.

There is no such thing as a perfect trainer, and so a scientific mind-set has to become a solid foundation for analysing, evaluating and improving our art. Even this approach can't guarantee us a masterpiece, though. As Melody reminded me, there are still going to be those egg-on-face moments that add a healthy dollop of humility to anyone's colour pallet!

✦

CHAPTER EIGHT

NATURE

In Cambridge, New Zealand

W<small>E WERE GETTING</small> down and dirty with nature in New Zealand, camping each night by beaches, lakes or mountains and cooking noodles on the camping stove. We were literally 'tramping', because that was the local word for hiking, and the term seemed more than appropriate in many ways. Luckily for us, matted hair was known as the 'beachy' look, and was apparently all the rage. We had also picked up a couple of giggling German hostages – sorry – *hitchhikers* to bully into swimming in ice cold lakes with us, and were generally having an awesome time getting to know Mother Nature at her most magnificent.

New Zealand is a great place for seeing how people interact with nature. One morning we had shared our campsite with hiking ninjas who were dressed in black from head to toe, remained poker faced as they ate astronaut food and made a martial art of tent origami. On the other end of the scale were the happy hippies, feeling most at one with nature by bobbing along through it at a leisurely pace in their colourful camper vans, and providing a home for the nation's unwanted possums within the trusses of their dreadlocks. Mankind's relationship with nature is certainly complex. There is a satisfaction in being able to tame it, climb it and bungee jump into it, while maintaining an underlying desire for some elements of nature's forces to always remain beyond our control.

Cambridge, on the North Island, is almost like a shrine to what can be achieved when man is able to harness the horse's natural potential. The streets are literally paved with stars of New Zealand's equine elite – including one of my favourites, Mark Todd's fabulous mount Charisma. The town provided me with a fascinating glimpse into the interface between man and nature that occurs through Thoroughbred racing as Thoroughbred studs are its biggest equine industry. The studs' slick management systems churn out vast numbers of blue-blooded athletes with a regularity and efficiency that apparently has nature bridled and harnessed for maximum profit. But if the racing crowd really wanted full control of the speed machines they create and invest in, surely they would all turn to Formula 1 or motorbike rallies? But there's something about the unpredictability of nature, the individuality of the horses, that makes the racing game all the more alluring.

Foals are a beautiful example of nature's little mysteries. However much the birth is planned and paid for, it is Mother Nature who really holds the cards when it comes to breeding. Man must just sit back and watch, with a gambler's interest, to see what nature has in store and which traits will emerge. Nowhere is the untold potential of the clumsy creatures more palpable than on a Thoroughbred stud, where each little wide-eyed tip-toer could become a multimillion-dollar racehorse. This is, of course, unbeknown to the foals, thank goodness, who are not only investments waiting to ripen or plummet, but who also are first and foremost individuals, blissfully busy discovering the world, learning what it is to be alive, and how best to operate the unfamiliar stilts. I haven't had an awful lot to do with foals; they're something of a mystery to me. So when I heard of two ladies who specialise in handling and training huge numbers of Thoroughbred foals on studs in Cambridge, I had to find out more. How would such a manufactured, industrial realm of horsemanship collide with nature's wild side during the taming of these young spirits?

I felt very privileged to have the chance to accompany Leigh Wills and Sally King on one of their working days. The sheer numbers of foals these two have handled is incredible, and when you combine these figures with their active enthusiasm to learn, it's no wonder the ladies had honed their expertise into an extremely effective and thoroughly developed system.

Leigh, a born and bred Kiwi, had successfully evented in younger years, and had founded Equus Equitation, a foal-training business, in 1999. Rather than disappear into the background, the ladies wore T-shirts in the business colour of hot pink, with Equus Education and their names picked out in embroidery. Leigh asserted that this made them easy for stud staff to spot and identify from a distance, but I have a feeling Leigh quite liked looking pretty snazzy too. I have been brought up better than to guess the age of a lady, and in Leigh's case, I wouldn't have much of a hope of getting it right anyhow. She had a youthful, healthy energy, a go-getting attitude, a smooth tan, and shiny blonde hair in better condition than the majority of horse people seem to keep it (myself included). It became clear she also had way more horse stories than could possibly have fitted into the life-span she looked the right age for. Sally, British by birth, had joined Leigh in 2005, a younger recruit, with dark hair tied up out of the way. Sally emanated patience when she worked with the horses, and moved with fluidity and grace. Like Leigh, she had the square-standing stance of people who use their bodies at work and love their job. Both ladies were strong but never braced, confident but not arrogant, with a great sense of humour, and I found them fantastic company.

At the first stud of the day, the initial job was working out where the mares were, with the help of giant whiteboards that mapped each horse's whereabouts within the town-sized property. Leigh and Sally consulted their files to ascertain which mares they need to work with that day and where to find them. We then picked up the equipment we needed and headed off in the car around the stud, which was in 'best kept village' type condition; there was very little evidence whatsoever that horses ever poo. The mares and foals were turned out in numerous paddocks, about three or four in each field, with plenty of space, immaculate fencing and ankle-deep grass. Each mare wore a tag around her neck to identify her. Munching away, I'm sure it didn't bother the horses whether the staff can be relied on to remember their names, but it certainly took a bit of getting used to that the horses were farmed in such large numbers that they seemed to be tracked like post-office parcels.

Leigh and Sally's job was to halter train the Thoroughbred foals, to train them to lead, to be handled and to have their feet picked up. They begin this process at three to six weeks of age, since this is when foals naturally begin to spend a bit less time with their mothers and a bit more time being curious and adventurous. This was the first example of the way the ladies have decided to plan their training to work with nature, rather than against it.

In each location, Leigh or Sally would catch a mare, bring her into a quiet corner of the field and then spend about five to fifteen minutes training the foal, before returning the pair and fetching the next. They explained that over many days, each foal would be handled several times, until they reached a level of handling and attitude that ticked the right boxes and meant they could 'graduate' from the programme. Before Leigh and Sally arrived, the studs did not have a system for handling foals at all and generally left them until they were weanlings, at which stage it was a bit of a wild and rugged sport getting those first halters on and early handling underway. Horses and handlers had been hurt, but since Leigh and Sally's involvement in training the foals at a younger age, no staff or horses had been injured during the same processes, so from the stud's perspective, the investment was a sound one.

Leigh and Sally's approach continued to work with, not against, the mare and foal's instincts. For instance, they had found a way of taking the work to the mare rather than the mare to the work, thus negating the need to battle with her natural herd instincts. Leigh and Sally carried a blue padded mat around with them; it had Velcro to attach it to any fence line so that they can create a safe place to handle the foals without having to move the mare away from her companions and into unfamiliar surroundings. It looked like a piece of gym equipment and was used to help absorb any foal gymnastics rather than have them bounce off or get tangled in the fencing.

They also make good use of the naturally calming effect that firm pressure had on the foal. When the foals were worried about being touched, or fretful in general, Leigh or Sally would move their bodies closer to the foals and, if needed, put their arms around them to offer a firm hold. The firm pressure seemed to instinctively relax the foals, in a powerful way that quite surprised me. The reaction I saw reminded me of a film by Temple Grandin, an autistic woman who explored the use of squeeze chute systems to calm autistic people, having seen the calming affect a chute can have on cattle. We also saw at first hand the calming affect that swaddling has on a human infant when the method was skilfully deployed by Sally with her gorgeous baby, Ollie: one air-boxing grouch was instantly transformed into a very content sushi roll!

Leigh and Sally used a foal's proximity to a mare as an indicator of how close to stand themselves. A foal gained comfort from the physical pressure of mum's side against them, and simultaneously would accept the firm pressure of the human on the other side. As the foals became brave enough to stand on their own feet and in their own space, they didn't need the close contact with their mares and were also able to cope with a more distant, obvious touch from the human too. I have to say the whole thing was conducted so calmly and with such skill that it looked very easy – but I was not fooled – the foals were as reactive as little deer, and I am sure any horse person's skills would be honed by working with such quick reflexes and heightened senses. One half-step in the wrong place and you may as well be the other side of the paddock for how far it will get you, and the foals can change so quickly and dramatically that you need to keep your eyes peeled, without walking on eggshells or acting like you are stalking prey. Both Leigh and Sally had embodied a relaxed but ever-ready way of conducting themselves. They seemed able to physically absorb any wriggles or worries that a foal had, without allowing the little one to leap away and become fretful, but without causing panic with the restraint either.

Perhaps the most beautiful use of nature's helping hand was in the way that the ladies worked with the mares. Although not employed to train mares, Leigh and Sally had found it hugely beneficial, and rewarding, to get mum on side and give her a nice time too; this makes good use of the foal's natural tendency to mirror the mare's adrenaline levels. Since their smooth-running system relied on mum standing in her parking spot and keeping calm, the mare handler had the lovely job of pampering mum in any way she liked. They'd found one genius way of doing this using salt licks, which was a drool-worthy treat without encouraging the nipping and barging that comes with tit-bits or handfuls of food.

One grey mare was very interested and perhaps concerned about what was going on with her exquisite dark bay filly. Every time she turned around to see the filly, Sally, who was standing close to the foal, would give her a reassuring stroke and let her touch noses with the foal. At one point, the mare put her nose onto the foal's back, breathing warm air and ruffling the fuzzy bay coat. Smoothly, Sally made use of this contact point and placed her hand next to mum's nose on the filly's back. The filly twitched an ear back to check what the new sensation was, but accepted the touch with no worry or resistance. It felt really special to see such subtle ways of using the mare to help, rather than hinder, foal training, and I could have watched Leigh and Sally for days – I was quite transfixed.

The biggest lesson for me, though, was that of the individual temperaments that nature assigned to each foal before we even meet them. I suppose it's easy as a trainer to focus on the things we can change, the way that management and training can manipulate and alter the behaviours a horse shows. Most problem horses I come across have a history, and 'raw' horses are so much easier to train and start than remedial ones; all this means it's easy to blame human conduct for all the horse's problems and at the same time congratulate human brilliance when the horses do well. But New Zealand seemed the ideal place to reflect on the sheer power and potential of nature and the studs provided unmistakable opportunities to witness the unique expression of each young student. It certainly got me thinking, more than ever before, about the massive effect our horses' natural, raw temperaments have on the lives they will lead and the worlds they will live in.

It was really quite wonderful to see the difference in the foals' personalities at such a young and naive stage. While some clung close to mum and peeped out timidly from behind her tail, others were nosey, or casual, or 'stressy'. Having spent all morning watching Leigh and Sally coaxing fairly delicate little beings into becoming active participants, I was totally flabbergasted by the sheer balls of one little guy who wanted to use me as a climbing frame while I fetched his mum in from the field. He tossed his head like a little stallion and had no problem whatsoever getting up close and friendly. The chance to experience this natural variety is a rare one.

Leigh told me that as soon as training begins, the natural differences in the horse's personas become harder to spot. It becomes complex to sort the nature from the nurture and to know who each horse naturally was. She told me of one, very rare, filly, who had shown pretty aggressive signs during early handling. The filly had changed quickly with training and would now appear happy and quiet to handle to any observer, but Leigh wondered whether this tendency would show itself again at later stages of her life.

Really we know very little about horses' individuality and the genetic or learned makeup of their temperament. We struggle enough to know how to holistically describe human personality!

I have seen systems for horses that divide them into right- and left-brained, or that label them based on their breed and sex. One personality test currently being explored by scientists rates horse personalities against five scales: dominance, anxiety, protectiveness, sociability and inquisitiveness. That sounds quite comprehensive when you read it, but it doesn't take long to think of a horse who you would struggle to define using only these parameters. Another scientific method for investigating one dimension of temperament is the novel-object test, whereby an umbrella, for instance, is flailed at the horse to see how they react, but this of course only gives a very narrow understanding of who the horse is and how they will cope with training (I'm sure that 'flailed' is not the scientifically accepted term, but you get the drift).

I often like to ask owners of spooky or grumpy horses to observe them in the field to see whether the traits are still present when people are not; this can shed light on the horse's true demeanour as opposed to learned associations with human contact. But the truth is it's really hard getting to know horses (as it is people), and no test can really give you a short cut that comprehensively sums up each individual's nature accurately.

What I had learned from Leigh, though, is that it really does make the most sense to do something totally novel if you want to learn about a horse's untrained reactions. Imagine if you could apply this when buying a new horse. If we consider horse viewings as speed dating, since you need to get to know him pretty quickly, the challenge of the meeting is to figure out which questions to ask the horse during the speed date! Perhaps one of the best ways to get to know the horse quickly would include teaching him a really novel task, or putting him in a really novel situation. You would quite possibly learn more about him this way then seeing him in his usual routine.

It was Leigh who inspired this line of thought when she told me that the work with the foals has made her realise that she would always buy a horse for his temperament rather than his ready-trained behaviours. Of course, we all know a quiet horse is better for some jobs and a hot one for others – but that's only the very tip of the personality iceberg. An easy first step to becoming a world-class horse trainer would surely be the ability to recognise a world-class student, but it's actually really difficult to decide exactly what type of natural personality would be ideally suited to various equestrian pursuits.

Do you really want a super-intelligent horse, or would he just talk *you* into the advantages of going around the fences? Do you really want the bravest horse you could find? How would you go about distinguishing between bravery and lack of reactivity because, for most jobs, reactivity is important. There is certainly much still to study.

Leigh is compiling some impressive research, which among other things is looking at equine behavioural traits that are present at just three or four weeks of age, and how likely these behaviours are to show up again later in development (as well as how likely these horses are to go on and win races). This seems like such foundational, important research that in some ways it's terrifying that it isn't already better explored. Imagine the stress that could be saved if we could work out a horse's ideal job, and best training approach, from just a few months of age and save wasting his time and mentality by pushing him into the wrong start in life. I am excited that this type of research will continue to shed light on a horse's individual behavioural tendencies and the way they develop through training, and I look forward to following Leigh's results.

So we must never underestimate the importance of innate temperament. It would be arrogant and ignorant to think that we are ever shaping a totally blank canvas in our horse training efforts. I was mulling over this very point as Hannah and I made our way up a rather large and beautiful mountain, pretending to be much fitter than we are, when we came across a couple making their way back down. They were a friendly pair and stopped to chat for a while before heading on. He was tall, German, with a big toothy grin, and his two-month-old baby girl strapped to his front. Well this threw a spanner in the works of my mind, since how on earth could I fail to notice the radical start in life this little person was getting? This child had literally climbed mountains before she could walk – how could that fail to give her a lift in life? If she went on to be a fabulous mountaineer, it would be pretty hard to ever distinguish whether she was bred or trained to climb, and no doubt each element plays a part.

A few days later I met a lady with a London accent – she stood out like a red telephone box in the room of Kiwis, despite the fact she had lived in New Zealand for over twenty years. Why was it that she had not altered her accent to fit her environment? She certainly wasn't born ready to address the Queen of England, but her early education had instilled in her a way of speaking and a way of being so deeply that it felt now like the natural raw material she was made of.

These two examples of the lasting impact of nurture offer some hope (or warning) that our training might be absorbed so thoroughly that it too, could feel totally natural to the horse and become *part of* who he really is, rather than a layer of learning on top of his true temperament.

Leigh and Sally hope that their training is more profound than instilling a finite set of learned behaviours. They hope to alter the horse's whole outlook and enable them to better cope with new situations that they will encounter in the future. Each youngster may have his own mind, but his attitude to life is shaped dramatically by the lessons he learns. The first few touches each horse receives are therefore precious: for the foal, because he will carry them for life; and for us, as a rare chance to view the raw reactions of the foal without the baggage of previous training. Never will there be such a clear window to glimpse the untrained temperament and reactions of each little creature. From this point on, nature will tangle with nurture as the young horses begin to form patterns of thought and behaviour, and we try to get along with both. Who he was born, and what he has learned, will become knotted together in how he reacts for the rest of his life.

During our travels there were two other times that the wildness of nature had me perplexed, and I hope you don't mind me digressing briefly to talk about other species. The first was in Bali. We were staying at a small fishing village on the coast, and had borrowed flippers and snorkels so that we could take a look at life on the coral reefs. This was going to be my first time snorkelling, and I was brimming with excitement. There was an occasional tourist boat that took people out to deeper water and better corals, but we thought this was clearly just a money-making scheme since the reefs could be seen just a short wade out from the white beaches.

Flippers are really only any good for actual swimming. For any other activity, they are definitely inhibitive. Wading through the shallow waves with clumsy high steps like a fishy clown, and brushing some of the floating rubbish aside, I wondered if we had made the right choice. We had been advised to stick to the sandy paths that led out into the coral and to avoid the dead coral, which sadly lined the beach and was razor sharp. At this stage, that was easy. Once we got to about waist deep, the walking was getting ridiculously difficult and it seemed easier to float on our tummies and paddle along with the flippers, so we put our masks on and flopped forwards into the water.

Instantly I was transported. I gasped so hard I almost sucked water into my snorkel. I had just no idea how much life was down there. I had thought we would need to swim much further out before catching the odd glimpse of a fish or two, but the life beneath me was teeming and I found it quite overwhelming. Had it been there right by my legs all this time I had been wading? There were fish like Nemo and all his friends from the film. One was bright blue, with a mauve underside and yellow lips. Another was big and ugly like a moving boulder. Another long and thin like the blade of a sword. Some came in great shoals and swept across gracefully like a chorus of dancers. Others pottered busily about amongst the coral. It was hard to keep tabs on them all, and new ones kept appearing all the time. I realised how little I understood them – this may seem an obvious comment to make, but they were nothing like horses *at all*. I couldn't even guess what any of them were thinking, or which ones were predatory, or protective of their space or if they were poisonous. They had neither eyebrows like humans, nor flexible ears like horses, which made any sort of emotional reading impossible, and it dawned on me that I had absolutely no idea what sort of emotional experiences fish could have. It seemed to me that they were unfazed by me entirely, and sometimes they would swim past my mask and along the side of my body. I felt so cumbersome and unmanoeuvrable in the water compared to their agility that it would occasionally give me shudders as they darted in and out of my vision, around my body.

Amazed, I looked for someone to share the experience with and realised Hannah was out of sight from beneath the water, so I lifted my head to look for her. As I did my knee came down and sliced into coral stinging instantly. My instinctive reactions to pull my limbs close in to me only resulted in more scrapes and grazes, by which point my snorkel had taken in water and was making me splutter. For just a second, I couldn't put my feet down and I couldn't get my breath back.

Eventually I got myself reorganised and decided to head into deeper water to avoid a repeat. In the deeper water, I found Hannah, swimming right down low and popping up occasionally for air, as happy in the water as a seal. But in the deeper water, visibility was not so good and the fish were bigger. This meant that quite quickly a midnight blue emptiness could be broken by some small alien beings travelling very purposefully in my direction. As I began to spot bigger and bigger fish – some who could surely easily eat a lap dog – my mind also wandered to my coral injuries, and I began to entertain the idea that there could be a shark somewhere sniffing my blood. I reconsidered and decided the shallows were definitely a better option so I left Han to dive about like a porpoise and went back to floating around feeling absolutely entranced by the otherworldly beings in the shallow water; entranced but also clumsy, ridiculous, ignorant and vulnerable.

By the time we came in from the sea, we were both sunburnt and there were many more scratches, but I would repeat it all again in a heartbeat given half the chance. I know tons of people reading this might well have snorkelled plenty of times and made less of a fuss about it. But I am sharing it here because the experience for me was profound. I gained new insight into how much there is that we don't understand about nature, and how ruled we are by our own natural instincts and restrained by our own bodies. Rather than feeling like the human race was the ruling species, I suddenly had the perspective that there is so much about other animals' life-worlds that we will never be able to really grasp and understand, and so however hard we try, the true nature of horses, the way they really think and feel, exists in a different sensory and cognitive dimension to our own.

The second time nature overwhelmed me was in Bolivia, in the rainforest, where we were based for two weeks helping at a wildlife refuge called Inti Wari Yassi. My job was to clean out the capuchin monkeys that were housed in quarantine, to feed them and provide them with 'enrichment'. Enrichment means hiding food in bamboo, or freezing fruit juice, or anything else we could think of to try to make up for the fact they had nothing to do all day. The capuchins were all ex-pet monkeys who had been rescued or given up to the sanctuary. Realistically, there was next to no chance of release into the wild for most of the monkeys and, because of the sheer numbers that ended up at Inta Wari Yassi, the conditions for the monkeys were pretty cramped. Because there was no hope of any sort of naturally functioning social group, most of the monkeys were kept in cages on their own or in pairs, but some, who could be trusted not to attack each other or passing staff, were allowed out on runners. This involved a dog collar around their waist that was attached to a length of strong cord with a karabiner clip at the other end. This clip could be attached to one of many ropes that ran through a playground-type structure of wood, so that the monkeys could run around on the wood and reach each other to play or groom.

On my first day, I heard plenty of horror stories about injuries the monkeys had caused volunteers in the past. Capuchins are small, but absolutely made of muscle; they have strong and clever fingers, and huge sharp teeth, particularly the males whose jaws reminded me of a pit bull's. The first capuchin I met was Pepper. Her coat was a dark, chocolaty brown, the wrinkly, grey skin on her face made her extremely expressive, and her long tail seemed to have a life of its own. When I saw her for the first time I was taken with her human-like fingernails, her bright button eyes, and her contemplative expression as she looked directly at me. Like with the fish, it struck me that I had no idea what she was thinking, or who she was, or how her mind worked – even though, unlike the fish, she did have lovely grey expressive eyebrows. I also knew that volunteers came in and out of her space weekly, and I could guess that life as a pet hadn't worked out too well for her. I had no interest in feeling like I had the right to want to cuddle Pepper, or touch her, or do anything to her at all really. I got to work on cleaning the cages and left Pepper and the others to their own devices.

As the days went by, I watched the monkeys interacting with each other and with the staff and volunteers, and I began to get a feeling for the likely rhythms of their behaviour. If someone went to pick a monkey up, this would always be met with fury. To be manhandled without consent, as though they had no rights over their own bodies or plans for where they wanted to go, made the monkeys irate. Most of the horror stories I had heard on arrival focused around volunteers who had thought they were pets or cuddly toys. While they couldn't be wild animals any more, they were always going to be wild animals at heart and could never be truly tame.

One little chap, whose name 'Conico' meant rabbit, was only very young and runty, with buck teeth. I loved to watch him busying himself in the undergrowth. When he found a wasp, he would roll it up in a leaf, and squish the leaf up and smash it about so that when he opened the parcel, he could eat the wasp juice and avoid the sting. He obviously had a knack for solving problems. While I was cleaning near him one day, he brought himself over and pushed on my lap until I sat down. Then he reached across and picked up my hand with both of his, sat in my lap and plonked my hand down on the earth. He watched my hand intently for a moment or two, and when I did nothing, he went back to my hand and pushed it back and forth on top of the earth.

I couldn't understand what he wanted, and after a few more attempts he scampered off and came back with a twig, which he put in my hand and then tried shoving it about again. I tried digging a little with the stick, which at first seemed to fill him with glee, but then he went back to pushing my hand in circles across the top of the dirt, not in the little hole I had made. Finally, I got what he wanted and started drawing circles and shapes in the soil and he was fascinated, watching closely without blinking and putting me back to work with a gentle shove of my hand if I ever stopped. When I had to get up to go he seemed distressed, clinging on tightly to my clothes with his infant like fingers and making all sorts of distressed noises that were horrible to hear.

And finally there was Dawn, whose baby had been killed by an escaped male just days before we arrived. Even without the gift of verbal language it was clear she was in deep grief. She was listless and lifeless, curled up doing very little, staring blankly at the floor and her facial expressions were so similar to those of our own species when we are desperately sad, both her eyes and mouth down turned. On one of my breaks, I decided to sit near Dawn and be kind to her. I had no idea what kindness might be for a monkey. I wouldn't have been so presumptuous as to assume I could stroke her, and throwing a ball or whatever would clearly be an insult to her intellect. We were not allowed to give food outside of the set routine and her appetite was almost non-existent anyway, even at meal times. But I hoped if I just sat with her and thought about how to be kind, something might come to me, and no harm would be done if it didn't.

After a few moments, Dawn came over and gently jumped up onto the rock behind me. I felt her strong fingers fighting with my hair and she pulled out my hairband, taking half my hair with it. I thought it must be that she wanted my band to play with, as Pepper had been leaping on people and stealing hairbands off them all week and had quite a collection. But she reached over my shoulder and dropped it into my lap, and turned her attention back to my hair. Firmly, she pushed my head down so that my chin was on my chest and then began grooming, picking through the roots with her finger and thumb, and sorting the cleaned hair to one side with the flat of her hand. I'm not sure what it was she kept finding that led her to occasionally thump or slap the top of my head quite hard, without warning, but I can only hope that whatever it was she managed to kill it and remove it. The grooming lasted about ten minutes before I had to leave to get back to work.

Every day after this I would go back on my break and Dawn would groom me, though she never let me groom her back; on one occasion I tried and she firmly pushed my hand away and showed me her teeth. The deep, thoughtful expression in Dawn's eyes, below her heavy brow, was no less complex than that on the face of another human.

I found caring for the capuchins hard work emotionally. Their lives had been so messed up by human intervention, and nothing we could do at this stage could really put it right again. Some species, I think, are just too wild to be happily tamed. Without language, even species that are very similar to us, like the capuchins, are beyond our comprehension, and beyond our control. We can't make them into the happy, calm pets that many people wish they could be. There are, of course, also animals that thrive in domestication, and have evolved to be more at home in human households than anywhere else, like the good old Labrador dog or Persian cat. They live with the family full time and, for the most part, even in their wildest moments, they are really not too dampened by the domestic life.

Horses, for me, are somewhere between wild and tamed species. They are not so wild that they cannot enjoy domestic life, but they are not so tame that many of them cannot survive perfectly well without us either, as we had witnessed with the brumbies of Australia. Even our domestic horses live most of the hours of their days without us about, and the truth is they are probably quite at peace grazing in a group when we are not there. They don't live in our houses with us as part of our pack or family. There is quite a bit of wilderness still left in the horse, compared to our pet dogs and cats for instance, but luckily for us many individuals seem to thrive in a domestic setting and to readily accept the infringements that this entails, as long as the training and management makes a compromise by working with the natural instincts wherever possible. The one thing I can tell you, having watched Leigh and Sally's work, was that however planned your horse's birth might have been, however docile he is now, he was born wild, untamed, and untouched.

So, the New Zealand leg of the trip had me reflecting on the natural world at large and concluding that nature is certainly powerful: I had lost three cameras to volcano dust, water and weather damage, spent my time acting as a walking sand-fly snack bar, and at one point was very nearly slapped in the face by a jumping salmon. It was clear that we need to work with our horse's nature rather than against it because, like weather to a sailor, nature can be the wind in our sails or it can sink us. If we can learn more about exploring each horse's natural temperament, perhaps we can do a better job of selecting the right partner for our chosen equestrian career, and the right training approach for our chosen partner. Despite the massive impact that our training can have on our horse's mentality, at the end of this chapter I'm quite pleased to feel ultimately overpowered by nature. I believe that the horse's nature is still beyond our control and our comprehension, and that each horse harbours some individual, innate consciousness, that makes him who he really is, too deeply rooted for human meddling to ever truly comprehend.

CHAPTER NINE

KINDNESS

In Vicuña, Chile

WE LEFT A GREEN AND FERTILE NEW ZEALAND, crossed the International Date Line and arrived earlier than we had left in the starkly different landscape of Chile. I was particularly taken with El Valle de la Luna (Valley of the Moon) near the town of San Pedro de Atacama, which certainly seemed to live up to its name. The moon was bigger and closer than I had seen it before, and it looked more tangible, like a golden Christmas bauble hanging just out of reach. The stars were abundant, dusted generously across the night sky like sugar. Every patch of darkness, when I came to look closer, was full of distant stars, and so many shooting stars that I totally ran out of things to wish for. During daylight hours, the landscape itself was like the surface of another planet: dry, yellow and red. The high altitude made the air thin and thirsty, and the hot wind dried out our skin and burned our lips. In some areas the sand gathered in sweeping high dunes, downhill running racetracks for the brave or stupid, or those chasing windblown hats. In other places, grey-blue sandy rocks formed cliffs and ledges from which huge cacti grew. This all set a stage for the most abstract feature: red rocks stretched up out of the ground, artfully sculptured by the fingers of the wind into twisted figurines like frozen dancers.

The people in Chile certainly lived up to all stereotypes: wearing ponchos, Chilean cowboy hats and eating a lot of beef. But maybe that's because most of them were tourists! In fact it seemed so full of typical Chilean delights in the sandstone town that I felt as if we really had stumbled across 'Chile-Land, the theme park'. Still, I'm not one to get grumpy about the tourist trade; with our backpacks and alpaca wool jumpers we were definitely part of the flock. We met some lovely people in San Pedro and the local people were hospitable and happy to be as Chilean as your money was green. But we weren't just in Chile to marvel at the rock formations. We were after a real-life Chilean cowboy – the genuine artefact – not the type you could hire from one of the tourist trekking groups. Luckily we found just what we were looking for two days south of San Pedro de Atacama in Vicuña, which was humming with excitement as the New Year celebrations approached.

The villa we stayed in was just beautiful. Like many in the region, it had a giant, heavy ancient door that opened onto a central courtyard room with a tiled floor and no ceiling, so that you could see the stars at night. Our hostess was wonderfully friendly, and so excited to hear about our horsey adventures, though there were no horses in her life now. She chattered away at such speed in Spanish that we couldn't really follow much, but I guessed the general gist as she beamed and pointed proudly at the computer screen. She showed us picture after picture of her children riding horses, horses she remembered from when she was a child, and unknown horses that she had just taken photos of because she liked them. Best of all, she knew a local rodeo-horse trainer, one Ramón Luis Alvarez Ojeda, who might allow us to meet him and learn about his methods. We got straight in touch via email, and while we waited for a reply, there was nothing to do but join the rest of the village in getting festive about the arrival of the New Year.

We hired bikes and went for a lovely ride around the empty desert valley until Hannah punctured a tyre – but luckily for us she managed to do this just yards from the only house we had seen for miles. Only it wasn't a house, it was a Hare Krishna temple, and the commune were more than happy to help with the tyre as well as giving us some fermented fig drink to cleanse us spiritually before we got back on our way. How on earth do we swing this type of luck?

That evening we had obviously missed out on the etiquette guide and were foolish enough to book dinner for 9pm – so geekily early, it turns out, that the only other people eating in the whole place were the DJ and the waiter. We knew that socialising started late in Chile, but it was a bit of a surprise that no one even bothers coming out for midnight. We were starting to assume the whole town was empty and head back to our room when the live music finally began from a stage in the plaza – at about 2am. Everybody, of every age, came out of their houses and danced together – Dads danced with babies, grandmothers jiggled about joyously, teenagers flirted, and married couples embraced with the sort of public display of affection that makes most of us Brits turn pink. We had found ourselves a friend for the evening in a chap who was cycling around the whole of South America, sleeping out in the desert with his tent. The three of us threw caution to the wind and terrified the locals with our version of salsa until the early hours of the morning, at which point, I have to add, the grandmothers and babies were still going strong.

By some small miracle Hannah woke up at 9.30am, and decided to check emails. Ramón had replied, inviting us to meet him at 11am. He was an hour's bus journey away and I was still nestled up like a sleeping dormouse! We got up, got out, somehow managed not to miss the bus, and then we had time to think, look out the bus window and wonder where we were going. We were getting a little used to that churning feeling that comes when you have no idea what on earth you are entering in to, but were filled with substantial relief when we spotted Ramón waiting for our bus to arrive. There was definitely an air of something wonderfully familiar about him – a faint aroma of one my best friends from home, a horse trainer, ex-rugby player, marine sailor, deep-sea diver, general action man, and all around awesome fellow called Jim Goddard! Ramón was tall, broad-shouldered, well-weathered and strong, with a short greying beard and the sort of authentic, open smile that doesn't often come with such manly looking men. On meeting, he wrapped us up in a warm bear hug, and we were instantly reassured.

Somehow Ramón managed two near-impossible things in just one day: he got me drunk and he got me wearing rotating spurs of a most unsettling nature. With such powers of persuasion I'm not surprised he can also train a horse or two. There is a challenge before me in relaying honestly everything I experienced in order to share it with you, at the same time as leaving you with the same respect and warmth for Ramón that I feel. This is a challenge because the ethical decisions Ramón negotiates are worlds apart from my own and, I suspect, from many of my readers'.

But the day started with us, yet again, repeating a pattern of horsemen's dodgy vehicles all over the world: we found ourselves squeezed precariously into a Jeep that had seen better days, legs wrapped around the gear stick and hanging on tight while we jump-started it down the hill. Ramón informed us with a smile that luckily he lives among plenty of hills so with a bit of planned parking, car starting is never a problem. We set off up the dirt track, leaving dusty clouds in our wake, into the foothills of the sandy mountains to meet Ramón's herd. The best news of all is that while we might have been over optimistic about our own language capacity, Ramón had vastly understated his, and so we were able to talk fairly comfortably in English, which occasionally drifted into Spanglish or mime. We had been relying largely on the wonders of Google-translate to communicate fully with Ramón before meeting him. It's a double-edged sword: on the one hand who knows if we would have even organised ourselves a meeting with a Chilean cowboy (or 'huaso') without cheating; on the other hand, we had potentially set ourselves up for a really awkward moment where our tactics caught up with us. We were worried that we would be restricted to repetitively squawking 'que?' in the style of *Fawlty Towers*' Manuel, while the cowboy lost patience and galloped into the distance on his noble steed. Luckily we were spared this nightmare by Ramón's good humour.

The first job was to water the horses, out of huge vats, carried in the back of the Jeep. Each horse was led to water and allowed to drink his fill. I have heard some people say that being the source of water for your horse can help to improve the relationship between you. I'm not really sure whether it does or not, but as I watched the horses' eagerness to gulp the cool water quickly down, I was pleased that in the UK, we don't have to find out, as we can supply our horses with water all the time without too much trouble. In fact, to us, it would be seen as an infringement of the horse's basic rights not to have water freely available. For Ramón, taking water to his horses was a necessity and not a training decision, but as long as they got watered regularly, he didn't see it as anything to be worried about.

Is it unethical for horses not to have water available all the time? I know that science has shown an increased risk of colic and other problems for horses who are not regularly hydrated but in Ramón's situation, would you excuse this treatment? Where would you place the ethical boundary regarding watering? For instance, how dirty can water get before it is cruel? If horses are roaming over hundreds of acres, is it cruel that they have to wait and travel to get to water?

I know, I know, I'm being annoying. But my point is, these things are never as simple and clear cut as you first think, and I am using this watering scenario to unsettle your assumptions on ethics, so that you can learn about Ramón with a bit of an open mind.

I came to the conclusion that it is a bit of a slippery slope; there are some things that are clearly cruel – tying a horse to a post and beating him up, for instance. There are some things that are clearly not – healthy horses grazing in a social group on plenty of land, for example; not many could argue with that. But there is a *lot* of stuff in the middle, and each of us tries to make ethical decisions about our horses based on our own emotions, social pressures, traditions, and information from various sources (some of which is not at all accurate). I bet there is at least one thing you do that *someone* you know would argue is unethical, and at least three things a friend of yours does that are not quite right in your opinion.

So, the good guys in my book are the people who are at least *trying* to be ethical (whatever that means to them) and trying to figure out what is right. It was clear from the moment we started talking with Ramón, that he was one of these guys, so I decided from that point on to be open minded (within reason) regarding Ramón's construction of ethics. I decided to play devil's advocate to my own first instincts, and to try to look at cruelty and kindness from a different perspective than the one that come most naturally to me. (Don't worry, readers, no horses were beaten during the process of this chapter.) But there were some situations where my own ethical boundaries were stretched, which helped me to work out why I am OK with some things, and not with others, and how I cope with the foggy area in between.

As we waited for the horses to drink, Ramón showed us the strengths and weaknesses of his horses' conformation according to Chilean standards. Wide chests, good bone at the cannon, short, boxy feet (which are apparently better for sure-footedness on the death-defying terrain), a wide forehead, straight face profile and strong neck were all preferences. His horses were around 15hh and looked something like a mustang crossed with an Iberian horse. While they were not worryingly thin, their ribs were just about showing, but most were marked by bald patches or white hair from scars, evidence of the rough lives they had led.

When it came to getting hands on with the horses, from the very beginning the equipment was nothing short of an adventure. Even the tack shed was the epitome of macho cowboy swagger; handmade from an old iron 'pisco' vat (pisco is the local grape-based spirit). This old rusty container, about double the size of a standard fridge, was crammed full of well-worn saddles and leatherwork. And the clichés kept coming. Ramón's grooming implement of choice was the blade of a knife. Ideal, he said, for removing dust from the coat, at the same time as feeling the skin for thorns from cacti. I guess he was not dealing with sticky British mud or furry winter coats; I can't see a knife doing much to help with that. Ramón had previously got in a bit of trouble for carrying his knife on his belt, so he had come up with a new storage system and was keeping a whole kitchen drawer worth of sharp implements and blades, dropped casually into his boot.

One youngster was tied to a tree for most of his days, by a 30-foot rope tied around his front fetlock (or as Ramón called it, 'his hand'). I asked about how he was trained to accept the restraint from his fetlock, and Ramón said that the first time they put it on they walk the horse forward until he meets the restraint, at which point it is very ugly and he scrambles about until he learns not to pull. He explained that it is very important to use a front leg otherwise there is more chance of leaving permanent scarring and potential ligament damage – as one of his other horses had (from a previous home), which he showed us.

Well, I can tell you that I didn't like the look of that little chap tethered by his leg to a tree. I can imagine he was bored and lonely, and I shudder to think of the injuries that could occur if the horse struggles against the rope. But, I keep my own horse in the enclosure that is most convenient for me, using electric shocks that run through the fencing – that would probably seem pretty barbaric too if we weren't so used to it. So I dropped the moral high ground and asked Ramón why the youngster was tethered in the first place. Ramón's reasons for using the tether were pragmatic: there was no suitable fencing (wood is not easy come by here), the youngster was causing trouble and biting the backs of his working mares, he was only staying short term for handling and training, and had some damage on his face caused by previous handling, which meant tethering him by a halter was not an option. It has to be said he looked fairly patient, he was not stressed or pawing the ground or showing any sign of pent-up energy or anxiety. He was just munching on his hay in the shade of the tree. He was being worked every day, and judging from the length of rope, his physical confinement would be much less than a horse who was stabled, he had shelter from the sun and the 360-degree view was much better.

After learning about the tethering, I was also a little ill at ease watching Ramón show us how to lie one of his horses down. I don't know why this trick doesn't really do it for me; it just feels sort of strange and dominating to have the horse lie down for our own entertainment or to enable our egos to feel in full control. To be fair, the beautiful bay horse he demonstrated it with really didn't seem stressed about it, and

Ramón emphasised that it's important not to bully them or force them to lie down but to train it a stage at a time. His aids to ask the horse to lie down were gentle. He lifted the horse's leg as though to clean out his hoof, and then pointed at the ground. There was no force involved in what we saw, and Ramón smiled like a circus performer and praised the bay horse lavishly as the latter sighed and flopped himself down to the ground.

Ramón is quite convinced that after this training the horses trust him more and are more obedient in other areas of their working lives. I'd love to know if this is really true. I've heard it said a few times before but I'm not sure if there is any fact in it or if it is just anecdote and justification for a rather swanky trick. Either way, it was interesting for me to recognise my own reaction as really quite uncomfortable with the whole thing, more so than the horse was.

Perhaps there is no logical reason to be so squeamish about it, after all, there are loads of other horsemanship practices that teach horses to do unnatural things – like jump narrow obstacles or hack out alone, or, oh yes, carry a rider at all. So it can't be the 'unnaturalness' that bothered me, and if the training *was* incremental and gentle, then what was my problem? To be honest, as I saw Ramón lie on top of the horse, it didn't impress me at all, even though I know it must have taken plenty of time and skill to teach. It just looked wrong somehow, and when he asked me if I wanted to sit on top of the lying heap of horse, I politely declined – it sort of felt like the victor of a fight showing off his spoils while the loser is laid out in such a vulnerable position. Logically or not, it didn't sit right with me. It *felt* unethical, and a little bit creepy. Ultimately, however well informed we are, I think most of us make decisions based on a foggy sort of intuition rather than on any logical grounds and it was good for me to recognise that my ethical judgments might not always be grounded in logical, welfare-based arguments.

Next it was time to tack up. Chilean saddles were similar to Australian stock saddles or old cavalry saddles. They are built on a fairly narrow solid tree, have a high cantle and a very padded, deep seat, and are used with three blankets underneath. The stirrups were like beautifully crafted clogs, which I guess provide the added security of the cup-type safety stirrups I've seen at home as well as the balance and ankle support of the wider stirrup treads that seem to be coming back into fashion.

Ramón showed me three types of headgear for the horse. The first was a leather strap that is tied around the lower jaw, underneath the tongue, and is tightened with a simple knot. It came from the native Mapuche tribes, who adopted horsemanship after a sort of equine spy schmoozed his way into the Spanish military, learned the basics, then stole a load of horses and took them back to his people to form their own cavalry troupe. Ramón told us that this device can be useful for horses who fight with their heads to retrain them, or for young horses, because 'while a metal bit might hurt the bone, this will only hurt the skin of the mouth'. What a bittersweet statement to hear. It horrified me to think that anything might damage the soft tissues of the mouth, let alone anything deeper than that. On the other hand I admired the fact Ramón emphasised that more pain doesn't equal better results in training, and was using the strap as a *gentler* alternative to a harsh bit. He showed me how to tie it and how to teach the horse to flex his head each way, and his hands were beautifully soft and generous in their feel.

I had been wondering about different textures for bits, having experimented a little with riding my own horses at home in material bits (aka lead ropes), freely held by the horses in their mouths with no headpiece. (I simply take one rope, feed it into the horse's mouth, and hold the other ends as reins. It stays in place only if you have trained the horse to be happy enough in their mouth to want to gently hold the rope with their lips/tongue, and you hold the other end with your hands, so you have a very close communication system, with no evasion at all.) The idea was to try to create a horse that wanted to hold the bit to feel the communication with the rider, but to take away the discomfort of the weight and bulk of the metal. It was never going to be a replacement for a metal bit for hacking, competing, etc, more of a sort of experiment into horse's mouths and potentially a useful training stage. I had been thinking a lot about approaches to mouthing since there is a horse at home who is very fussy with his tongue, and I was interested in the idea of initially mouthing young horses with something softer and less intrusive than metal.

A friend and teacher of mine, Sandra Williams, introduced me to the importance of texture in work with feral and head-shy horses, where she has found soft stimuli – silk scarves and feather dusters – may look daft but yield much faster results. Could the same be true of acceptance for the presence of a bit across the tongue and against the soft pallet? Would leather, fabric, even silk, be a quicker way to relaxation of the mouth? Or would it be irrelevant to the reaction when the 'real' bit is eventually introduced and feels so different, or worse still, would it simply create fussiness? I am yet to finish these experiments and explorations, but was inspired to continue by the use of leather in Chile.

The second piece of head equipment that Ramón introduced me to was a metal bosal. I've seen a bosal used a few times and had a bit of a go myself with Western trainers in England, and I have to say I think it's an underused tool. This visit reminded me to brush up my bosal skills when I got home. It consists of a stiff, round circle, wider than the horse's head, that hangs around the nose in such a way that, with the right technique, it can teach the horse to soften at the poll and allow his nose to drop so that his forehead is vertical. It makes this lesson very simple and clear for the horse, since when he does this, the wide noseband of the bosal hangs freely around his face, offering a true 'release', and when he lifts his head it bumps him on the nose or chin. Of course it doesn't in itself teach him to lift his withers, engage his hind legs, top line or bottom line (all of the things that most trainers want when teaching the horse how to carry himself) that's all down to the trainer and the whole training regime – but it's a useful extra tool for the toolbox.

Most bosals are made of leather or treated rope. Ramón's bosal was made of thin metal. I've seen some shocking after-effects of a metal noseband on remedial horses in England. Both examples I can think of had been trained in Spain, and had deep, bony scarring on the nose. They carried a huge amount of pent-up stress, along with a fear of lengthening their necks and moving forwards when ridden. I can imagine Ramón's metal bosal could cause similar distress and damage if used roughly. In fact, even used in the way I use a Dually halter at home, I dread to think of how a metal bosal would feel if it were used in its place. Ramón showed us how it can be used to teach the horse to flex his head in either direction and to back up, again with hands so soft that they could nurse sick canaries. He also showed us injuries this horse had suffered around the chin and face from his previous trainer who, in Ramón's words, fought with him all the time.

I asked Ramón how he had overcome this so that the horse was now responding so gently. He was very clear that, when the horse tried to fight, Ramón had to 'be in charge', and yet also that he had to be very soft when the horse was good. I'm pleased we only saw the very soft side. I do wonder exactly what the 'in charge' side looked like, since I am aware there is great skill in not slipping into fighting when prioritising a need to take charge and be respected. These two concepts, 'fighting' and 'earning respect' can sometimes feel very difficult to differentiate; one man's definition of being in control might be another's definition of dominating or forcing, as we had discovered with John Chatterton in Australia.

It is not just a matter of emotive language and moral values, it is also a matter of practical success – some horses just cannot be made compliant by getting bossy with them. Others absolutely need someone to step up and confront them and set some boundaries. There is an on-going matter of consternation in horsemanship across the world in trying to deduce which horses need what level of 'taking charge', and also judging morally when 'control' has gone too far towards 'domination', and 'respect' has gone too far towards 'fear'. It is sometimes a sticky mess to untangle, made more complex because sometimes what is right for the horse long term is not what is pleasant for the horse short term. And of course, everyone has their own slant on what is happening and will often describe their actions in the way that suits them (or their audience). I find it very useful to ask trainers and owners to describe exactly what they are doing, rather than use more generalised, conceptual terms of description, e.g. 'I am hitting the horse with the whip' rather than 'I am earning respect'. That makes it easier to know whether I personally would perceive them as being effective, ethical, neither, or both. So, when Ramón told us he 'took charge' I would have liked to know exactly what this meant, as I have seen all sorts of actions described this way, some which I would absolutely condone, and others which I would not.

Finally we put on the bridles. When I say we, I mean Ramón, because I couldn't even figure out how on earth the bits were supposed to integrate with equine anatomy. They had high curved ports in the middle of the mouthpiece, and metal rings, a little bigger than a jam-jar lid, threaded with beads. The reins were attached via long shanks, and the whole bit was made of a dark metal, perhaps iron.

It turns out the top of the metal ring goes in the mouth and hangs down below the chin. Ramón explained to me how the bit works, and there was more thinking behind this than my prejudice expected. The idea is that a well-balanced bridle will hang vertically in an equilibrium that allows the horse to be totally free from the pressure of the bit on the roof of his mouth or the bars. The weight of the reins and the weight of the metal loop act as a cantilever to keep this balance point correct. The loop is not there, he insisted, to act as a curb pressure point and push into the chin and, indeed, from the way it sat, it did look unlikely that it would act on the chin unless you pulled really, really hard (which I'm sure some people do). While I could see the bits were designed to offer comfort when no aid was being applied, it also looked as though the bits were designed to be pretty severe when the reins were used firmly. I think they would offer maximum impact on as many parts of the horse's mouth as possible – poll action, roof of mouth, tongue and bars.

So it was time to get our own equipment on and in the roasting heat of the day I didn't much fancy putting on chaps but with no idea what was in store I thought it wise to have my best kit on, so zipped my poor sweaty legs in and went for my riding hat. Ramón had a whole trunk full of cowboy hats to keep riders cool, but I didn't fancy testing out their shock absorption. As I pulled my own hat out from my bulging backpack, he raised his eyebrow and looked me up and down, re-evaluating his previous conceptions and wondering if I was simply going to wobble off and head dive onto a rock and ruin the day for everyone. Suddenly I had an idea. 'The thing is,' I said, 'I promised my mother.' Now this he could relate to. 'Ah yes,' he exclaimed with a smile, and then pointing a finger at my nose, he said sternly 'You must always respect your mother.' Brilliant, we were nearly good to go. But he had one more equipment surprise in store.

'Rrrrosie,' he called (with the most wonderful rolled r). 'Here are your spurs.' Oh my goodness gracious me, and Gordon Bennett! They were the same spurs that I had seen in a museum just days ago and had stared at in disbelief, face pressed up against the glass of the dark ages. Now they were here, in real time, and this guy wanted me to wear them. He saw my face before I had time to decide what to do with it. He smiled, 'Well, do you want to learn about Chilean horsemanship or don't you?'

I did want to learn about Chilean horsemanship. And I didn't want to be rude. After all, I thought, even though I have rotating spikes on my feet, I'm still me. I know I won't lose control of my legs and start spurring away as if the Lone Ranger has possessed me. And, when I poked them tentatively into my own fleshy bits, they weren't half as sharp as they looked. The rotation actually made them *less* severe than a solid point – something I hadn't expected. Horses all over the UK are kicked in the belly with every stride to keep them going, and a lot of my work back home involves teaching horses to respond more positively to the legs. I have never worn spurs as part of this training, and I have always been pretty resistant to wearing them, feeling naturally repelled by anything that could make my aids more painful to the horse.

But now I was forced to have a quick rethink. Spurs are often used in dressage, for example, as a way to make aids more precise, rather than simply stronger. I know that the texture of physical pressures on the horse can have a big effect on the response that those pressures are likely to get. For instance, try pushing your horse with the flat of your hand, compared to poking him with one finger, or pushing him with the bristles of a dandy brush. While the strength behind each pressure might be similar, the feeling of it is different and the horse will respond differently. He might be more ticklish with the brush, lean into the poke more, and move away from the flat hand best (for instance). Having poked the spurs and reassured myself they were not actually pizza cutters, I was willing to try riding in them to see if the feeling from the spur was very different for the horse than from my calf or heel, and if this made it easier for him to offer the right behaviour. I knew I had good control of my legs and wasn't going to spur him by accident, and I was confident that I had a good feeling for what level of spur use would be uncomfortable or painful. Used lightly and with the right movement, the prongs ran over the top of the skin like the wheels of a toy car, and seemed to tickle.

After all, I told myself, we are more than used to metal in the mouth, why should metal on the heels be such an ethical problem in itself? Surely the boundaries are all about how the equipment is used, and if it makes it easier for the horse to get it right, then perhaps it is actually a more ethical option. I certainly wasn't going to know without at least being open to trying them. And there was one more interesting point about the spurs: the fact that they jingle. Aside from making me feel like a Morris dancer, Ramón said this has a real use. The horse hears the spurs jingle before you touch him with them, and so learns to associate the noise of the jingle with moving away from the spur. This gives him an extra chance to respond to the light aid, and means the spurs themselves have to be used less often. So, if I ride through the streets with bells on my fingers and bells on my toes (she shall make music wherever she goes) you know I am simply following the example of the Chilean cowboys. All jokes aside, I do think that audio stimuli are vastly underused in training and it was great to see this real-life application.

So it was time to meet the horses and mount up. The mare I was riding – Chigüilla – was a three-year-old bright bay, with a lovely long mane, a large but pretty head and a lot of forelock. Her name meant 'useful bag' (don't ask me) and Ramón had high hopes for her ability to canter sideways, essential for Chilean rodeo. Hannah mounted Guinda, a stockier, older mare whose name meant 'cherry', and Ramón hopped up on his mahogany bay stallion, Galanzo, who looked more Iberian than the others. Ramón told us he could be quite the challenge and his name meant something along the lines of 'big flirt' (like horse like owner, Ramón told us with a cheeky wink).

Another man rode up on a beautiful smoky-blue dun gelding. Ramón had invited him along to show us how it's really done since he comes from generations of horsemen. I was impressed that the men could very easily manoeuvre their horses close enough for a manly embrace from rider to rider. By way of an introduction Ramón declared, 'This is Antonio. He is a great horseman but his wife left him yesterday.' To my spluttered response, 'Oh, gosh, I'm sorry,' Ramón replied, 'No problem, he didn't like her anyway. Let's ride!'

Ramón gave us a quick briefing on basic Chilean controls. He explained that Chilean horses are more resistant than English ones; they don't feel as much pain. An English horse (he laughed as though it was *hilarious*) you only strike once and the next day he's all *spooky*. But Chilean horses, you can strike them today and still strike them again tomorrow! This was an undoubtedly surprising compliment to pay to the Chilean breed, and one that I couldn't get my head around at all.

The aids were largely as I've experienced before, legs touch the barrel for forward, along with the voice aid 'Vamos!' (We go!); and one-handed neck reining for steering. The reins should be held tighter than I expected as I immediately took up a Western length, but Ramón corrected this until there was much less slack in the reins. The most important thing, he told us, is that the horses know you are in charge, so if they don't go, *kick hard*. Even though he told me to kick in a way that didn't use the spur at all, but instead bought the calf into contact, I knew for sure I was going to be doing no kicking of any kind, so I needed my little mare, who was used to this style of training, to think I was a pro and move off light signals from the very beginning. Luckily, my time with IH has taught me to use my body language and energy levels to make myself seem important, so I knew just what to do. I adopted my best Chilean cowboy voice, picked up my reins, looked at the horizon and meant business: 'Come on then, Handbag,' I declared, 'Vamos!'

The trip up to the training arena was steep and twisted over crumbling paths and dusty slopes, and the view was stunning. A chinchilla leaped across the sandy mountains, darting between the rocks. The arena itself was basically a flattened top of one of the foothills, with no walls or fences, the sun was burning in the bright blue sky, and we began working the horses with a backdrop of red and yellow mountains above and green rows of pisco farms below. Antonio demonstrated some of the manoeuvres necessary for Chilean rodeo while Ramón explained the sport. The descriptions would have taken my breath away if the altitude and the hot wind had left me with any to spare.

The point is for two horses and riders to manoeuvre a bull by literally pushing the horse into the bull and shoving him about. The pattern in which he must be moved is quite specific, and there are more points scored depending on where the contact takes place between the horse and the bull. The horse mustn't smash into the bull, but must push into him. One of the manoeuvres involves stopping the bull very quickly, which can often lift him off his feet and throw him into the air. Obviously the huasos need horses who are trained to be balanced, light on their feet, obedient, manoeuvrable, and easy to control. So, while I don't need to lift a bull off his feet, I knew the potential relevance to my own work so I kept my eyes and ears peeled.

One of the key movements that a horse and rider need to perfect is a sideways canter – or cross gallop as Ramón called it. The aim is for the horse to be straight, and to move quickly totally sideways (eventually with his chest against the flank of the bull). In some very basic ways it's like a dressage full-pass, in that the legs cross and the horse moves sideways, but the focus is not on the rhythm, softness and poise of the horse so much as the speed, accuracy and power of the movement. Ramón showed us the early stages of training, which looked a lot like what we would call shoulder-in. I had a little go on my young mare, who was still learning but very willing, and then we practised some stops.

Ramón taught his horses to stop by weight aid alone, by leaning back before pulling them to a halt. The horses responded quickly to the weight aid and so in theory he didn't need to use as much rein contact to control the speed once the initial training was in place. Speed control using the horse's mouth causes all sorts of problems in the UK, with some horses becoming strong in their mouths or needing constant holding back, and others becoming tense and fussy in the mouth, and so I could really understand the value in preparing an aid for braking that didn't involve the mouth. Although I had some trouble getting used to the volume of the aid: 'Lean back,' Ramón said. 'No lean back more. Lean back more …'

I could feel my ponytail brushing my mare's rump before Ramón was happy that I was in the right position. It was certainly way out of the tidy position that is encouraged in Britain. I wonder whether exaggerating the weight aid would make it easier for the horses to learn, and perhaps later it could be made more subtle. However, I know from some of the lessons I have had back home how important it is to be a balanced burden for your horse to carry, and I do wonder if throwing the weight around like this might be a hindrance to the horse when they are trying to adjust their own speed.

I obviously didn't look as clumsy as I felt with the new tack and techniques, because Ramón then offered me a ride on his stallion, who we had heard could be quite a challenge. As I mounted up, Ramón said, totally deadpan, 'Now, really be careful, Rrrrosie, because it is not so simple with a stallion; if you fall off up here, we'll never catch him.'

Right-oh, heels down then, I thought. But actually the stallion was a pleasure to ride, eager to move and quick off the aids, if a little sharp. I was determined to earn my rodeo stripes and master this sideways canter thingy. At first, I followed Ramón's advice, which was generally to up the volume of the aids, more outside rein, more inside leg. I was aware that I had the unfamiliar spurs on, and that the bit had the potential to be very severe, so I was tentative with my aids and Ramón was asking me to be firmer. We were moving sideways about as gracefully as a supermarket trolley might – shuffling across the arena in a sort of perpetual ten-point turn. I looked down, and realised how hard my little horse was trying, and how disorganised we both were. I decided to take a break and watch what Ramón did, rather than what he said.

I noticed that despite the sauntering cheeky cowboy persona, Ramón was actually very together. He was emotionally grounded. I never once saw a sign of anger or urgency in his aids. He was psychologically composed and balanced. His aids were, for the most part, small and clear. I believe both Ramón and I had been undervaluing the extent of this core horsemanship and paying too much attention to the times when he did use bigger or stronger aids or corrections. In fact, there was a whole load of subtle stuff going on that we had both been neglecting.

Right, so how was I going to do it? I cleared my head and remembered a position-based lesson that I had with Julia Fisher, a riding coach back in England. Although the position required here was different, the core stability, accuracy and clarity of the aids were the same, and recalling the session took my brain and body instantly back to a powerful, gentle place. At first I just cantered and felt the horse's body moving beneath me. I felt his feet hitting the dirt and his back springing under the saddle. I began to imagine what it might feel like when he cantered sideways, and how my body would have to adapt to that movement. Then I moved the outside rein against his neck, absolutely sure of the effect it would have. As we moved swiftly sideways across the arena, I saw Ramón raise an eyebrow, surprised and impressed. 'Give me one month,' he said, 'and I could have you ready for rodeo.'

While I was dead chuffed with the compliment, I was pretty pleased that our time schedule meant I had to politely decline. I'd heard that the best way to stop a bull charging your horse is to kick him in the head, and I felt there's a difference between stretching and challenging your ethical boundaries, and abandoning them altogether.

The ride back from the arena covered heart-stopping terrain. The descents were long, on loose dry stones and rutted ground, and so steep that you could feel the horse leaning back onto his hocks, sliding down on his hind legs, and using his front feet to brake. It felt like an age to slip and slide to the bottom of each precipice. Apparently, Ramón canters down these hills, which frankly makes the Derby bank look like child's play. I simply had no idea that horses were capable of these feats, and have a whole new level of respect and confidence for their potential sure-footedness.

I told Ramón this when we got the bottom of the slope in one piece, and he pointed out that the horses are sure-footed as long as the riders don't mess them up. He showed us the scarring on the muzzle of Hannah's mare, Cherry, and also the way her tail was totally limp and immobile. This was the result of a terrible fall. Ramón had been taking an inexperienced rider out, and she was nervous of a high path on the side of a slope, that was narrow and getting narrower. At the last minute the girl (who was riding a different horse) decided to turn back, as she did so she knocked into poor Cherry, who was the packhorse that day. She stumbled and couldn't regain balance, and with the weight of the pack pulling her down, she tumbled and rolled all the way down the mountainside. Ramón was sure he had lost her, but when he reached her she had survived with terrible injuries to her face and apparently no feeling left in her tail. She had been so brave and sure-footed during the day; it was hard to believe what she had been through. Horses can be so unbelievably forgiving.

A little later into the ride home, when Ramón turned around with a naughty look in his eye and asked, 'Hannah, she gallops, yes?' I said, 'Well no, actually. She has cantered once or twice but she is still learning so probably not a good idea today.' Ramón was grinning. 'Well today, she will gallop!' then before I had time to respond he smacked Cherry on the rump with the flat of his hand, kicked his own horse on and yelled, 'Now… go!'

The stallion I was on had started running before Ramón had finished the words. There was nothing to do but go with the flow, the unfamiliar terrain whizzing by under the horse's hooves as we hurtled round the corners of the mountain track. I hoped Han was holding on tight and I let go of any ounce of control of the situation, feeling like I was flying. Then Ramón shouted 'Now … stop!' with some level of urgency, and I had no idea if we were about to fly off the end of a cliff, but we all pulled up without a problem. Han looked a little windswept but not too rattled (she's got some guts, that one) and we found that the ranch was just around the corner. This is not how we do health and safety in England.

We arrived back at the ranch so thirsty that my saliva had turned to mud, my skin was baked by the sun so that I felt paper thin, and we were ravenously hungry – it was now 5pm and we'd hardly eaten since last night's celebratory dinner. 'Nobody died from not eating lunch,' Ramón smiled as he dismounted. 'Well, maybe not *yet*,' I thought, suddenly feeling close to expiring, and rather lightheaded in the baking heat now I was back on my own two feet.

We decided to take Ramón for a drink at his local pub, and he kindly(?!) ordered us a pisco sour (which is made from raw egg white among other things) and it went down like window cleaner. It was a real treat to talk to someone so passionate about his horses and their training, and I hoped that Ramón could not tell the pisco had already made my lips feel like rubber.

As Ramón talked us through the way his training differs from more typical techniques, I realised how lucky we were to have found him. Many local trainers use a method of breaking in youngsters that can lead to injury or even death. They tie a horse by the neck to a strong post and hit or spook him until he gives up struggling. Sometimes horses die from asphyxiation as they struggle against the rope that ties them to the post. Ramón discovered that not only was this not necessary but also that he didn't need to fight the horses much at all. One example he gave of this was some body-language techniques he had seen on a Monty Roberts video that enabled him to move the horses about on the ground using his intention and gestures rather than resorting to hitting them. It was clearly important to Ramón to find more ethical methods and to think outside of the mainstream techniques that were around him. He was proud of his training and the relationship he had fostered with his horses.

I liked Ramón so much that as we moved on to talk about problem horses, I could feel myself moulding his answers into the ones I would really have liked to be hearing. But by now the warmth of the pisco had worn off, and it has to be said that Ramón's approach does revolve largely around being firm or tough. Though he distinguishes this from brutality or fighting, I think this is somewhat of a sliding scale and one man's gentle is another man's rough. At times, when he felt the horses weren't listening to his aids, he backed them up pretty firmly with a strong kick or a solid pull. It just shows how tough the really rough horse people here must be, as Ramón, who was proud of having shown us his gentle techniques, seemed on the tougher end of the scale in British training standards.

What is interesting to me is that his horses seemed to tolerate this with far less stress and detrimental effect than I would have expected. Is this because, as Ramón says, Chilean horses are bred tougher and more resistant to stress and pain? Is it because his corrections were carried out consistently and clearly, with good timing, and without an inch of anger, emotion, guilt, frustration or any other baggage? Or is it because there is a whole load of other, more subtle, horsemanship that Ramón is using alongside his tougher side; skills he may not even be consciously aware of that perhaps make for a successful overall programme. I don't know. Perhaps it's a combination of the three. He is an open-minded, thinking horseman, who believes in sharing the training tools that are so often kept secret in his society, and making things easier on the horse than those around him choose to. He is a horse lover, and yet not dependent on the horse's affection towards him for his self-confidence and peace of mind, which means he is less likely to be offended or made emotional by the horse's behaviours.

He is relaxed, clear, quick and predictable in what he asks of his horses. These things mean he has horses who follow him about the corral, stand quietly to saddle and bridle and brush, are polite to mount up and willing partners to ride. While I won't be trying out the spurs on any of the horses back home, (I know I'd be eating dirt if I even thought of wearing them on Harvey!) I am so glad that I had the opportunity to meet Ramón, learn from him, and through some big differences in language and culture, develop a real fondness for him. I hope that this chapter has encouraged you to explore your own ethical boundaries and where they come from. This chapter in our adventure certainly helped me to develop a little tolerance for differences among others who are also trying to negotiate the difficult task of working out the best way to be both ethical, and efficient, in our treatment of equine companions and workmates. Of course, we all want to be kind to the horse, but I realised there is room for a little kindness in our judgments of others who may have started their horsemanship journeys in very different places from those we started in.

CHAPTER TEN

✦

SMALL STEPS

In the Pantanal, Brazil

IN THE PANTANAL, the hazy, orange light makes everything look as though it is dripping with runny honey. Each wet season, a tide of cattle drifts across endless landscapes, escaping seasonal floods that are bound only by the horizon. Farms are so remote they are reached by boat, hovercraft or plane, which skim over acres of floods and marshland, interrupted only by the occasional island of incredibly dense jungle, an oasis for the abundant wildlife. Biblical proportions of mosquitoes coat every living skin surface like iron filings relentlessly smothering a magnet. Jaguar attack, cobra bite and tropical disease post a very real danger to the vast herds of cattle and horses that exist here. From an aerial view, I imagine the landscape of the Pantanal appears to be teeming with life, every patch of earth wriggling with movement like an oversized insect colony. There is strange and colourful wildlife beneath your toes and in your hair, watching you from the trees and the long grasses. Caymans (little crocodiles) bide their time, plotting, without blinking, in every puddle. The entire economy rides on the back of the horse, and the cowboys who raise them, watch over them and work with them, have inherited the wisdom to do so from generations of horsemen before them.

We were based in the depths of the Pantanal for a week, at a working 'fazenda' (farm), earning our hammock space, rice and beans by sharing training knowledge and techniques with the cowboys.

We had been expecting some level of difficulty with this leg of the trip. Never mind the geographic isolation; we'd been warned that the macho cowboy culture in the region would not be welcoming to outsiders, women, or people with new ideas. As a vegetarian horse whisperer who was travelling with my female partner, I was pretty conclusively all three of those things. On top of that we had a new language to deal with. Having finally started to feel at home with South American Spanish, Portuguese sounded like it was being played backwards from inside a washing machine. My mouth simply did not seem anatomically prepared to make those sounds.

It had been a twelve-hour ride on the 'death train' (so named because of its history transporting yellow fever victims) and a four-hour border crossing, queueing alongside the grumpiest German tourist you can imagine, followed by three hours with our backs against the wall in a high-pressure sales situation with a man 'who could help us meet horse people in the area' until it dawned on us both that we were about to be conned. The realisation kicked in three hours too late, but at least we got out losing nothing but hope. As I sat in the humid, peeling yellow hotel room in Corumbá, I tried to come to terms with the fact that we were not going to meet the horse people of the Pantanal. We had sent countless emails. There had been red herrings and dead ends, and now con artists too and, ultimately, it was just too hard to get in touch with the fazendas and find one that wasn't under flood water, that could be reached and, moreover, that *wanted* to be reached.

It was literally at the eleventh hour that an email came back offering us the chance to stay on a working fazenda for the week – but for about ten times our weekly budget. So far, we hadn't paid for any of our horse experience – and with seven months in total away from home, we simply couldn't afford it. I felt confident that I could earn our bed and board rather than play the tourist, if they were at all interested in sharing techniques and learning from each other but, as we'd been told, there wasn't necessarily much evidence to think this was the case. Han wrote an optimistic email back, asking to stay for nothing, and I took some painkillers and tried to sleep off my dull, sweaty headache.

Somehow, and I still can't quite believe it, it came together. By luck or fate, the fazenda agreed, since the owners, João and Olivia, were actively looking into alternative training methods for the horses and so were happy to have us come and stay.

The following morning we were up early for the journey. Since the floods were late in their area, the fazenda could be reached by off-road driving rather than boat, but the journey from the nearest tarmac road was a long one. As we clattered about violently in the back of a pick-up truck further and further away from any hint of civilisation, I looked over at Han and jokingly said, 'Well, look, if we don't like it we can just leave!' My bravado came from nervous tension; this journey was nothing a breadcrumb trail could navigate us out of. We were absolutely in the hands of our hosts, and in the middle of miles and miles of nowhere.

João was a smiley, moon-faced man, with a dark beard, not very tall but strong and confident. He had learned his horsemanship from his father, who had trained horses in Portugal for bull fighting. João now owns Xaraes, a rather swish hotel offering wildlife safaris to tourists and, six miles on into the bush, a working fazenda, with 3000 head of cattle, 100 horses and a barebones farmhouse, which looked like it was from the Wild West of North America.

Ever-graceful Olivia, whose English was better than she thought it was, became translator between João, his two employed cowboys, Seu Ze and Seu Izidro, and us. João explained that Seu was a respectful prefix, a little like 'sir'. The fact the cowboys were never referred to without it showed the value of their knowledge and skills. He told us that the methods of training wild horses at this fazenda used to follow the local norm of tying them to a post and scaring or hurting the horse to make him struggle and fight until exhausted before saddling up, mounting and trying to stay on. Five out of ten horses started this way were wasted, through injury like asphyxiation from the rope, or because it was so traumatic that they 'went crazy' and never made successful riding horses. I had known before we set off on our trip that it was likely horses were still trained this way in many parts of the world, but it was shocking and saddening to face the realities of this cruelty as we talked to this lovely guy, who until three years ago had used these methods.

João told me that now, though, there was a movement to re-educate cattle farmers in a new, more ethical and efficient way of training the horse, run by an organisation a little like a farmers' union, which offered free courses to its members and taught a method known as 'Doma Racional'. Since João and Olivia had hosted a course in these techniques two years before, they noted their horses didn't buck or jump about as much, so as well as being safer, it was kinder on the horse and more efficient in terms of number of horses wasted. João agreed to show me the method on the last day of our stay. In the meantime, I would be able to watch the cowboys' daily routine, and also work with some wild horses to show my own approach.

So, at the end of the first day, we bunked down for my first night's sleep in a hammock (Hannah was already pretty hammock savvy). The barn we were staying in had mosquito-mesh sides, no electricity and was about a mile walk away from the main fazenda. We were certainly feeling close to nature. As Olivia showed us around, we loved her turn of phrase: 'Sometimes it's nice to close the toilet seat so you don't get frogs in it', and 'Sometimes it's nice to lock the bathroom when you are finished so you don't get animals in there.' At night, the infinite star-scapes were serenaded by mythical noises; an otherworldly nocturnal main street of wild boar, coyote, buffalo and howler monkey. It felt surreal knowing that somewhere nearby, there were giant anteaters, and giant otters– apparently almost the size of a human. The moths were as big as British garden birds, and the caymans' eyes glinted in the torch light as I tried to catch a glimpse of the creatures responsible for all the odd noises. If I hadn't been so exhausted from our epic journey, I don't think I would ever have slept at all. But we found a nifty way of tying up the mosquito net like a cocoon around the hammock, to stop anything crawling in from any side, and I went to sleep in my little swinging pod, heavy with travel tiredness, wearing a head torch so that I would be ready to turn it on in an instant should a snake, spider, jaguar, cayman or anything else come too close.

It was largely a successful plan, though I learned my first swamp-forest lesson that night: that the last thing you want when woken by a giant moth visit is a light on your head – it makes things much worse. The Giganta Moth was desperately in love with my headlight and, in his eagerness, shoved his hairy legs up my nose and in my lips and in my hair. I had, until this point, slept so well that during the clumsy awakening, I had forgotten I was in a hammock at all, and couldn't understand why the world was swinging so violently as I tried to escape from my well-tied mosquito net. Yet again I had to be rescued by Hannah, who is so at home in the jungle she would happily bunk up with the howler monkeys in the trees.

At six the following morning we were up and waiting at the fazenda, as instructed. The hub of the farm was a small undercover, open-sided yard with white-washed rails, on which saddles sat, hooks for ropes, and chairs for sitting in the shade later in the day. To one side was a store room, containing all sorts of dusty, odd-looking equipment, including a musical instrument made from a buffalo horn, bottles for the orphaned goats, leather-working equipment, and a freezer full of medicine for the animals and bottles of ice water to keep the cowboys cool. In the front yard was a stable-sized enclosure, a larger corral with a tall post, and a huge wooden tank with a tap above it. This was used to give the horses a drink and to wash them down after work, and it also had become home to a growing family of what we later learned were genuine 'killer' bees. Whether they lived somehow in the thick wood of the drinker, in the soil beneath it or the tree behind it, I do not know – and I didn't try to investigate! But they surrounded that water drinker much of the time and I gave it a wide berth.

As we waited, we became aware of movement on the horizon. It was a group of horses, cantering and kicking up dust. At the rear was Seu Ze on a stocky sorrel horse and Seu Izidro on a large and beautiful mule. As they came closer it was obvious the horses were a group of young males – the way they occasionally tussled which each other and rough and tumbled, grabbing each other's ears, or knees for a few moments before getting left behind and falling too close to the cowboys, and then racing to catch up with the front runners. They came in a beautiful muted range of colours – chestnut, bay, grey, dun – several with dorsal stripes or zebra marks down their legs. They were about 14hh and from their roguish, ungainly gait, and the babyish curls still left in the very ends of some of their tails, I assumed that most of the group were between two and three years old.

They were herded into the corral and their expression changed as they recognised their confinement and proximity to people. They began to swarm and dart, like panic-stricken shoals of fish worried by a seal, with occasional lone mad dashes for safety. Seu Ze and Seu Izidro jumped off their own mounts and moved the wild horses about in the corral; they were looking for one in particular. When they found him, they worked with expert body language to separate him from the group and secure him in the smaller enclosure. Then they looked over at me and pointed to him. I guessed he was to be the first horse I was to work with.

I collected some things to give him time to settle and then approached to peer through the wooden boards. He was a lovely, rich autumnal shade of chestnut. His nostrils were flared and his eyes were busy and worried. He stood glued to the back wall, as though wishing he was camouflaged against it, but his coat was lit up like gold in stripes down his body from the morning sun flowing through the gaps in the wooden boards.

I learned that he was three years old, was called 'Morango', which means 'strawberry' (apparently a masculine word in Portuguese and so a strong, manly name in this part of the world!), and he had recently been gelded. The castration operation here, like in many isolated locations around the world, is completed without sedation or anaesthetic. It involves lassoing the colt, tying his legs so he falls down, and restraining him during the procedure. This is often the first close contact that young wild horses have with people, and requires several strong men to match the strength of the struggling horse. Seu Ze was a true expert 'peão'

(Pantanal cowboy) and knew the rope tricks and techniques that made this process as quick and stress-free as possible, but there is no doubt that it was still traumatic. One of the biggest threats to these horses is tick-borne diseases, so tick management through cutting the mane and painting medication into the ears, was also common before the horses had been regularly handled or trained. Every horse went through the process of being lassoed and tied to the post to have this done, a quick and forceful procedure that often left the horses more fearful of human contact than when it was unknown to them. In Morango's case it had left with him an extreme phobia of ear contact. I later learned that it was because he was the most difficult horse on the place to medicate with the tick medicine that he had been chosen for me to show what I could do.

I was surprised that other than the extreme ear fear, Morango was quicker to learn than I would expect given his recent human-related experiences. After ten minutes or so he was not only accepting but enjoying the scratchy rub from a long stick on top of his withers – in the spot he would be most often groomed by other horses. It didn't take long before I could slowly work my hand up the stick and begin grooming him with my fingers, working my way into all the grubby, itchy spots at the base of his mane, and watching his expression change from fear to curiosity to relaxation. After the first fairly easy one-hour session, he left the enclosure with his new halter on looking a little bemused but none the worse for wear. It is policy here not to ride horses within ninety days of castration, so starting under saddle was not an option, but over the next couple of days I continued to work on his general handling confidence, leading and catching ability. He was such a sweet little horse, and I loved the way he seemed to concentrate carefully and really think so much about everything we did.

I became a little addicted to trying to alleviate the problems with his ears. I taught him to lower his head when I rested my hand on his poll, then I cupped his ear, and used a stick with a sponge tied on, to get him ready for the medicine paintbrush. He was very specific about his fears. He practically told me how his ear had been pulled, from which direction and with which hand, because every now and then I would change what I was doing and notice a huge improvement or set-back depending on whether I had re-awoken a memory or tried something new and untainted. He absolutely enchanted me with his bravery and willingness to try. I would move my hands, or the stick, into a slightly more challenging place, and he would hold his breath. Rather than react explosively or defensively, he would wait, thinking perhaps, looking at me, and then finally, daring to trust, he would bob his head downwards an inch or two, as much as he could bear, and I would take my hands away and tell him he was ever such a brave Strawberry!

Eventually, after several sessions, he was ready and allowed me to paint the medicine in his ear. João had come to watch. He seemed impressed at first, but then began talking fast in Portuguese. I wasn't sure what he was saying. He seemed to be trying to instruct me to do something. Eventually he came over and took the medicine paintbrush, gesticulated to me to hold Morango's ear, and put the paintbrush right down his ear – and I mean right down – he must have been tickling his ear drum! Despite the fact that I had not prepared Morango yet to cope with two people, one of whom he surely remembered from past tick treatments, or for the depth of the medicine in his ear, he stood stoically for the treatment and trusted me to hold his ear gently still. I knew he had given me more than I had earned, and I was so proud of him and grateful for his courage.

The next colt they gave me to work with had a reputation as the wildest on the place – a gift to João, a tobiano colt. (Tobiano is the name given to a specific pattern of coloured and white patches. I have only recently learned that this colouring was named after a Brazilian revolutionary, Tobias, who left Brazil after defeat in 1842, and, with his men, went to Argentina riding horses of this specific pattern.) He was still entire, and easy to spot by his unusual colouring and wild behaviour, darting around the corral crashing into the other horses while trying to scurry to the back to stay away from people. His name was Tubaino, a word play on his colouring and a local fizzy drink (like Coca Cola but with more sugar!). His small ears and bright eyes reminded me of a British native pony. He was quick-witted, sensitive and a bit of a worrier, but eager to learn how to get it right. He was intelligent and fun to train. He quickly developed a wonderful attitude to work and ability to figure out the lessons I put before him. After three hours' work spread over three days, Tubaino was easy to tack up, long-line, leg handle, lead, catch, mount and I was riding him about in a loose and wobbly walk, steering softly. The approach I had used was to repeat many short exercises on rotation, a little long-lining, a little short-reining, a little mounting, a little leg handling then back to short-reining or long-lining again, like circuit training. I have found the repetition helps all the exercises feel familiar, and the horses seem to relax into them rather than wonder what new thing you will do next.

Between each training session, we drank 'terere', the local iced tea, from a cow horn, watched some of the cowboys work or waited for more horses to be herded in from up to six miles away. Hannah and I initially made every social blunder possible during the rituals around drinking terere, but our hosts kindly educated us, and good job too, since drinking terere with the cowboys was to form a large part of our daily routine.

The main rules are as follows. The terere is prepared and offered by one person, who acts as a host. The cow-horn cup is almost full of herbs, and a little iced water is poured onto the herbs for each drinker and slurped up through a straw. The host will offer it to everybody present in turn, moving in a clockwise direction from one to the next. If you would like terere, you take it when offered, and drink everything in the cup before handing it back to the host. Slurping as much as possible is good manners and means you like the drink. The cup moves in cycles around the group, with each person drinking five or six times in total, but it is the host's job to keep offering until nobody wants any more. If you would like to be included in the next cycle, you hand the cup back without saying anything, a struggle for our good English manners. If you have had enough, you hand the cup back and say 'thank you' and you will be excluded from the next cycle.

At first it took me a while to get used to the fact that the pace of work is so slow, with tea breaks between each activity, but once the day's heat took hold – around 40 degrees – I understood the rationality of this rhythm. My usually steadfast rule of wearing my riding hat at all times around horses melted away in the scorching heat. Even taking a cold shower (with at least three frogs) could not get rid of my heat-induced migraine at the end of the second day.

I was overwhelmed by the holistic and varied knowledge of Seu Ze and Seu Izidro. Seu Ze reminded me of Morgan Freeman to look at, and I could certainly imagine him in a film. He was the epitome of manliness, immaculately dressed in clean jeans and a half-buttoned white shirt with a colourful woven belt, quietly eyeing you from under the rim of his hat, gun on his hip, knife in the back of his trousers, and loyal dog sitting at his feet worshipping him like a god. He had a quiet way of moving and being around animals and a wisdom that seemed to somehow encompass all animal movement on the place – wild or domestic. We saw him working leather, feeding orphaned goats and cows, moving groups of cows and horses from place to place, tracking jaguar, medicating wounds, milking cows … the list goes on and on. And he carefully watched me work from under that hat rim without saying a word.

The third colt presented to me was also recently gelded and was very shy, not dashing about wildly like Tubaino but staying quiet and shrinking between the other horses like a shadow. He was a smoky grey dun with zebra stripes down his legs, and his name, Lombãu, meant big wolf. It was a big name and the little chap struggled to live up to it, shaking and quivering in the corner of the corral once he was separated from the comfort of the herd and, though he didn't react explosively, his heart rate remained a little high. In fact it remained high throughout the session, and he seemed to be holding his breath, looking nervous and withdrawn, with a little quiver appearing once or twice on his flanks or chest. Most wild horses that I have worked with begin to replace fear with curiosity fairly quickly, and start to actively enjoy a good scratch before the first session is through. But, although he didn't leap, jump or give me any problems, Lombãu stood cowering, shrinking beneath my gaze, and it was heart-breaking to see.

The low-level anxiety didn't seem to be improving much even after many repetitions of the same, simple exercise. During the sessions I gave him lots of little breaks where I left the pen entirely, to see if it helped him relax, and I broke things into tiny steps. I decided to take things very slowly with him. I didn't know why he was not looking as happy as the other horses, though the difference was subtle.

Han was itching to get involved in the horse training. Until now she had spent her time mostly trying to help translate when Olivia was away and sorting out our banking and future travel plans. She did a lovely session with Lombāu just stroking his neck and withers and trying to give him a comfortable, peaceful experience.

Olivia too was tentatively thinking about getting practically involved. Olivia's story reminded me of more than one of my clients back home. It seems all around the world there are women who have suffered heartbreak through horsemanship. Years ago, she had incurred a terrible fall and broken her back. The horse she had been riding had been declared dangerous and was shot before she had come round, and Olivia felt responsible. Olivia struggled with the residual emotional torment of fear and guilt from this incident, twisted up with her uneasiness regarding the way the horses were trained at Xaraes and her inability to help them, as she knew no better way. When she talked of how she missed riding, it was as though a part of her was missing, but through both confidence issues since her fall, and guilt surrounding the way the horses were trained, she could no longer enjoy it and hadn't ridden for years. Her guilt and confusion was so troubling that, despite living amongst so many beautiful horses, Olivia tried not to watch them out of the window, tried to avoid thinking of them and when it was time to castrate, medicate or train, she tried, in vain, to banish them from her thoughts entirely.

Lombāu, I thought, could be her perfect project, as she could take plenty of time with him, being kind to him, and really form a bond that both would benefit from. He seemed safe and unreactive but worried and shut down; perhaps both horse and human could thrive, and heal, if they could spend gentle time together. I put this idea to Olivia and she took the project on very thoughtfully. That afternoon she spent some time alone, standing with Lombãu, talking with him, and not putting any pressure on him at all. This was the first meaningful time Olivia had spent with horses since her fall.

On the third day, as Han and I walked to the fazenda just before dawn, we became aware of a moonlit shape moving on the path in front of us. At first we thought perhaps it was a giant anteater and crept forward slowly with excitement but as we got closer we knew something was wrong. The movements were that of a struggling animal: trapped, jerky and unnatural. The dark dawn light was blue and foggy so we had to get incredibly close before suddenly we knew what was in front of us – it was a horse. In fact it was Lombãu, and he couldn't get up.

He could hardly even raise his head and neck but he was kicking and kicking with both back legs, straining against the weight of his own body as though it was made of heavy iron and just would not leave the ground. Since he had seemed so withdrawn and worried during training the day before, I wasn't at all sure that comforting him or getting any closer to him would help him to relax – in fact, his eye was rolling towards us in fear as he desperately tried to move. At first I thought it must have been a big-cat attack, or perhaps a snake bite, but I glanced around his legs and couldn't see any injury, blood or swelling. His only symptom seemed to be his inability to get up – all the legs were paddling away and working, it was just as though he was magnetically stuck to the ground and unable to summon the strength or coordination to break the magnetic force and right himself.

Shocked, we rushed on to the fazenda to tell the cowboys, who seemed saddened but perhaps not as urgently motivated as I'd have liked. We showed them a photo we had taken on the phone to be sure they understood the predicament. They did. And in their own time, they made their way out to Lombãu to drag him into the shade as the morning sun grew stronger Later, we came to understand there is no sense of urgency because there was nothing really to be done. Lombãu had been taken ill with a protozoan that induces paralysis; it had probably come from a tick.

The atmosphere on the whole place was sombre over the next two days. We got on with training the other horses, and Lombãu persevered with his own struggle for life, and there was little any one could do to help him. If we had just got a little further through training then I would have gone and sat with him and sponged the sweat from him and kept the flies away from his face, but I knew that despite our best efforts so far, he wasn't really seeing a value in human contact yet, and being approached by the very creatures you are afraid of while paralysed has to be something from a torturous nightmare. We were all helpless. There are no emergency vets here; the nearest is several hours drive away. João had given an injection of a new trial medicine that he hoped might give him a chance, but this illness had claimed the lives of many other horses including Lombãu's father, and so his chances were slim. Finally, on the fifth day, his condition had deteriorated and João decided to put him to sleep.

That afternoon was cloudy, clammy and grey. I saw Seu Ze and João heading over to Lombãu on the quad bike. I tried to focus on the horse I was working with. But when three gun shots sliced through the heavy, dismal atmosphere, I caught Han's eye, and I thought of Olivia and felt wretched. Nobody wept or fussed, or asked each other how they were feeling. Everybody got on with their work with quiet thoughts and heavy shoulders. Black vultures stained the grey skies, somehow looking lonely in their constant circling, despite their strength in numbers. Olivia kept busy and out of the way. There was no good opportunity to ask her how she was or offer much support, but I tried to smile in her direction to communicate some level of empathy. Horses die from tick-related disease, cobra bite and big-cat attack regularly here, and I just hoped that Olivia was better hardened to life and death in the Pantanal than we were.

Gradually, over the following days, the atmosphere lifted, like a window opening in a stuffy room, and I felt able to enquire a little more about Lombãu's illness. I asked whether the withdrawal during training might have been an early sign and João thought that it could have been; sadness and nervousness are often early symptoms. Despite a deep regret for his suffering, I was relieved that we had taken things slowly with him and not been tempted to go any quicker.

I know, in my heart of hearts, that if I hadn't had other horses to work on who were progressing quickly, I probably would have put more pressure on Lombãu to show the cowboys what I could do, especially since he wasn't really doing anything evasive or being difficult to handle, or anything that suggested a very high level of stress, he just seemed consistently pessimistic and withdrawn. Thank goodness this wasn't the case, and thanks to Lombãu I will always aim to remember to take note of the subtle signs, and treat even low-level stress seriously.

I was allowed to choose my final student from a group of fillies. I'd love to get better at knowing how to select a good student from watching their interaction in the group. I have to say in all honesty I simply picked the biggest filly, hoping she would be well grown enough to cope well with carrying me, and that for once I might not look too tall! Her name was 'Primavera' (meaning 'spring', as in the season), and from the very beginning she lived up to her chestnut mare stereotype and showed a fiery temper, biting or kicking out if she was confused, worried or irritated. I needed a few extra tools to work on the back legs, and had to take extra time to chill her out about the girth area, and to get her happy with the idea of being handled and generally on side. While certainly willing to voice her opinions and register her complaints, she also learned very quickly and appeared to really enjoy the lessons that involved using her body and moving about – long-lining, short-reining and riding – with a seemingly inbuilt confidence about the job. This meant that when I had time for an extra session, I chose to work with Primavera and her riding work progressed to trotting about, wearing the full Pantanal get-up – a deep saddle with a front and back girth, and several sheepskins between horse, saddle and rider. She looked and felt fantastic, but I felt like I was perched a very long way above her!

During all the sessions, I had very little idea what João and the cowboys thought of my training work. João had watched almost every second, and had been asking questions, and it seemed our opinions on many things matched. But his face was hard to read, as were the faces of the cowboys who watched from a distance. I had half a clue about their ideas when they watched the way I mounted Tubaino for the first time. I made progress by leaning over first, releasing the pressure often by getting down and doing lots of bending work on the short reins. Seu Ze exclaimed that the technique would be good for the mules. At first I wondered if this was an insult, something about me being too slow and careful and soft, and being better suited to a less athletic animal. Later, I learned this was actually a compliment since the mules are the hardest to start, and often put up the biggest fight. They are well known for their ability to buck and kick during training. I was so pleased when Olivia told us that João had been impressed and had announced that despite his doubts before watching me work, I *did* know horses after all. João seemed surprised that so far, the horses had put up no resistance, and stood still to be tacked up, or clambered on and off. When I mounted Primavera for the first time, he spoke up. 'If she bucks now,' he said, 'she'll buck till she dies – she is not at all tired!' But I have never had a horse buck on the first ride yet; and Primavera was easy to read since she was quite happy to communicate with a dirty look when she wasn't happy with something, so I felt quite happy that riding would be no problem. She proved me right and the ride went ahead with no trouble.

I was surprised, however, by which things impressed the cowboys. For instance, they mentioned a problem getting young horses to accept the rain covers – huge sheets of waterproof material that cover the rider and horse during the rainy season. While they told me about this I was holding Morango, so I asked them to pass me one and showed it to him. Sure enough he leaped back, leaned back on his haunches and looked at me like I was brandishing a tiger. I folded it up, wrapped it in a saddle cloth, which I had already introduced to him, and popped the parcel up on his wither and took it away a few times before allowing the parcel to fall undone, the saddle pad to fall away, and the sheet to gradually get bigger as I moved toward him and away from him with it. Within five minutes I had him swamped in it, and Seu Ze laughed in disbelief, saying, 'He looks like an old horse'. This trick impressed them as though I'd pulled a rabbit from a hat, which seems odd to me as it feels like an obvious approach. I suppose they were probably equally bemused by how impressed I was with their 'everyday skills' with the bull whip and lariat.

On our last day it was time for João to show me the Doma Racional methods he'd learned on the course. I'm going to tell you now that you may well not like reading about these methods, because I certainly didn't like watching them, and indeed, if you want to skip the next page and head straight to the conclusions of the chapter I don't blame you at all. He worked with 'Açúcar' (meaning 'sugar'), a three-year-old grey, Arabian-looking filly who had already had a little handling from a visiting trainer a few months ago, and so was fairly easy to catch and touch. João put a bosal onto her head and with the help of Seu Ze, he tied the rope from the bosal to her tail, and then he stepped out of the corral and left her there. I remember at this point getting the sinking feeling that the 'kinder' method we had been looking forward to learning was going to be a bit of a let-down. The rope was perhaps ten inches shorter than her length, requiring her to bend her head to the side. At first she struggled, trying to get her head straight and, finding her tail pulled, she would throw her head up, spin round, try little half rears, and scuffle about. It was strange and horrid to see such staggering, unnatural movements as she tried to free herself and work out new ways to balance.

Gradually, she worked out the way the rope worked, and seemed to alternate between walking in incessant tiny circles, chasing her tail like an endless revolving door, or standing leaning her head into the halter, her tail pulled round to her side, a glazed look in her eye. After thirty long minutes, João approached her gently, talking to her and handling her with nursing hands, and shortened the rope by another few inches. This set her off again struggling and then circling, confused and trapped, straining her eye towards the group of fillies in the next-door corral. Later again, João approached and tightened the knot, now her neck was held bent over half way towards her own shoulder, and again she twisted about searching for freedom before returning to the repetitive circles. By this point the rough material of the bosal had worn away the hair on the front of her nose, leaving the skin raw and red.

I didn't know where to look. I had made a commitment to learn about local methods of horse training whether or not I agreed with them. I am aware that sometimes, within methods I don't agree with, there is something practical I can learn and employ in a more ethical way back home, so it always pays to respect any successful horseman enough to watch them work with a notebook handy. I also believe it is only through watching and learning about current techniques and cultures that we can hope to make any meaningful difference in the future. If you don't understand where people are coming from, and what they currently do, you don't really know what it is that needs changing and how to go about doing it. So I was determined to watch and learn about this new 'kinder' technique that was being taught to all the fazenda owners across the Pantanal.

João had watched my methods for the whole week, and was polite and open enough to show me his own way of working, which he had already made very clear he was hoping to change and find a more ethical alternative. He was doing the best he could with what he knew, and, while it is a hundred miles away from what I would call ethical training, he was using the cutting edge of 'ethical horsemanship' that was available to him. There was no point in getting judgmental or being rude to João, but I could hardly bear to watch Açúcar's torment. I kept reminding myself that this was the kinder alternative; it was progress from *crueller* methods that existed before, and that this would have happened to Açúcar whether I was there or not. But I felt awful for Açúcar as she stood in the corner of her corral, by the gate, head twisted round unnaturally, dust-smoke to her knees from her struggling, and a huge, hot and heavy sky above her. To one side of the corral was nothing but open spaces and horizon, horses in the distance, and the freedom she had grown up with. To the other side was the group of fillies she had been herded in with, including Primavera whom I had trained, and they all grouped together and watched Açúcar intently.

The next time João approached he swapped the rope to the other side of her body, and the whole process was repeated from the new side. At lunchtime, she was untied for a break and a drink, but in the afternoon, the whole process was repeated. This time the rope from her tail was tied onto a bit in her mouth rather than the bosal.

At the end of the day, after about six hours in total, tied in the various positions, she looked exhausted. She was then tied to the post and tacked up in the whole kit. She flinched just a little as the large saddle and pads were put on her back, and she leant backwards like a stretching dog as the back girth was tightened. Then João turned her loose in the corral and encouraged her to run about in the tack freely.

Once he was satisfied that she was moving OK in the tack, she was tied in the small stable-sized enclosure and João mounted up from the ground, first halfway up and then on and off a few times, before staying on, untying her and encouraging her to move around the pen. At first she crouched down as he took his weight in the stirrup, unsure of which way to run or what to do, but after a few repetitions getting on and off she stood still to be mounted. Without necessarily knowing it, João was successfully using pressure and release (or negative reinforcement) to show her the weight of the rider was OK. It was hard to get her moving around, though – she did not understand leg aids, rein aids or voice commands, and so clumsily stop-started in bursts of worried energy or periods of planting to the ground and ignoring everything.

Once she had done a couple of circles and shown no sign of bucking, João rode her a little in a bigger space. He managed to manoeuvre a couple of haphazard circles before she headed for the gate area and sort of shut down there, refusing to move forwards or backwards, or even to turn her head. She became a horse made wholly of heavy, dead wood. I have heard of the concept of breaking a horse in, but I have never seen a horse who looked so thoroughly broken spirited. João gave her a stroke and then dismounted. He did not look proud of himself, and Açúcar was so mentally tired she couldn't even move out of the way of the gate as it was being opened.

Unbelievably, the following day would involve riding her straight out with a lead horse across the farm. João says this generally goes OK, but is more dangerous than the first day since the horse is not as tired. It is a testament to the generosity of the spirit of horses that the youngster must simply figure out how to respond to aids 'on the job' from this day on.

Clearly this technique is stressful for the horse, but I tried to look at the whole thing objectively, and draw out some of the positives of the Doma Racional technique. It is promising that there is an organisation that offers education for farmers and cowboys in methods of training that differ from the old technique of a certain style of sacking out or beating the horse, and I feel so grateful to have landed up in a fazenda that is part of the new exploration of training methods and openness to change. However, the only actual progress from my point of view is that this technique does not require any aggression directly from the cowboy towards the horse. It is significant to me that the horse has a hard day *but not a hard master*. While it might be argued this makes little difference to Açúcar, who struggled with the rope as much as she might have struggled against a man, I argue that it *is* different. This is because I *hope* it will change the people. João told us that there is a culture of human aggression toward horses, a need to 'win', to 'overcome', 'break his spirit' – this Doma Racional technique allows and, in fact, encourages the farmers and cowboys to become the horse's ally, his friend, to be soft and gentle. It takes away the need for the violence to come from the human, and I believe that this may well start to heal the culture and change the people.

South American horsemanship has a reputation in England for being harsh on the horse, yet João himself was much more compassionate than I expected in the way he moved around Açúcar. His body language was calming and gentle. His ego did not come into the equation. He didn't seem to have a point to prove; there was no sense of pride in her awful experience, and he wanted things to be easy on them both – he just thought this was a tough thing that she just had to go through, like the tick medication and the castration. To João life here is tough, and horse training is part of that toughness.

It had taken six to seven hours to get Açúcar ready to ride, and my two ridden horses took just three to four hours (spread over three days) to take from wild to riding. At this stage they also understood some of the aids nicely and were mentally engaged and accepting the process, but it took conscious careful work, involving techniques, timing, judgments, etc. The training system I use has evolved around horse owners in the UK, where most horses have an owner who is willing to dedicate time and money to invest in low-stress training. Every horse has some potential to become a competition horse, or a perfect hack, and it is important that he learns to be obedient, soft, trusting, etc. There is no room for error and no tolerance for stress or exhaustion. The Doma Racional technique has developed to take up little of the cowboy's time. Though the process takes all day for the horse, it's only a few rope adjustments during the working day for the cowboy, who can go off and get on with other things. It's also really easy to learn; every horse is treated the same; it is not a process that requires much feel, and so anyone is enabled to start their horses without beating them and with less injury to horse or rider through this method. While it seems like a dreadful leap back in time to us, it is at least a sign that traditions are beginning to become unsettled, and mind-sets are beginning to change.

João and Olivia seemed to be incredibly forward-thinking compared to others in the area, and they would have been happy to employ someone to train the horses in a more ethical way. But there was nobody around to do it, and no learning opportunities available, though João said he had been watching me closely and was going to try long-lining and short-reining the young horses himself. While it would be easy to condemn João for the training he had done with Açúcar (not to mention the methods he used before Doma Racional), it seemed to me that he was a pragmatist and not a bully. He didn't want to fight with the horses, or hurt them, but if there was no one who specialised in horse training around to employ, he needed ways to train the horses that did not require much of his cowboys' time, and that the cowboys were able to do. While there are attempts at movements toward ethical horsemanship like Doma Racional, and while there are people who want more ethical horsemanship, there is still hope that things will move forward but, for the time being, the practical and ideological isolation of the region holds progress back.

On the last night, João and Olivia invited us to supper and asked if we would stay on to train more horses. We knew we couldn't stay; the next leg of our trip was already planned, and we had more horses to meet and commitments back in the UK to return to. As we prepared to leave, I kept catching the eye of untrained horses we drove past, spellbound by the unknown potential and personality in each one, and terribly uneasy about the type of training I knew lay ahead of them. I felt a magnet pulling me backwards, a heaviness about leaving, and a big part of me wishing we could stay. I once heard a crazy theory that every time someone makes a decision, a separate universe is born in which the alternative decision is lived out. As we left, this potential other universe seemed almost tangible. I could picture what would become of us if we were to stay in the depths of the Pantanal training horses for farm work, turning Tubaino into the greatest cow horse that ever lived and meeting all the wild ones that were still mysteries to us. But I knew it wasn't to be in this reality. We had other places to go. Of all the places we had visited so far, this was for sure the hardest to leave, and our hearts were heavy as we packed away our hammocks, enjoyed our last shower with the frogs, and said goodbye to João and Olivia.

I could only relieve the sadness of leaving by pondering on the lessons learned. I had been struck by the harshness of life here, the very real and regular confrontation of death and suffering, the struggle to medically manage the bodies of fearful animals in a time-effective way. However, I was also amazed by how peaceful life here was – untouched horses and trained horses living in groups on massive expanses of land, eating food they were designed to eat. I have to say the four I worked with, three chosen as challenges by João and one I picked at random, were really very easy students compared to the average Warmblood or Thorough-bred at home. It could be the breeding, management, feeding or herd lifestyle, or the fact that no training is better than inconsistent training, I don't know, but they really were very sane and trainable horses; they behaved as though they had read the 'how to be trained' handbook.

I was surprised to learn that in this part of the world they don't even have a word for crib-biting and had never known a horse to weave. Even more surprising was that they had *never* had a horse with colic. While jaguar, cobra and protozoa caused suffering and death, our own man-made plagues of stereotypical vices and colic were entirely alien to the horses of the Pantanal. This hit me pretty hard when I had to use mime to explain vices to a cowboy, who tutted and shook his head in disbelief. I guess it's all a matter of what you get used to and come to accept as normal. In reality jaguar attacks and stereotypical behaviours are shocking as novelties but frighteningly easy to become accustomed to.

While mulling over this idea of novelties standing out against the mundane, it occurred to me that one of the challenges of training is ensuring that horses too learn which things are everyday occurrences and can be ignored (e.g. being mounted or approached) and which things to recognise and respond to (leg aids, rein aids). This is ideally illustrated by Pantanal horses who must learn to yield to the pull of a rope on the head but resist the pull of a rope attached to the saddle when a cow is roped.

It was interesting too to notice which things stood out to the horses as dangerous and cause them to spook. When I arrived, as I initially encountered the very busy undergrowth, I asked whether the horses spook at the numerous caymans, and João seemed surprised at the question. 'No,' he said, 'not unless they tread on one.' It's incredible that in the Pantanal, where the horses actually *were* prey, wild pigs, rustling bushes and reflections in puddles, didn't make them jump. Even though there really was a jaguar in the bushes and a snake in the grass, the average horse seemed *less* spooky than the average horse back home.

João found it unbelievable that we have horses scared of cows and goats in England. The long working hours, slow, easy pace of work, and relaxed rein contact in the Pantanal all help to produce mature riding horses who are arguably amongst the most relaxed and willing working horses I have met. There were no stress behaviours in the mouth, no jig-jogging, no evasion; they mooched along looking quite at ease. It would be negligent to think we have nothing at all to learn from this.

It seems that it is accepted as normal in some places, like the Pantanal, that raw horses show difficult behaviours during training unless repressed by fatigue or restricted by ropes. I hope that my few days at Xaraes were at least novel enough to stand out to the cowboys and sow some seeds of realisation that the 'normal' struggle involved in medicating or training horses is *not* inevitable, and that raw, 'unbroken' horses can be very compliant, not defiant, creatures if given the chance. I hope this adjustment in mind-set will have reflected in some tangible way in their daily handling. In return it certainly made me realise that spooky, sharp, hot, uptight horses are not the norm of the species, and if the average horse in such a dangerous context could be so peaceful then ours should certainly look as relaxed in their safe and mollycoddled lives at home, and we should keep looking at our breeding, management and training in the hope that even our hot-blooded competition horses can enjoy a more grounded mentality. Otherwise what's the point in being safe and well cared for if it leaves you feeling paranoid, stressed and twitchy? Might as well live with the caymans and get a good night's sleep! I was reminded of my lessons in India, and I'll certainly be employing the idea of making resting and working worlds more similar for horses in order to maximise on their ability to be settled and brave.

It's so rewarding when the learning goes both ways. We heard from Olivia by email a few days later that João had been using one of my training ideas since we left and found it revolutionary. Can you guess what it was? Getting on from a mounting block!

Ah well, at least it's a small step (no pun intended!).

◆

CHAPTER ELEVEN

BEAUTY

In Itapira, Brazil

ON THE BUS TO ITAPIRA, on our way out of São Paolo, I looked at the carnival carnage out of the window. It was the morning after the night before, and the city was trying to wake up and return to normal. There was glitter and sequinned debris all over the streets, a four-foot high unicorn head had been abandoned by the side of the road – apparently fallen from a float. The odd partygoer was still making their way home, blurry-eyed, sleepily dancing down the street, and still partially clad in the remnants of some unidentifiable fancy dress. Curled up on the bus, we were not feeling too bright and shiny ourselves, since Hannah had really got the carnival fever the night before, gone totally native, and refused to come away from the trance-inducing samba beats until the early hours of the morning.

Friends from university who were working in São Paolo had got Saturday tickets for the carnival parade at the 'Sambadrome' in São Paolo the night before. The Sambadrome is an unimaginably large structure, featuring a mile-long track with grandstand seating rising up on either side. Its sole purpose is for the mobile parties of dancers and floats to jiggle their way festively past hoards of exhilarated spectators. Each samba school parades with its own theme song playing repetitively, and teams of dancers and floats all dressed to fit in with the school's annual theme. These themes are not as simple as the fancy-dress parties I have been to at home, and included topics such as 'celebrating 50 years of Korean immigration', which featured troops of dancers dressed as atoms and a lot of Gangnam-style moves.

Each samba school was made up of hundreds of participating dancers, organised into various matching outfits and routines, and about twenty breathtaking floats. These floats, built onto the back of lorries, were enormous and incredibly complex, with people hanging off poles or dancing on podiums, movable parts, multiple layers of stages, and glitter cannons. It was joyous to see that the troops of dancers included just about every type of person you can think of: old, young, overweight, skinny, short, tall; they were all swept along with the party fever and grinning madly in their extravagant outfits, thrilled to be part of something so big, and so moving. The elation was contagious. Each team had a few glamour girls, with feather tails, high-heeled shoes, lavish make-up, big hair, and tiny outfits, who jiggled about in a double-time samba that made their skin ripple and their assets bounce, before jumping to a finishing pose, hand on hip, for the crowd's flashing cameras. I was struck by the fact that I found everything about the parade appealing, not just the floats, and the outrageous outfits, and the obvious months of cumulative work that led to this moment, but also the dazzling smiles, the singing, the inclusivity and the abundant feeling of happiness that was emanating from the rows and rows of giddy participants.

Having attended the world's biggest party, in a country known for its obsession with personal aesthetics, it was no wonder that as we drove out of the city my mind started to ponder the concept of beauty, and the way that, in horsemanship, we often get lost on a wild-goose chase in trying to obtain it. When we get our horsemanship right, riding feels like a rhythmic, cooperative dance, and yet often this dance is sabotaged by our misguided efforts to get the horse looking the way we think he should.

I love the amount of equestrian art that is on show around the globe.

Almost every city and town we visited had equestrian statues in the town squares, paintings in the galleries, murals on the walls or sculptures in the parks. There is no doubt that people have found the horse's image to be a powerful muse, and a fantastic medium for expressing all sorts of concepts and ideas.

For instance, there is a theory that memorial statues of ridden horses symbolically tell you about the manner of the rider's death. If the horse has both front feet raised off the ground, the rider died in battle. If he has one foot raised, the rider sustained injuries during battle and died some time later. If he has both front feet on the ground, the rider's death was not battle-related at all. Though it doesn't take much research to find exceptions to the rule, I found myself wondering what else the artists were thinking of as they crafted these beautiful figures.

Many of the brass or stone horses, to my eye, look tense or panicked in the pose that has been chosen. They often have their mouths open in resistance of the bit, their nostrils flared, their eyes wide. When I study the cold stone figures, I wonder whether this immortalised behaviour was common of battle horses once. It may even have been misread as eagerness for battle, since I can imagine the horses in these statues bolting forward with their comrades on either side, running out of blind terror rather than in blood-thirsty bravery. The image of a stressed horse may have become celebrated as a totem of nobility and courage.

Wild, half-crazed, hard-to-control horses are often idealised in painted artwork too. These are the horses often depicted as the mounts of the gentry, jogging on the spot, half rearing, tongue lolling and rolling eyes, sometimes looking more dragon than equine. The sheer power of the untameable horse somehow adds value to judgments about the person on his back. Smaller, quieter, more sedate horses are shown in peasant scenes doing more humble jobs; the wildness itself seems to be a mark of prestige.

I know from my owners back home that beauty is certainly in the eye of the beholder, with some preferring an Arabian's dished face, and others a cobby Roman nose. For some, nothing but a long-legged Thoroughbred will do, and others still melt at the knees when they see a high-stepping Hackney pony. Each breed's body and temperament has been sculpted by mankind over generations to appeal to a certain aesthetic, as well as to fulfil a certain role.

The aesthetic ideal that we came across next in Brazil was the eye-catching world of classical dressage. Dressage, as a discipline, has military roots. The idea was to train the cavalry horse to be under utmost control, so that the rider could manoeuvre quickly on the battlefield. The pinnacle of this training is reached when the horse is able to perform various 'airs above the ground', such as the courbette, where he balances on his hind legs with his forelegs raised off the ground in a low rear, or the capriole, where he launches forward in a deer-like leap. These moves were supposed to have been very useful on the battlefield for positioning the rider so that he could attack foot soldiers or for leaping into lines of men and knocking them down. The horse should be balanced, poised, and instantly obedient to any aids. Though I am impressed by the training the cavalry must have put in, I find it hard to believe the front line actually looked like a choreographed dressage test, with riders piaffing about while striking soldiers down neatly. I can't help thinking it was probably pretty chaotic trying to control horses in the carnage of an actual battle. Sadly, though quite understandably, horse behaviour doesn't seem to have been at the forefront of war records, so it is hard for us to really know.

Lusitanos are related to the ultimate warhorses. Their ancestors existed on the Iberian Peninsula as far back as 20,000BC and by 900BC they were renowned for being exceptional horses for battle. The descendants of these horses were developed as the Andalusian, a breed that was first recognised in the fifteenth century, and, apart from war, its various roles in human lives have included bullfighting, stock work and driving. It wasn't until the 1960s, though, that the Lusitano breed was officially given its name, when a separate stud book was developed for the Portuguese strain of the Andalusian horse.

The image of an Andalusian or Lusitano horse has been linked to romance and nobility for generations. They are often dappled grey, powerful yet elegant, famously photogenic, with thick, strong necks and flowing wavy manes, ideally suited to carrying white knights on romantic quests, or galloping mystically through the waves on a stormy beach. They became an idealised image of courage and romance, linked closely in art and in folklore to the brave soldier and the good prince. The romance of the breed has continued to grow so that now, rather ironically, many women would be quite willing to chuck the poor eligible prince aside to get their hands on one of these horses, who are descended from living weapons for men, but have become gentle soul-mates of swooning women.

São Paolo in Brazil is something of a mecca for the breed, with many breeders and enthusiasts based in the region. We had been invited to visit the Interagro stud in Itapira, the biggest Lusitano stud in all Brazil, which breeds and trains horses for many disciplines, and exports them all over the world.

It was a bright, sunny morning as our hired car turned off the main road and down the long, red dust track that weaved between the sweeping hills. Martina Brander, the head trainer, rode up on her marble-grey stallion just as we arrived. She dismounted and handed the horse to a groom as we manhandled our luggage out of the car. Thinking of aesthetics, I had tried to tidy up for the occasion but the truth of the matter was that we had now been away for several months, and the sole of my boot was taped to the top with duct tape, which contrasted significantly with Martina who was the epitome of professionalism, together-ness and confidence. You could have guessed Martina's profession from a distance, her elegant, statuesque frame, strong posture, steely thighs, smart, belted grey jodhpurs . . . it all exuded sheer dressage-ness

Our visit, like everything else on the farm, was spectacularly well organised and left us feeling spoilt rotten. We were well fed, attended to and even given goody bags of branded Interagro merchandise to take with us when we left.

Interagro was built on lush rolling hills that once supported a coffee plantation. From the top of the hills, the red-tiled roofs and white stone walls of the stud farm just about peeked through the vibrant trees that thrived in the fertile soil. Some 450 horses live at Interagro, with beautiful, airy loose boxes and stalls arranged in a number of small yards, and then acres and acres of grazing for youngsters, stallions and broodmares, as far as the eye could see. The horses were ridden or driven around this peaceful haven on ready-made tracks, which encircled a purpose-built lake.

It was lovely to drive around the farm and view some of the young-stock. We met a bunch of two-year-olds who were loving their youth. They were all greying-out from whatever colour they had been born, which meant their coats were each the shade of a different coloured beach pebble. They grabbed each other's knees and cheeks and ears, playing rough and tumble, and romped about and raced until they were so tired they all flopped down, flat out in the long grass and fell fast asleep.

I also enjoyed watching some of the youngsters in training. One of the trainers, Paulo, worked with Fernandel and he had the most lovely feel around a horse. Paulo was strong, athletic, and relaxed, with good timing but never hasty, and I was thoroughly content as I watched the young horse learn. Fernandel had been in training for only five days, and was accepting touch all over, getting used to tack and leading nicely. Paulo used a rope to familiarise him to touch all over his body, rubbing it around his neck, barrel, belly and legs. He was one of those people who turn me green with envy – he could lift himself effortlessly onto a horse's back without seeming to jump or push or pull; as if a magnet just sucked him up there. He sat up on Fernandel's back, bareback, first with both legs one side, then astride him, before dismounting on the offside and then getting on with something else, so it was all no drama. It was certainly beautiful to watch a job done well and, much like the dancing people at carnival, it was the emanating positive attitude of the trainer and of his horse that made the scene appealing.

Our first opportunity to see ridden training close up was to watch and then try some 'working equitation' at the fabulous purpose-built arena, which had an incredible view over some of the grazing pastures. In the sport of working equitation, the horses and riders negotiate a series of obstacles, which require utmost accuracy and control, mostly at the canter. And, wow, can these horses canter! Largely because of their bull-fighting heritage, Lusitanos have the potential for the most amazing, balanced, agile canter that allows them to turn on a sixpence and weave around in tiny shapes without breaking rhythm. The sheer power in the ample muscle of their hindquarters as they pivoted round obstacles, or made the transition from halt to canter and back again, was astounding. And despite the sculpted bulk of muscle, their feet hit the ground as lightly and carefully as ballerina's slippers.

I really liked the idea of the working equitation. These horses were beautifully fit for purpose and able to use their bodies in the most supple, powerful way. With the focus of training on the manoeuvrability of the horses, rather than on a judged aesthetic, the training was all about how the horses felt to ride and how they were able to use their bodies like athletes. Of course, it just so happened that in completing this training, they were strengthening core muscles in their stomachs and backs, and muscles in the hindquarters, they were relaxing their mouths so that they could respond to the bit, and they were looking fantastic by most contemporary aesthetic judgments. Just as with humans, there is something beautiful about the body of a creature that is toned, flexible and fit.

The obstacles divide difficult manoeuvres into tangible aims, and make training more bite-sized and more fun for both horse and rider, so I couldn't wait to have a go. The horse that I rode, Baramir, was a real pro, which was a total delight because it meant I could focus on my own skills and riding and try to learn as much as possible from him. Between you and me, my dressage skills are always a work in progress and while I would ride young or tricky horses in front of any audience, I was apprehensive that while riding these magnificent, highly trained horses, the vast limits of my horsemanship would surely be exposed. To be honest I was worried about how I might look to these highly trained riders. But the working equitation gave the perfect opportunity for developing dressage skills without feeling under pressure to constantly look the part, since the focus is on the obstacles rather than the aesthetics, and yet your skills are improving all the time. It was so refreshing not to feel pressure to be conforming to the perfect image while working on dressage.

It also helped that what my instructor lacked in terms of English language, he made up for in sense of humour. He was such a good laugh and though I often didn't really follow the joke, his cheeriness was contagious. It started with our names, Hannah was christened Hannah Montana amongst many giggles, and my name left him totally tongue tied. For a while he struggled away with the 'R-o' sound before having a eureka moment and declaring my name would now be Raisin. The language barrier also had the pleasant effect of simplifying his commands and advice, which stopped me over-thinking. 'Do you have any advice about how I should do the weaving poles?' I asked, hoping for comments on seat bone position or something for the multiple flying changes (which means the horse can change his leading canter leg without breaking rhythm). He beamed at me and pointed at the weaving poles: 'Flying chance, flying chance, flying chance, flying chance,' he said, I didn't correct his error since I felt flying chance was perhaps more apt then flying change anyway. 'Go!' he exclaimed. Right then, I couldn't over-plan, so I got on with it and found that everything fell into place quite easily, flying chances and all!

As we walked about after the session, I was thoroughly inspired by the feeling of attentive development and thorough workmanship that permeated the whole place. Everything was done beautifully, everything was immaculate and no one seemed to be in a rush. When I spent time talking with the riders, they were full of respect for their coaches and thoroughly committed to their own improvement. I was amazed to see so many stallions stabled in close proximity and yet so many relaxed faces over the doors, and I was told that vices were rare. The horses we saw were well-mannered and relaxed during grooming and tacking up, and it was refreshing to hear Martina describe the way that time is invested in young horses to get them used to the mounting block, to scary things before an auction, and practising loading well before they needed to travel. It was also lovely to hear how emphasis is placed on finding each horse the right role, as he grows up his strengths determine his discipline, and he is partnered with a trainer who gets on with him. This sort of thoughtful and conscientious, individualised training impressed me in a project of this size, and is surely borne out of a system that dedicates time and money towards producing skilled staff, holistically trained horses, and a slick operation. It was good to see that the money wasn't only being spent on blingy browbands or fashionable bloodlines; it was going into things that made a difference to the horses' personal wellbeing. Though it has to be said, the prestige of an Interagro Lusitano comes at quite a price tag, but why shouldn't it with all the thought and training that has gone into their development?

Even if we don't have all the resources of Interagro at our fingertips, money has a part to play in the aesthetics that many of us are chasing in our horsemanship. Horse acquisition itself can be a clear case of conspicuous consumption; with certain breeds or types bought in order to demonstrate class. If that doesn't sound like you, then it might be another aspect of your personality or status that you hope to demonstrate through the horse you choose to ride or own. His breed and appearance will buy you membership to certain cliques, and help you to obtain certain aesthetic ideals that you value. I wouldn't suggest that image is the ruling force of *all* your horsemanship choices, but there might well be a grain of truth in the fact that you can display a little something about who you are, or who you want to be, based on how your horse looks when you ride along on him.

If you think this isn't you, then try finishing the following sentence. 'I would be terribly embarrassed if I was seen: riding a pony/riding in draw reins/trying to catch my horse/with my horse dirty/on a donkey/ with my horse spooking/getting off/falling off/with my saddle on backwards.' The embarrassment is only there if you are ashamed of the image of yourself that might be portrayed, so if you can imagine feeling it, it shows that you too would like your horse and your horsemanship to help portray a certain, successful, version of yourself that you are happy to be judged by.

In a way, horses can act as an extension of our own bodies; or rather we can, in effect, become parasites on their bodies to obtain the self-image that we most like. When you ride a beautiful horse, and he is going in a beautiful way, you feel part of the beautiful picture, which is frankly a wonderful feeling. I know I feel more beautiful on a well-schooled horse than I ever do on my own two feet. When we are riding, our horses can become a big part of our own self-image. This phenomenon means that it is not only our own bodies that we are willing to mould and moderate in the quest for achieving beauty.

Martina demonstrated exactly the best side of horse-human combined beauty with her mount Attalus, riding in the grand indoor arena, the sunlight streaming through the open sides and a little speckled owl watching with an aloof expression from the rooftop. I was a lot more impressed than the owl looked, since Martina frankly made it all look effortless. One thing I particularly like about watching Lusitanos do dressage is that their conformation sets them up to find the frame fairly easy, with that strong, ready-arched neck. Attalus' powerful back and hindquarters lifted him from the ground as though his heavy barrel was filled with helium; his ears flickering back to listen to his rider, his tail swinging loosely with the rhythm of the dance.

When it was my turn to have a go, I knew there were a few things I was dying to try out. I use a lot of dressage-ish schooling with the babies and remedial horses at home. I enjoy working on developing a loose rhythmic stride and a light mouth, and I find improving lateral work is often indispensable for certain problem behaviours like spooking, napping, rearing. But I have never been properly taught to do anything that I consider really flashy, like tempi flying changes (skipping), or half-pass (moving sideways and forwards), so other than playing around on my own horses, and watching Carl Hester longingly, I'm pretty raw in terms of fancy footwork. I was really looking forward to seeing how some of these things felt when done properly, and to seeing whether I was capable of finding the right buttons, hopefully without messing up too much of the wiring in the process!

The session didn't disappoint, I rode more half-pass and flying changes than ever before. It was a real treat to ride such a balanced, supple mount, though I had to work much harder than I'd expected to, and while my body may have gained some level of composure and subtlety, my red cheeks and watering eyes betrayed the struggle that was going on beneath the surface.

I was surprised by how much effort I needed to put into maintenance: maintaining impulsion, maintaining rhythm, maintaining bend, etc. The way I ride the youngsters, there is very little physical effort required; I pride myself on their lightness. The aim is to train them to keep doing what you asked of them until you ask something else. But during my lesson, in order to keep everything together, I needed to use my legs every stride, especially during lateral movements. On top of that there were constant mini adjustments, little more bend, little more speed etc. I felt as though I was clutching too many ping-pong balls in my hands, and in danger of sending one pinging, then dropping the lot! It would be easy to conclude that the horses should be trained in a way that doesn't leave them so high maintenance, but I know that the truth of it is that Martina didn't need to work as hard as I did, and so some of the issue was that my own mistakes were making problems I then had to work to iron out. Indeed, as the session was coming to an end and just before my legs fell off, it came together rather nicely and suddenly felt rather easier – and dare I say it, something near beautiful.

I have seen a similar scenario many times before, where one rider or handler needs to work so much less than another, and to the frustration of all concerned, even if the second rider was able to copy the exact aids of the first rider, he might not get the same results.

It was really good for me, though desperately uncomfortable, to be on the other side of the fence and recognising this dynamic as it feels to a student. I believe it's a mixture of mental presence and clarity, physical balance, timing, accuracy, feel and confidence that leads the horse to be able to clearly understand and accept your requests, which is easier said than done. So if your head is in the wrong space or your balance is off, the buttons may not work, even if you do manage to push them all accurately and at the right moments. This is because riding a horse is a dialogue with a living being, not a complex computer game. Learning the controls is not anywhere near enough. When these things are not coming together, the rider sometimes has to work so much harder until they find that missing piece. Ideally you need a coach with a seriously skilled set of eyes to spot what you can change and, harder still, find an effective way of communicating it to you. In the absence of such a rare guru and as long as the horse does not suffer, I believe sometimes working a bit harder is a stage you just have to be willing to go through. Finally that feel comes to you, like that elusive rising trot sought for by all bumpy beginners and suddenly, as if by magic, it all clicks together.

My final treat of the day was to ride in a Portuguese saddle. When one of the grooms named Carla led my beautiful bay mount, Profano, around the corner, I felt honoured; he had been turned out impeccably and looked as romantic as any knight's horse could. The dark leather headpiece and breastcollar were adorned with brass medallions, with one plaque of leather and brass square in the middle of Profano's elegant face. His black mane was braided and his bright bay coat gleamed like a new penny. The saddle needed plenty of clearance during mounting and dismounting, with a very high cantle at the back of the seat, as well as sturdy support at the thigh, it would have been hard to fall out of. It was also fairly hard to sit *on* though, pretty solid under your bottom! Profano was a little sharper than the other two horses I had ridden at Interagro, and more sensitive to lateral aids, so that the main challenge was keeping him straight through his movements. This was especially true for his flying changes, which I became a bit addicted to; I desperately wanted to do justice to the beautiful horse and turnout.

Martina was very astute in her comments, and I believe she was quite right when she said, 'Rosie, you cannot ride him like he is a baby. You must learn how to ride a trained horse so you know the feeling you are aiming for with your babies.' She had a good point; my muscle memory is totally geared toward riding in a way that gets horses forward, loose and relaxed, and I needed to learn how to get it all a bit more composed and controlled and together. This reminded me of a scalding lesson I once had as a child. I had been riding bareback, cantering around to the back of the ride on a little Shetland x New Forest pony and grinning with the delight of it. The instructor was not so delighted, however, and exclaimed in an exasperated voice, 'Oh my God! Rosie, you ride like a wild animal. You are never going to fall off, but you are never going to look presentable either. Will you just *try* to have a bit less fun and be a bit more *tidy*?!'

I left the Interagro Stud aching. My legs ached, my back ached, my fingers ached. My bum really ached. My first thoughts were that we can't expect to be part of the beautiful picture if we don't get our own bodies in the right shape to be able to do the horses justice. But then I began to wonder whether a young dressage horse might ache after a session as much as I did, and I questioned whether it was really a case of 'no pain no gain'. I mean, now that we don't actually need militarily prepared horses, why are we still chasing that holy grail of the perfect outline, flying changes, half passes and the rest?

Across time and space, people have done, and still do, some pretty horrific things to horses in the name of beauty. Think of Black Beauty and the bearing reins that held his head up high. Even on a more domestic note, we all know an old wives' tale or two about the imaginatively awful things done to horses to get them looking 'right' for showing or selling. How can we be so sure that our picture of the perfect dressage horse is not something our grandchildren are going to find abominable a few years down the line?

My friend Sue Palmer, IHRA and physiotherapist, has helped me to understand that certain ways of moving the horse, and encouraging him to balance himself, help him develop the core muscles that make carrying a rider more comfortable and less damaging. Some dressage work certainly falls within this beneficial category. And I know from experience that certain types of dressage schooling can encourage the horse to become more relaxed and obedient to the aids, making him safer and happier as a riding horse also. So I know that some work under the umbrella of dressage really is good for the horse, to the best of our current knowledge.

But in all honesty, most people are not thinking of their horse's mind or body when they are working to ride him with his head in the desirable position. Often owners chase this aim in the same way the carnival dancers manicured their nails, because it seems like the right thing to do; the culture and the idealised image steer them in this direction. I know this, because I have felt this pressure myself and have asked the horse to come into 'an outline' when I spot a certain person watching me ride. While I have nothing against riding a horse in an outline per se, sometimes, in the moment, I have done this out of pride and ego, not as a deliberate training choice that holds the horse's mind and body as priority. When we remind ourselves of the type of horse-human image that we are trying to portray when we ride, it is getting your horse in an outline that, in most horsey circles, notches up the level of competence that the horse-rider image portrays and buys acceptance and respect within certain cliques. It sometimes has very little to do with creating the right fitness or the right attitude, and it has more to do with vanity.

I thought back to carnival, and to the equestrian art, and the crazy things we humans do in the name of beauty. It was clear to me that we have to be really careful that when we are training our horses to move in certain ways, and idealising certain postures, we make sure we are chasing the wonderful feeling of dancing and not getting tempted toward the quest for the image. From my time at Interagro I learned a really valuable lesson, that the best type of dressage forgets what the horse and the rider look like, and works on how they both *feel*. The pinnacle of dressage is not the capriole as I once thought, we are not in the military and thank goodness our aims are now different. Good dressage today is all about a different holy grail, when both horse and rider *feel* great to one another during riding; both should feel fit for purpose, flexible and relaxed, communicating through subtle aids and able to manoeuvre in perfect balance with one another. I think this is a noble aim, and one that is worth a little bit of hard work from both me and my horse, since I truly believe it is in the best interest of us both in the long run. We should aspire to be those carnival dancers who love the dance, and to encourage the same from our horses too.

So, the attention to self-development of my own body began immediately, since we left Interagro and shortly found ourselves volunteering at a Hare Krishna yoga retreat near Buenos Aires in Argentina for a week. It was a cheap bed and a chance to fitten up before we returned home in just a few weeks time. It involved five hours of gardening a day from 5am, and in return we got organic home-grown vegan food, a boot-camp type training session each day consisting of running, press-ups, sit-ups, and an hour of yoga each evening. Now, if you thought the dressage bought me down a peg or two about my physical capabilities, you don't even want to hear about the yoga! I had no idea it required such strength, I thought it was all about standing on mountain tops with your toes pointed, wearing billowy clothes, and *relaxing*. Wow, it was pretty tough and, sadly, I was that comical figure, the yoga virgin, falling over at the back of class. While all the elegant elastic girls were poised in 'flying swan', I was quivering and toppling out of 'down-facing dog'. Still, I was doing it, and that's something to be proud of. I was sticking my fork in the ground each morning. I was doing sit-ups each afternoon and I was stretching myself into positions each evening that meant I got to say 'hello bottom' to my own derriere.

And now, every time I walk past one of those horsey monuments I reflect on the tragic irony that even the horror of horses in battle can become an idealised, 'beautiful' image. It reminds me that we just can't trust our own aesthetics without analysing them carefully for ethical implications; sometimes you need some distance to see the ugliness in things that look beautiful when you are caught up in the culture and the context. I know it is important to check with myself that my own ego isn't resting on the way the horses make me look, and to remind myself how beautiful horses are when they are muddy, woolly, wild and free, without any sort of human sculpting needed.

CHAPTER TWELVE

✦

LOVE
In San Antonio de Areca, Argentina

Our final equine stop introduced us to the testosterone-filled world of Argentinian polo, and got me thinking about how horses benefit, or suffer, from the amount of affection afforded to them in their various worldwide vocations.

We had travelled on a very long bus ride from Buenos Aires to the 'gaucho town' of San Antonio de Areco, a couple of hours north-west of Buenos Aires in Argentina. The town was incredibly pretty, built alongside a wide, gentle river, with sandstone buildings that were painted matte terracotta, or sky blue, and had iron railings with vine-like gates. Avenues were lined with trees and the sun shone generously. The dirt roads were tomato red and the nurturing weather encouraged an absolute abundance of greenery.

In this area, the cowboy rodeo culture was strong, with a competition called 'jineteada' often pulling in the most crowds. Jineteada is a little like bronc riding in North America, in that the basic premise is for the determined cowboy to cling on to a horse that is trying to dislodge him. As in North America, it's all over quickly, with rides lasting just six to fifteen seconds in order to get a score, and the score is higher if the horse bucks better. But in San Antonio, the 'ideal' is for the horses to leap up in the air off their hind legs, like a rocket-launched rear, rather than buck and spin. How is it that even 'wild', 'untrained' horses are obviously influenced so that they throw the rider in keeping with the local aesthetic for bucking? I guess that they probably breed deliberately to create horses who buck in the local style (as they do in North America), and it also seems the specific method of clinging stubbornly to the creatures backs is likely to encourage a certain type of jump. The Argentinian riders use much more rein contact than their North American counterparts, pulling the horses heads up to encourage the skyward leap that will get the highest points.

As a hub for jineteada and gaucho culture more generally, it seemed like San Antonio was an unmissable stop while we were in Argentina, though having seen plenty of photos I wasn't sure I really wanted to see jineteada for real. While it looked very dramatic, I could see it was going to be tough to learn about the experiences of the horses involved. We met a chap called Kevin in our hostel, and I was actually quite relieved when this chance meeting turned the direction of our San Antonio stay away from jineteada and toward another Argentinian equestrian mainstay, polo.

Polo originated from a game called 'pulu' in India, with the first polo club formed in 1834. It was brought to Argentina with the British settlers, and had spread in popularity, with the local gauchos proving skilled in the sport. Argentina became a mecca for polo, with more 10-handicap players than any other country in the world. The basics of polo are that each team of four can score points by hitting the ball through the other team's goal. The game is divided into chukkas, and generally riders swap ponies in between chukkas since the pace of play is fast and tiring. The main rule revolves around the 'line of the ball', which is an imaginary line that extends in the direction the ball is hit and on beyond the ball. The player that last hit the ball has right of way and no other player should cross this line, but they can ride alongside him and hook his mallet out the way, or bump their own pony into his to knock him out of play.

Our new friend, Kevin, was in his twenties, from North America, with a typically dazzling all-American smile, and he had been travelling through San Antonio when he came across Patricio and his polo yard. Fascinated by the sport, and entranced by his first few close encounters with horses, Kevin had stopped travelling and stayed put to volunteer at Patricio's place and learn what he could about the game. He was starting to work out that maybe it was the horses that he loved more than the game itself, but he was happy to introduce us to Patricio and Patricio, in return, was more than happy to be the subject of our attention for a few days.

The polo yard was a good walk from the hostel, a fair way out of town and down a dry dusty track that was home to a pair of little owls who were remarkably unfazed by us and fluttered from perch to perch ahead of us as we followed Kevin's hand-drawn map and made our way to the yard.

Compared to some of the polo operations in Argentina that can involve hundreds of horses, Patricio's polo school was a small venture. It consisted of a well-kept polo field, some grazing land, two tying-rail areas (one for each team) and a building that contained a tack room, changing rooms, showers and a swanky looking club room complete with bar. This set-up was the brainchild of Patricio and his cousin, who everyone called 'El Negro'. We only saw El Negro once, riding bareback at a fast canter with about six other horses in tow; he was pretty impressive. The idea was that by spending a bit of time indulging rich clients from Buenos Aires with polo lessons, the boys could afford to support themselves in their addiction to this expensive sport. At Patricio's place there were daily lessons and a game most days of the week until the European season began in February and Patricio would head to Italy to play professionally.

When we arrived, Patricio gave us an upside-down grin from underneath the horse he was shoeing. The others, around thirty of them, were tied to rails and dozing in the sun. If the polo world decided to make a calendar of good-looking guys, Patricio would be 'Mr January'. He had smoky eyes, chiselled cheekbones, a shadow of stubble broken by a small scar that suggested a devil-may-care approach to health and safety. His mop of dark hair was pushed back out of his eyes, and I wondered whether he looked this good naturally or whether he had spent longer in front of the mirror than he would probably be willing to admit. Much of the time, he wore a red beret at a jaunty angle, apart from when he was on a horse with a polo stick held aloft like Zeus' thunderbolt. He had a sparkling wink and a hint of cheekiness in the curling corner of his mouth that implied perhaps, despite his good looks and daring horsemanship, he didn't take himself too seriously. This was debatable. We certainly couldn't say Patricio was unaware of his appeal or his own achievements.

Once he had finished with the horse's feet, Patricio chatted with us while one of his grooms tacked up a horse for him to ride. He told me the youngsters arrive here already broken in and training revolves around getting the young horse used to the ball and stick, and creating a fit horse, with a good mouth and a quick turn of speed. He then vaulted up onto the leggy bay gelding, and kicked him straight into canter, finding his stirrups as he went and glancing back over his shoulder at us with a cocky smile as he accelerated down the pitch.

Draw reins that ran to the D rings of the saddle, rather than the more common European position of under the girth, were used to help keep the horse's head straight during one-handed steering. Patricio rode a series of turns and figures of eight in canter (with changes of leading leg) halt-canter-halt transitions, sometimes with tight turns (a little like Western rollbacks), all designed to imitate the manoeuvres necessary on the polo pitch. Although he looked as if he was stuck to the horse with super-glue, the riding style is undeniably different from either Western or European riding positions. Even at speed, the position looked quite casual and loose – limbs in disarray with no real tidy lines, in fact he looked perpetually untidy – but somehow he absolutely moved with the horse, never unbalanced. He alternated between an 'armchair' seat, with his legs well forward from his hips, and standing up in his stirrups leaning over the horse's neck. He clearly loved riding at speed, and I got the feeling he quite liked an audience to be galloping past too.

When he rode over and gestured from beneath his well-shaped

eyebrows for his polo stick to be passed to him, I asked a little about his training approach, and his reply was so painfully, confidently simple, that I felt a bit daft. The conversation went a little like this:

Rosie: 'So what do you do if you have a horse who doesn't stop very well?'

Patricio: 'I stop him.'

R: 'How do you mean?'

P (raising eyebrow): 'With the reins.'

R: 'I see. Very interesting. And how did you teach him to do flying lead changes so smoothly?'

P: 'I change direction. He changes legs.' (Yawn.)

R: 'And does he do lead changes well from the beginning or do you have to do something specific to help him get better?'

P: 'He gets better.'

R: 'Super! And how do you get him used to the ball and stick?'

P: 'I use the ball and stick. He gets used to it.'

You know that feeling when you can tell you are being really quite annoying but you can't quite figure out how to stop? This was the feeling I had when talking to Patricio about horses. I really felt like I obviously knew so little about things that I couldn't even choose a sensible sounding question to get conversation started.

Of all the relationships I had forged with horse people during our travels so far, I had never felt quite as foreign as I did when trying to learn from Patricio. I imagine this has something to do with my gender as well as my nationality, as Patricio himself said, 'Of course the males are better; they are more intelligent, braver, stronger, can concentrate for longer and have quicker reactions. With horses and humans.' I think he was joking, at least a little bit, but then again all of his sincerity seemed a little like he might be laughing at me, and all of his jokes seemed a little too serious – so it was hard to know.

But it wasn't just gender politics, our horsey lives were just worlds apart. On one occasion I asked him why many of the horses are ridden in two pairs of reins, I had assumed this would be something to do with the action of the curb rein lowering the head, that it might be some nuance of the equipment that was right for this job. I was yet again reminded of the gulf between us when his answer was 'In case one pair breaks during a match'. I mean, really?! I can't even imagine pulling so hard as to need a contingency plan for breaking one's reins on a Pelham bit in the horse's mouth. I have only once had a pair of reins break, when I was a teenager riding an ex-racehorse on the gallops – but I blame that entirely on my own attention to detail when cleaning tack and it is not something I would expect regularly enough to factor into the tack choice for the entire polo team. Either he was darn hard on his horses' mouths, or he didn't really know or care why two reins were used.

I have to emphasise that Patricio's response cannot be taken as representative of the polo world in general. When I posted elements of this chapter as a blog online, I was overwhelmed by the effort that some readers went to in order to explain to me their own approach to polo. There really are some very thoughtful and conscientious individuals in the polo world, and then, on the *other* hand, there are some, like Patricio, who are good at looking dashing and galloping very fast in front of the camera. And yet perhaps I have gone too far in portraying Patricio's appeal as only skin-deep. Patricio was kind enough to allow us to watch him, and he seemed well liked and admired by both the young apprentices whom he taught with good humour (one even sporting a matching red beret), and by the paying elite. Perhaps, given longer to get to know him, we would have found more in common.

But it was not just that our training cues or tack were different, we didn't share the same base interest that I had done with Ramón, or João or McLean or any of the others. While Patricio was certainly skilled on a horse, and not deliberately unkind towards them, it clearly wasn't a love of horses or horse training per se that led to his enjoyment of the sport.

These horses were not pets. Maintenance of their health and fitness revolved around keeping them polo-ready, like well-oiled machines. Some of the teaching horses, for instance, were known collectively as 'los gordos' or 'the fatties', and I'm not even sure that they had individual names. I am sure it didn't matter to the horses what they were called, but it was a sign of what they meant to Patricio. It was hard to talk horses with Patricio, because he didn't really seem interested in them. He was interested in the world of polo that they opened up for him.

After watching plenty of riding and lessons, and even a few casual games, on the final evening we watched a serious polo game, under a moody sky that developed into one of the most aggressive thunder-storms I have ever seen. The earthly rumble of galloping hooves, the shouts of the players and the whip-cracking noise of the thunder made for an incredibly high-adrenaline spectator sport. The sky was black with cloud on one side, and burnt ochre orange on the other, there was an end-of-the-world feel as though the stakes of the game were of super-human consequence. When the ball was hit and the horses lowered their necks, flattened their ears and surged after it, I could see why the speed of the sport is so intoxicating. I couldn't really tell who was winning, but Patricio always seemed to be first after the ball when it was sent flying, the pack just behind him shoving and bustling to get a shot. After the match, the sweaty riders patted each other on the back and dismounted noisily before handing their blowing horses back to the grooms.

The players then swaggered into the clubhouse to shower and re-dress in expensive leisurewear, before congratulating themselves with a drink as their adrenaline levels returned to normal. Meanwhile the grooms raced around in the thrashing rain to put the horses away, sometimes riding one bareback and leading several others at once. In the clubroom, Patricio was in the thick of it, hosting the clients, sitting expansively on a leather sofa and generally being dashing.

We could see all this through the window of the clubhouse from the tack room where, once the horses were away, we sat sheltering from the rain with the other outsiders: the grooms, Kevin, and his visiting girlfriend. I was pleased to spend the time with the grooms, who were kind enough to be patient with my Spanish. I asked one whether he liked polo. 'It's OK,' he shrugged, 'it's good work. Patricio is a good boss.' I asked him whether he liked horses. 'Yes,' he said, lighting up instantly with a warm smile. 'Any horses.' He paused as though considering a few individuals. 'I like them all.' And I felt a sense of relief for the horses I had met. This was odd of me, since the groom is doing the same job whether he likes them or not. Why did it bother me so much that Patricio didn't seem that into his horses, and why was I so pleased that his groom was? Does it really make a difference to their quality of life, given that they are kept healthy yet hardworking anyway, whether the people around them like them or not?

Interestingly, the lessons I learned about love and affection for horses while with Patricio and his staff reflected the lessons and messages acquired throughout the trip. My first instinct was to conclude that affection does matter. It's hard to believe that some equine scientists still argue that human emotions and relationship concepts are irrelevant to horses and are just our way of over-complicating things to make the relationship feel more like a human one. I believe that horses, as social animals, are likely to know if the people around them care for them. After all, they are experts at reading body language. From there it is not such a very great leap to suggest that, as herd animals who are emotionally aware, they might prefer a loving owner or carer to a nonchalant one. But there is something immediately preventing me from jumping to this conclusion, and that is the lives of the tourist horses we have seen across our travels.

The first were the horses who dance for tourists and at weddings in Rajasthan. We met some, along with their owner and trainer, during our visit to the Mawaris at the beginning of the trip. Everybody who watched them dance loved them, we were told. They were applauded and congratulated, admired and adored at their various functions, festivals and events, as well as earning good money dancing for tourists on the street. The mare that we met was almost white, but with small patches of pale grey, including one patch over her left eye. She had pink skin and a long nose, giving her a mousy looking face. The owner was a sinewy old man, with small, serious eyes and an extravagant moustache.

He was subtle in his approach, standing at her side and holding her head up with one hand while pointing a long stick at her legs with the other. From the way she reacted to the positioning of the whip, I would be pretty confident in guessing that the 'dancing' action she offered had been trained by whipping the legs while restraining the horse from moving forward. It was a little like piaffe, but the movement was faster, tenser, with an uneven, panicky rhythm. Her teeth were grinding on the bit, her eyes rolled back in her head showing a white rim while she quick-stepped. There was some skill involved in the training, since the timing must be good in order to reinforce the movement when it happens and in order to phase the aid down to just a point of the whip, but skilful or not, it was a sort of trained panic. I could not understand how anybody with an affinity for a horse could look at the overall picture and find it an appealing aesthetic, even less how they could take a photograph of her dancing like this because of the love, affection or admiration they felt for her. The truth is, that she only looked afraid and stressed to my eyes because I have been lucky enough to have an education that leads me to believe that I know what her expressions mean. To another's eye, however loving, it could go totally unseen behind rose-tinted glasses.

I also think of the horses on Java, carrying tourists up to the top of Mount Bromo. This was one of the 'non-horsey' travelling adventures on our trip. We were hiking to the top of the active volcanic crater of Mount Bromo. It felt like we'd landed on the moon, wading through deep ash, rolling dunes and a hot wind. The air was so thick with dust that it coated everything, eyelashes clogged together, breathing began to sting, lips became caked and yet another camera choked to death. The smell was noxious, chemical and pungent, and every instinct in my body knew that this was an unhealthy place to be. It was a challenge to make it to the top, and even though the site was spectacular, it took endurance to stay there for more than a moment or two before beginning the long retreat. For those who didn't fancy the walk, or who wanted the 'complete local experience', there was the option of riding a pony to the top instead. For some, this was another chance to get close to the species they loved. The ponies, only about 13hh, were cantered about at the bottom of the ascent as a way of advertising them. We watched one overweight woman being helped onto the back of a little dun pony who had his eyes more than half closed to avoid the dust. His whole body swayed as hers was manhandled into the little saddle, and then his owner set off leading him up the long incline, fetlock deep in sand and further and further into that poisonous air, as the rider asked what the pony's name was and started chattering away to him affectionately.

We saw horses for tourists all over the world on our travels, and it seems their human appeal does little to guarantee any sort of consistency in the standards of their welfare. When I think back over the owners that I have helped with horse training in the UK, there really seems to be little to suggest that loving a horse is in anyway a substitute for clear and consistent training. My heart has gone out on many occasions to owners who care deeply for their horses but find their devotion apparently unreturned when the horse behaves dangerously or unwillingly despite it all. It seems incredibly unfair to tell these owners that actually the consistent boundaries of some fairly mechanical competition or dealing yards create much happier, more settled horses, than the emotional baggage that comes with a novice owner who adores her equine friend. It's not how you feel that is important; it's what you actually do.

Patricio's horses were in fact pretty well trained. By that, I'm not condoning the way their mouths are pulled about for tight turns; what I mean is that they knew what was required of them and so I observed very little stress or struggle in getting them to do the things needed in daily management and riding. The training they received seemed consistent. I could argue that consistency is, if anything, easier in the absence of large emotional attachments. After all, there is no jealousy, no being offended or insulted, less hurt, and so less retaliation, temper, less frustration. There is less emotionally riding on the actions of the horse (excuse the pun). It is easier to respond in a detached, consistent and clear manner if you view the untrained horse as an unfinished project rather than an uncivilised family member or an abusive friend.

The physical aids that we apply, the management regime we choose, the food we give him and so on are going to have a much bigger impact on his welfare than the affection we feel. Affection, without knowledge, can be terribly misdirected making our actions useless or harmful against our best intentions. Of course, it goes without saying that the ideal would be if we could combine knowledge and affection, from which we can attempt to develop empathy, and make choices that are practical and positive in our horses' daily lives. This combination, however, seems to be a difficult one to achieve.

These musings about emotional and practical skills made me think back to the beginning of our trip, in India, where we had the good fortune to witness the teachings of the Dalai Lama, twice. The first came about because one of our many lucky encounters had led to us getting seats at one of the Dalai Lama's audiences in his temple in the mountain town of Daramasala. I say seat, but actually it was a little bit of floor space amid hundreds of monks and religious students. We sipped a cup of very salty, buttery tea as hours of chanting lulled us into a sleepy trance. But it was at the second event, one hosted by our General acquaintance in Delhi, that I really recognised the practical value in what he had to say and decided to read his book.

He told a story about a time he had been asked to bless a new temple. During the introduction, the local elder had said that he hoped a blessing from the Dalai Lama would bring an end to the sadness and poverty of the region. The Dalai Lama had thanked the elder for his kind words but had asserted that the only thing that would help the community was the actions of the community itself. He implored the audience to focus on the way they treat each other more than the way they worship, meditate, or pray. The message was very much: don't walk past litter on your way to the temple to hear preaching about what's good for the world; begin being good for the world yourselves and pick the litter up when you see it. This pragmatism really affected me, regardless of one's religious convictions, it has to be said this guy was certainly talking some sense.

I found reading his book and listening to him talk really useful for my horsemanship-thinking. He is refreshingly optimistic alongside his frank realism. For instance, he firmly believes that everyone has the potential to change. To me, this is what I have heard Kelly refer to as a 'helpful' belief to have – not least since it suggests that horse people (from any background) can learn to understand horses' behaviour more effectively. From a horse-centred point of view, it also seems more useful to talk about a horse's undesirable behaviours as a temporary problem, rather than to assign that horse permanent negative-personality attributes. While I do believe each horse has a natural tendency towards a specific set of useful and less useful behaviours, as I explored at the foal stud in New Zealand, it's certainly going down a dead end once we label them by their less attractive features, as though they are permanent faults, rather than continue to search for ways to bring out the best in them.

The Dalai Lama asserts the equality of all human beings based on the fact that we are all trying to do the same thing: escape suffering and find happiness, in whatever way we know best. I've often found a similar approach useful for making mental peace with even those horses who seem willing to wipe the arena walls with me. All horses, I figure, are only aiming for comfort, safety or happiness. And who can blame them for that? It's our job to make sure they find those things in their working life. Most badly behaving horses simply haven't worked out a way to stay safe and happy that also fits with our agenda.

Sometimes it can feel like the world of horsemanship has so much to do still. I can feel as though our best efforts are not yet good enough at maximising the horse's ability to learn and cooperate, and I can reflect on the fact that I come across stressed, unhappy, confused and anxious horses at every turn. But despite the difficulties we all face in figuring out the best way to fulfil the horse's potential to be what we want him to be, I don't feel disheartened. This trip had shown me that there are so many good ideas out there, and so many good horse people who apply them in new and unique ways. If we can continue to find clever ways to deter the wrong behaviour, while making the right choices comfortable, safe and fun, and if we can do this with compassion and regular re-evaluation of our motives and our conduct, I think we are well on the way towards an ethical world of horsemanship that even the Dalai Lama might approve of.

When finally it had come time to catch the plane home, none of the films on offer could captivate my imagination. All I could do was cast my mind back over our months of adventure and lose myself in the colours, sounds and smells that were so absent on the sterile plane. As I remembered the people we had met and the stories they had shared with us, you'll be pleased to know that it seemed to me that most of the horse world is hoping for similar ends. I've rarely met a horse person, in any continent, who doesn't want a happier horse; whether out of love for him, or just because they are so much better company, or largely more useful when they are not distressed. It is certainly not just in the UK that people want the best for their horses.

This was ably demonstrated on our trip by Davendra's settling procedures and naming techniques in Rajasthan, the patience of some of the 'parent' lads with their Calcutta racehorses, the acts of collaboration at Athayasa and Naomi's struggle for collaboration with her staff and horses in Bali. Then there were John Chatterton's thoughtful efforts to rethink and reword training approaches, the rigorous search for underlying training truths at the Australian Equine Behaviour Centre, the exquisite handling of those beautiful Thoroughbred foals, Ramón's secret soft side, the comprehensive training of the Lusitanos and the best efforts of the peãos of Pantanal to turn around a culture of cruelty. It seems that wherever there are horses, you don't have to go too far to find at least somebody who cares about them and is really trying to get it right. At our final spot, in Argentina, I had thought that somehow this was missing. But I had been looking for it in the wrong place, distracted by the speed and flashy smile of the front man. In the end, it wasn't all that surprising that it was the underdogs of the polo venture who held the most affection for their horses. While some of the riders thought of the horses as sports equipment, the grooms knew them as individuals and handled them with affection and respect.

Finally, as I drifted to sleep in my tiny airplane seat, thinking about the importance of love in our horse's lives, I was reminded of a tender moment I had witnessed seven months earlier at the beginning of our adventure. In India, in the rural town of Fatepur Sikri, under the baking midday sun, my heart had been melted when I saw a gnarled old carriage driver, with a tooth like a tin opener, sitting on a wall, stroking his pony's ears and offering him half of his banana. The pony's gentle lips took the banana gratefully and after he had finished chewing, he rested the whole weight of his head on the driver's lap and dozed in the sun. I think it's helpful (for my peace of mind if nothing else) to believe we are mostly moving in the same direction, toward an ethical, yet practically efficient, relationship with our horses. It's just that some of us are starting from a very different place, and we all have very different things to offer.

USEFUL ADDRESSES

Charities whose good work we encountered during our travels

Friends of the Marwari Horse Bit Donation Scheme –
    http://friendsofmarwari.org.uk/pages/page9.html

Kaimanawa Heritage Horses –
    www.kaimanawaheritagehorses.org

Leg Up Trust – www.legup.co.nz

Save the Brumbies – www.savethebrumbies.org

The Brooke Hospital for Animals– www.thebrooke.org

Training organisations mentioned in the book

Equus Education – www.equuseducation.com

Intelligent Horsemanship – www.intelligenthorsemanship.co.uk

Interagro – www.lusitano-interagro.com

John Chatterton – www.johnchatterton.com.au

Ken Faulkner – www.australiannaturalhorsemanship.com

Monty Roberts – www.montyroberts.com

Parelli Natural Horsemanship – www.parelli.com

Paul Clarkson – www.paulclarkson.com.au

The Australian Equine Behaviour Centre (Andrew McLean) –
    www.aebc.com.au